DATE DUE

			PRINTED IN U.S.A.

NEXT TO GODLINESS

Next to Godliness

*Confronting Dirt and Despair
in Progressive Era New York City*

DANIEL ELI BURNSTEIN

UNIVERSITY OF ILLINOIS PRESS

URBANA AND CHICAGO

∞ This book is printed on acid-free paper.

Library of Congress Cataloging-in-Publication Data

Burnstein, Daniel Eli, 1952–
Next to godliness: confronting dirt and despair in Progressive Era New
York City / Daniel Eli Burnstein.
p.   cm.
Includes bibliographical references and index.
ISBN-13: 978-0-252-03024-6 (ISBN-13 : cloth : alk. paper)
ISBN-10: 0-252-03024-9 (ISBN-10 : cloth : alk. paper)
1. Street cleaning—New York (State)—New York—History.
2. Refuse and refuse disposal—New York (State)—New York—History.
3. Public health—New York (State)—New York—History.
4. New York (N.Y.). Dept. of Street Cleaning.
5. New York (N.Y.)—Social conditions.
I. Title.
TD819.N6B87   2006
363.72'91'097471—dc22   2005013685

To Jo

"Regenerate the individual" is a half-truth. The reorganization of the society which he makes and which makes him is the other part.

—Henry Demarest Lloyd

CONTENTS

Illustrations follow page 54.

ACKNOWLEDGMENTS

I thank Gerald N. Grob and Richard L. McCormick, who have been great sources of encouragement and historical insight. I also give special thanks to Steven H. Corey, a fine scholar of New York City and the urban environment.

I am indebted to numerous other friends and colleagues who have given me advice and encouragement as I worked on this project. I cannot name them all here, but I would particularly like to thank Samuel L. Baily, John Buenker, Alexander Callow, John Whiteclay Chambers II, Muriel Clawans, Phyllis Collazo, Deborah Cornelius, Dan Dombrowski, Dan Domike, Elizabeth Fee, Dan Fishman, Gary Gershman, Revelle and Louis Gershman, Glenda Gilmore, Bert Hansen, Robert Johnston, George Levine, Kriste Lindenmeyer, Clay McShane, Martin V. Melosi, Gordon Miller, David M. Oshinsky, Jim Parry, Philip J. Pauly, Jon A. Peterson, Kurt Piehler, Naomi Rogers, David Rosner, Gary Saretzky, Harry Scheiber, Traian Stoianovich, Joseph P. Sullivan, Nancy Tomes, Wendell Tripp, Anthony Troncone, and Richard Young.

Participants in Rutgers University research seminars in political history and in the history of science and technology offered valuable comments on earlier versions of chapters 1 and 2, respectively. I very much appreciate the support and encouragement of the Institute for Health, Health Care Policy, and Aging Research at Rutgers University, under the directorship of David Mechanic, and the Rutgers University History Department. I also thank the faculty and staff of Seattle University's Department of History for their support and encouragement. I am particularly grateful for the help afforded by the department's chairpersons with whom I have worked, Jacquelyn Miller and Thomas Taylor, and by the department's administrative assistant, Karen Lawrence. I am grateful as well to the deans and associate deans of Seattle University's College of Arts and Sciences who have encouraged my research endeavors: Connie Anthony, Paulette Kidder, Wallace Loh, and Steve Rowan. For their discerning guidance, I would like to thank my kind and thoughtful editors at the University of Illinois Press, Laurie Matheson and Carol Betts.

Needless to say, my work would have been impossible without the kind assistance of librarians and archivists. I am grateful to the helpful staffs of the Rutgers University Libraries; New York Public Library; New York City Municipal Archives;

New York City Municipal Reference Library; YIVO Institute for Jewish Research; City University of New York's Russell Sage Collection; and the Rare Books and Manuscripts Room, Butler Library, Columbia University. Special thanks go to Florie Berger and Arlene Shaner of the New York Academy of Medicine Library; Ngocbich Nguyen of the main desk at Butler Library, Columbia University; Karen Gilles, Jill Moerk, Bob Novak, and Holly Sturgeon of Seattle University's A. A. Lemieux Library; Jim Bobick of the Carnegie Library of Pittsburgh; and David Ment and Bette Weneck of the Special Collections Division of the Milbank Memorial Library, Teachers' College, New York City.

My grandfather, who revered learning, did not live to see me complete this work, but I am glad that he saw me on my way. Special thanks go to my parents, Myron and Muriel Burnstein, for their enduring faith in me and for instilling in me an awareness of the importance of history, ethics, and politics. More than anyone, my beloved wife, Jo, helped me through the long process of research and writing, with her patience, generosity, lively conversation, laughter, and wise advice. I dedicate this book to her.

NEXT TO GODLINESS

INTRODUCTION

During the nineteenth century, the United States evolved from a rural and largely homogeneous nation into one that was substantially industrial, urban, and ethnically diverse. In the process, the existence of overcrowded and ill-ventilated housing, unsafe workplaces, filthy streets, unsanitary drinking water, and other urban problems spurred reform movements that sought to prevent or alleviate these conditions through both private and governmental means. The episodic appearance of frightening epidemic diseases, particularly cholera and yellow fever, did much to strengthen citizen awareness of public health issues. Because filth in the air, water, streets, and homes was considered to be a major factor undermining the health and well-being of the populace, the term "sanitary reform" became practically synonymous with the drive to improve public health and indeed with social reform in general.

The mid-nineteenth-century social reform movements that were framed in terms of public health were part of a broad humanitarian trend taking root in the Western world at that time, with agendas ranging from antislavery to women's rights (and the drive for representative government in many areas of Europe). Proponents sought to foster conditions that they believed would allow more people to reach their highest potential as human beings or bring them closer to God's ways. American public health reformers throughout the remainder of the century drew inspiration and policy models from their European counterparts, particularly those of Great Britain, which had a generation's head start on the industrialization process and its side effects.

There, the sanitary reform movement had gained significant momentum following the publication of Edwin Chadwick's influential *Report on the Sanitary Condition of the Labouring Population of Great Britain* (1842), which graphically described the filth and other unhealthy physical conditions in the poorer neighborhoods of Britain's towns and cities. Through statistical reckoning, Chadwick correlated conditions in those neighborhoods with a higher incidence of disease, mortality, crime, and other indicators of physical and social distress. Concerned citizen's groups subsequently attracted many new members and did much to influence public opinion and educate legislators about the need for public health measures. While hindered by taxpayer resistance, long-held fears of centralized government, and many citizens' adherence to laissez-faire economic ideology, Britain by the 1880s made significant strides—for example, by installing urban sewerage and water systems, improving street cleaning services, and mandating rudimentary workplace safety measures and housing codes. In part because America's self-image was to a great extent predicated on the idea that an independent, prosperous livelihood was here for the taking (for those who would properly discipline themselves), the factors inhibiting the advance of public health measures in Britain held even greater sway in the United States. Nevertheless, by the end of the century, many Americans were aware that dismal surroundings made it difficult for poverty-stricken urban residents to maintain good health and a positive approach to living. Out of compassion, and out of concern that disease and disorder might spread, numerous middle- and upper-class citizens sought to reform urban social conditions, especially after the depression of the mid-1890s made it more difficult to ignore the depth of poverty and unrest in the cities.[1]

It is within this context, of an America beginning to come to grips with urbanization, and with the related influx of millions of immigrants, that we can more fully understand civic sanitation issues in late nineteenth and early twentieth-century urban America. This book focuses particularly on street cleaning and refuse collection issues that stirred considerable social and political interest in New York City between 1895 and 1917. These dates correspond with that period known as the Progressive Era, a period that witnessed an increased demand for change in the nation's social, political, and cultural institutions. It was in the cities that the movement for social reform helped spur broader acceptance of the principle that government should be used to address a wider range of social problems. New York, the largest American metropolis and the hub of immigration, attempted to confront many of its complex social ills, often serving as a model for other municipalities (and sometimes as a cautionary example).

The New York City Department of Street Cleaning (DSC) was responsible for the collection and disposal of household refuse and the sweeping of the city's streets. The latter was a formidable task in an era in which the production of consumer goods soared while many New Yorkers possessed no more than a rudimentary awareness of the litter problem. It was a task made all the more difficult by the pervasive presence of manure that tens of thousands of horses deposited daily onto city thoroughfares.

In a time of growing awareness of the physical and social environment's effects on both individual and community well-being, dirty streets were considered a real threat. To a significant extent, lay and medical opinions still subscribed to the rather holistic traditional association of dirt and foul air with disease and with a degraded environment in which despair, crime, and other marks of personal and community disorder could kindle or perpetuate disease. Conversely, conscientious personal and public sanitation signified healthful living and wholesome surroundings.

In part because of the meaning ascribed to dirt (and to cleanliness), we can examine street sanitation and related issues to better understand the attitudes of Progressive Era social reformers toward public health and moral order, individual and governmental responsibility, individual character and its relationship to the social and physical environment, and the integration of the poor—especially the immigrant poor—into the broader society. The view of health common to those times, with its emphasis on the role of both environment and behavior, strengthened activists in their belief that improved city services and regulatory efforts—for example, better street cleaning and more tenant-friendly housing codes—could help prevent the interrelated conditions of dirt, disease, despair, and disorder in the slums. Indeed, concern for civic sanitation was a key factor reinforcing an increased awareness that urban environmental conditions underlie many social problems, and the corollary assumption that such conditions can and should be ameliorated.

At the same time, concern for civic sanitation reinforced the reformers' efforts to influence the individual behavior patterns that most activists believed ultimately determined personal advancement and societal health. To reformers concerned with public health and sanitation, and to social reformers and urban activists in general, the level of street cleanliness was an important gauge for ascertaining whether the city was providing those conditions needed to help the poor attain a state of "decency"—that level of individual well-being and morality that would, in the aggregate, ensure a healthy and orderly city.

In effect, the progressives fashioned a comprehensive social vision that applied to practically all social problems. Because their view of sanitation and health played so significant a role in that social vision, the quest for clean streets serves as a valuable lens for understanding that vision as it applied to the urban experience and social reform. And because many of today's citizens would be able to identify with the Progressive Era social reform ethos, an increased knowledge of that period might serve as a foundation for growth in social consciousness in the present day.[2]

A sense of the emotional force that public sanitation issues possessed during the Progressive Era and the role that these issues played in building the social consciousness of the era's reformers is underscored in chapter 1, which examines the New York City garbage workers' strike of 1907. For one week, during a summer hot spell, the strike exposed people to piles of garbage that at times stood over five feet high in the streets, many years before plastic bags could be used to mitigate the resultant odors and filth. The anxiety created by the strike stemmed in part from the meaning ascribed to cleanliness, which was influenced by traditional medical theories that had endured from the decades prior to the

verification of the germ theory in the 1880s. In what was still the early stage of
the bacteriological age of medicine, holistic concepts derived from notions about
the miasmatic origins of disease and from a systemic view of the body reinforced
the special sense of urgency created by the strike. Even educated elites were not
yet convinced that disease could be fully explained by a model in which illness
was caused by specific germs invading specific areas of the body. Because despair,
intemperate behaviors, community disorder, and disease were considered an
interrelated ensemble that tended to arise when sanitation or other important
physical and social conditions were insufficient to provide for the well-being of
city residents, a garbage strike seemed to threaten an orderly way of life and the
ability of slum inhabitants to rise above the barriers of ill health, poverty, and
despair toward a better life.

Chapter 2 moves backward in time a bit, to the mid-1890s, to discuss the work
of the charismatic commissioner of the DSC, George E. Waring Jr., highlighting
the views of this early (and emblematic) progressive reformer concerning the
improvement of urban social conditions, as well as the symbolic significance that
his administration held for American reformers throughout the remainder of the
era. Waring succeeded in depoliticizing the DSC and in systematically cleaning
detritus-filled streets, even in neighborhoods that were at that time among the
densest areas of human habitation on earth—a task that had previously seemed
practically impossible to achieve. In attempting to improve services for impoverished immigrant neighborhoods, Waring stressed the importance of mutual
obligations, the assumption of a two-way or contractual arrangement between
the individual and society. Both the dismal living standards that characterized
tenement districts and the behaviors of individual inhabitants of those areas were
considered to be important components in generating social pathology, filth,
and needless disease. In emphasizing that improved sanitation required both
the upgrading of DSC services and greater cooperation from residents of those
neighborhoods, Waring recognized external reform of the urban environment
and individual reform as coequal components in addressing unhealthy conditions. A corollary assumption was that positive surroundings would reinforce a
more resolute character among the poor, since impoverished individuals would
then be more likely to believe that middle-class values and aspirations were
relevant to their own lives rather than only to the lives of people who earned
significant sums of money. The credo of mutual obligations touched a chord in
many middle- and upper-class citizens, helping to secure a mass base of support
for innovative social programs during the Progressive Era.

Chapter 3 explores the ambivalent relationship between New York's social
reformers and the mostly immigrant pushcart peddlers who crowded onto the
streets of tenement districts (particularly on the city's Lower East Side). At the
root of this ambivalence was a conflict between two public goods. On the one

hand, reformers knew that Lower East Side consumers depended on the peddlers to provide inexpensive food, clothing, and household items, while on the other hand, reformers and DSC and health department officials complained that the carts added significantly to the filth, congestion, and disorder of the streets, and that the food purchased from the open carts was liable to be laced with germ-ridden street dirt churned up into the surrounding air. Since most people assumed that cleanliness was a prerequisite in the rise of impoverished immigrants to respectability, middle-class comfort, and health, and that their ability to rise was a key to the maintenance of a stable, democratic society, the congestion and dirty streets generated by the pushcarts seemed to cry out for a reform response.

Nevertheless, there was conflict within the reform community, and between reformers and rigid conservatives, over pushcart policy issues. Many reformers wrestled with the dilemma of how to regulate the carts without sacrificing the availability of inexpensive consumer items in impoverished neighborhoods. Indeed, an examination of conflicts over pushcart policy can help illuminate changes within progressive reform thought during the latter part of the era, when the agenda of social justice for the poor became a more prominent feature in urban politics. The pushcart question also affords a window for viewing a process of evolution within Tammany Hall, New York City's dominant political organization, which sometimes joined the peddlers in opposing reform policies but at other times sided with the politically connected owners of permanent businesses who sought to block totally the presence of pushcarts in their neighborhoods. In addition, the issue of pushcart politics helps to illuminate the rise to public influence of representatives of independent working-class organizations and immigrant groups whose interests lay outside of the classic reformer–political machine dichotomy.

As anthropologists have noted in studying peoples in various parts of the world, cleanliness has been a powerful metaphor in many cultures, often signifying practically all that is considered wholesome and orderly. These cultures have, of course, differed in their definitions of what is and is not clean. A number of factors helped shape the progressives' definition of cleanliness, the special importance that they gave it, and their response to its presence. The Enlightenment-based theory that social problems arise from negative conditions within the social and physical environment certainly reinforced a sense of urgency about the glaring sanitation problems associated with the growth of cities, industry, and immigration. And, as noted, the lingering influence of miasmatic and other pre-bacteriological medical theories strengthened the focus on sanitation. At the same time, a general sense of optimism that was rooted, in part, in the technological advances of the age strengthened the will to tackle urban problems, as did the existence of quasi-millenarian religious ideals that were metamorphising into visions of near perfection for earthly society.

Given the era's emphasis on cleanliness and its association with wholesomeness, order, good character, and health, it is not surprising that reformers stressed the topic of civic sanitation in childhood education, which is the focus of chapter 4. By the 1910s, "juvenile street cleaning leagues," originally founded by Commissioner Waring, engaged tens of thousands of the city's children, from nine to fifteen years of age, in club meetings, cleanup drives, parades, and even supervised athletics. Juvenile street cleaning league members forswore numerous unsanitary habits, from littering sidewalks to spitting in streetcars, while they also sought to influence their fellow New Yorkers to do likewise. Advocates hoped that the leagues would spur citizen cooperation with the DSC and offer children from tenement neighborhoods an alternative to the youth street gang, which was a common symbol of the physical and moral threat that the slum posed to individuals and to society at large. Reformers believed that the leagues and related programs within a broad Progressive Era movement concerned with child welfare could furnish opportunities for positive socialization that most middle- and upper-class parents provided their own children as a matter of course. Ideally, through participation in interesting and enjoyable activities, and through explicit instruction in civic education, children would learn to reject delinquent and uncleanly behaviors that reformers believed threatened to erode civic order and public health. And the children's newfound sense of responsibility would presumably predispose them to become more thoughtful and assertive citizens when they reached adulthood. In an era in which the influx of immigrants heightened fears that the poor might adopt unhealthy lifestyles or radical political ideas, activists hoped that these programs would help ensure a more civil and stable society; but they also conceived of the leagues as a resource that children from squalid surroundings could use to help escape the slum neighborhood trap of crime, dulled sensibilities, and disease that inhibited prospects for self-actualization and social mobility. We can, in fact, see in the history of the juvenile leagues an interplay of Progressive Era social reformer motives, which were held in creative tension; on the one hand, the reformers worked, as a sort of societal superego, to build a more stable social order and influence the attitudes and behaviors of the child, while, at the same time, they hoped to establish greater social justice and enhance individual and group expression among the very people that they sought to influence.

In cooperation with the public school system, women's civic groups often took an active role in organizing the juvenile street cleaning leagues. Those women who were concerned about overstepping traditional roles by becoming involved in the public sphere frequently justified themselves by arguing that they were actually fulfilling their traditional role as nurturers of the young. Their activism was part of a broader trend in which activist Progressive Era women sought not only cleaner streets but also such goals as safe milk supplies, publicly funded playgrounds, and legislation concerning occupational safety and health, workmen's compensation, and child labor. The juvenile leagues provide a case study in the extension of the ideal of woman-as-nurturer to the public sphere. While some scholars claim that this extension may ultimately have constrained women's participation in society and politics as equals, in any case it did help to legitimize the principle that government should act when necessary to address problems of social welfare.[3]

In emphasizing involvement in public sanitation efforts as a crucible for the promotion of civic ethics in children, juvenile league activists operated from a perspective that was at odds with a different concept of freedom and the good society, one that placed more value on an unfettered individualism. In part because complex urban problems seemed to necessitate an increase in government services and regulations, there occurred during the Progressive Era a greater mass reckoning than ever before concerning the conflict between a broad social consciousness and individualistic values. The often implicit question was how to temper the latter values without losing their essence. Progressive Era attitudes toward public sanitation and the juvenile leagues illustrate both the nature of this long-standing division within American political culture and reformers' attempts to synthesize aspects of the two opposing sets of values in an urban industrial environment.

While this study focuses on issues of street cleaning and refuse collection in New York, it is certainly not an historical survey of those matters nor is it a survey of the DSC during the Progressive Era. Rather it is in the line of historical works that have investigated local matters in order to gain a richer understanding of issues that transcend the locality in question. The examination of New York's street cleaning experience above all brings into relief the progressives' ethos concerning the interrelationship of dirt, disease, and disorder; the way in which this viewpoint strengthened the urban social reform movement of the era; and the progressives' reciprocally oriented fusion of concerns for both the external needs of the poor and individual morality.

CHAPTER 1

The Garbage Workers' Strike of 1907

In every era, crises arise that embody the social and political tensions of their times. On June 25, 1907, the workers who collected refuse for New York City's Department of Street Cleaning (DSC) went out on strike in the Borough of Manhattan. The DSC employed approximately seven hundred fifty drivers in the borough. These men were responsible for loading residential trash cans onto horse-drawn trucks. The DSC also employed over twelve hundred street sweepers, and it was responsible for removing snow from the city's thoroughfares as well.

Within eight days the strikers reported back to work, but to a far different department. The DSC's commissioner had fallen into political disgrace, and officials of the city's health department had then taken over the administration of the leaderless DSC. Characteristics fundamental to urban America in the Progressive Era had contributed to a crisis atmosphere during the strike and helped to shape the eventual outcome.

A garbage strike in our own era is of course not without menace, yet such an occurrence during the early twentieth century was fraught with symbolic meaning that added to the public perception of endangerment. One issue that carried considerable meaning for Progressive Era citizens was that of political corruption. The sensitivity of reform-minded civic groups to this issue affected their attitudes toward DSC inefficiency. These civic groups wielded substantial power that, in turn, influenced the actions of Tammany Hall, New York City's dominant Democratic political organization, during the strike. Furthermore, civic group publicity about DSC shortcomings reinforced the significance of sanitation in the public mind. In combination with early twentieth-century conceptions of disease, the meaning given to sanitation by Progressive Era citizens was perhaps most important in shaping the fearful reactions of New Yorkers during the strike. Additionally, a profound faith in professional, and especially medical, expertise influenced the settlement of the strike as well.

Throughout the United States, an extraordinary public sensitivity to political corruption was a hallmark of the Progressive Era. In the years since the Civil War, America's major cities had witnessed dramatic increases in population and industrial growth. During such a transformative period, social relations were far from stable, as seen in the considerable labor unrest of the times. The manipulation of large enterprises, such as utility companies, for private gain reinforced the anxieties of a people often scarcely removed from the small-town or rural life of an earlier day. All of the social tensions of the age, the feelings of dependency and lack of control, seemed to coalesce in the public's outrage toward the wealth and power of the men and corporations perceived to be corrupting politics in the quest of special privileges.[1]

New Yorkers were hardly immune to the nation's anxieties about political corruption. During 1905, the state was rocked by investigations of gas, electric, and life insurance companies, which disclosed widespread corruption throughout the big-business and political establishments.[2] Within this atmosphere of public distrust, the DSC became the subject of an investigation by a special committee of the New York City Board of Aldermen during 1906. The aldermanic committee, chaired by two leading civic reformers, found numerous irregularities during the course of its investigation. For example, DSC horses were routinely condemned as unfit by John C. Wallace, the department's superintendent in charge of stables, and the department then sold these animals for a song to the Fiss, Doerr, and Carroll Horse Company, the city's largest commercial stable. Wallace reaped a reward under the table when Fiss and Doerr then sold or rented these same horses back to the department for top dollar. (The DSC rented up to seventeen thousand horses per year, at the fairly steep rate of two dollars per day.) Among several other serious accusations, the committee found evidence implicating the department in sweetheart contracts for the disposal of refuse in Brooklyn and for snow removal in Manhattan. The latter arrangement cost the city over a million dollars in excess charges in a single season.[3]

The committee's report paved the way for the removal of John McGaw Woodbury as DSC commissioner in October 1906. His successor, Macdonough Craven, came into office with a good public image. A man of distinguished family, he was a technical expert in waste disposal methods who was chosen from within the department. Craven had been hired originally by the charismatic George E. Waring Jr., whose tenure during the mid-1890s as DSC commissioner was legendary for its battles against corruption and inefficiency. Noting that Waring had been the only commissioner to keep the politicians from obtaining influence over the plump patronage potential of the department, the *New York Times* wished the nonpolitical Craven good luck, knowing that he could well use it. Unfortunately, the new commissioner soon found himself in trouble over his decision to retain Woodbury's improvident and inefficient snow removal system. A heavy snowfall in the winter of 1906–7 left the city's residents seething. After the snow season, the department came under additional fire because of poorly swept streets and lackadaisical garbage collection.[4]

Representatives of civic groups and settlement houses became increasingly vocal in their criticism of the DSC. The University Settlement, which took particular interest in the issue of clean streets in its crowded and impoverished Lower East Side neighborhood, issued a report noting that "the Street Cleaning Department . . . has allowed our streets to degenerate into a state of filth and unwholesomeness. . . . Heaps of rubbish before every house, the dozens of un-emptied garbage and ash cans, unswept streets, [and] crossings which are pools of black mud . . . [epitomize] the unsightly disease-breeding conditions of East Side thoroughfares."[5]

The Woman's Municipal League of New York (WML), a volunteer civic group, was particularly active in monitoring the DSC and promoting programs to enhance civic and personal sanitation. Because of ineffective garbage collection and street sweeping, the league warned that "in the crowded East Side . . . there seems to be every danger of disease developing."[6]

The WML was distressed that the DSC had failed to launch educational efforts to reduce the massive litter problem. Nor, its members added, were police officers being reminded of their responsibilities regarding enforcement of the litter laws. Contrary to Craven's assertion that budgetary restraints precluded a smooth-running operation, the influential civic group maintained that poor worker morale and worker inefficiency were the main problems, for which they held the commissioner responsible. The WML believed that these problems were inevitable in a system in which building janitors were forced to tip DSC drivers if they wanted their refuse removed, unfit men were foisted on the department through politically connected foremen and district superintendents, and effective worker training and supervision hardly existed.

League members therefore urged the commissioner to fight and "smash a well entrenched and hoary system," but they were clearly losing faith in Craven's ability to do so. Reflecting the common perception that the viability of the social fabric depended in no small way upon proper public sanitation, the civic group declared that "the results of his [Craven's] incapacity and indifference are written in filth and disorder all over Manhattan."[7]

With accusations of incompetence and corruption receiving frequent press exposure, the WML helped launch a campaign in April 1907 to arouse public opinion and force the DSC to fulfill its obligations. The league cooperated with the prestigious New York Academy of Medicine and the City Club, the latter a patrician group broadly concerned with governmental corruption and inefficiency, in forming a coalition of twenty-five civic organizations, known as the Streets Conference Committee. Members of the coalition built on investigations of the DSC already performed by the WML, presenting a completed survey of problems associated with city street cleaning and trash collection to the newspapers with accompanying recommendations. As the group most cognizant of the crisis within the DSC, the WML prodded the Streets Conference Committee, calling for Craven's dismissal in May, before the survey was ready to be published. Clearly, Craven was in political trouble even before the strike.[8]

On June 25, three hundred fifty drivers walked off their jobs on the East Side of Manhattan. The newspapers initially reported the strikers' vague complaints about layoffs, forced overtime work, and their feeling that the DSC deputy commissioner, "Big Bill" Edwards, overworked the men. An informal workers' committee had repeatedly attempted to confer with Commissioner Craven but were told to discuss their grievances with Edwards. After an unproductive meeting with Edwards, the drivers allied themselves with the Teamsters Union (Local 658) and struck.[9]

Craven informed the press that he would talk with the strikers, if they returned to work. Maintaining that the drivers' grievances were vague, he claimed that he had "tried hard to find out . . . exactly what the men want. Some of the men who are not very enthusiastic about striking do not know themselves." Craven predicted that the men would be back on the job the following day.[10]

Other DSC officials were more uneasy. The day of June 25 was sweltering, and it felt all the more so because until that date it had been the coolest June in seventy-five years. The temperature climbed to eighty-nine degrees, with high humidity. Eight heat prostration cases were reported in the city. Some DSC officials worried about the public health consequences of leaving garbage to fester in such heat.[11]

Concerns over public health mounted during the strike, partly because most people of the era believed that epidemic bacterial diseases were a constant danger lurking in the shadows. In reality, *endemic* diseases—maladies that were constantly present such as tuberculosis and childhood dysentery—were the chief causes of death in urban America. Nevertheless, partly because these ailments were ever-present in the environment, they did not seem as frightening as the great *epidemic* diseases such as cholera and yellow fever, which had occurred relatively infrequently even during their heyday in the nineteenth century. The very infrequency of the epidemics had added a fear of the unknown to the anxiety produced by their alarming symptoms, rapid spread, and extremely deadly potential. It had been only fifteen years since cholera had caused tens of thousands of deaths in Russia and only twenty-nine years since yellow fever had resulted in the death of 10 percent of the population of Memphis, Tennessee.[12]

By 1907, epidemic outbreaks could be successfully managed through quarantine and other public health measures that had been improved through knowledge gained in the study of bacteriology. Although most physicians knew this fact in an intellectual sense, many were not ready to accept it emotionally. After all, bacteriology was in an early and still somewhat tentative stage of development and, like the general public, physicians were conditioned by still-potent memories or tales of epidemic outbreaks. In this context, it is not surprising that newspaper coverage was sensational whenever cases of epidemic disease were reported in the Western world in the early 1900s. Indeed, the specter of unexpected waves of sudden death from cholera and yellow fever hung like a sword of Damocles over the Progressive Era consciousness. Thus a massive garbage strike in New York City was bound to kindle fears of a deadly epidemic.[13]

Public apprehension during the strike also reflected a general uncertainty about the etiology of disease. During much of the nineteenth century, medical opinion had been split between "contagionists," who believed that disease was transmitted from person to person, and "anticontagionists," who emphasized that poor sanitary conditions produced foul air containing noxious fumes ("miasma") that were responsible for much disease.[14] As nineteenth-century physicians learned more about contagion, many theorists came to accept a modified miasma theory, which some medical historians term "contingent-contagionism." In this schema, diseases were caused by contagia. But these contagia—which until the 1880s were usually conceived in terms of a chemical ("zymotic") fermentation process that poisoned and broke down body tissue—could take hold only in conjunction with foul air, unhealthy soil, noxious social conditions, intemperate personal lifestyle choices, or inborn constitutional weaknesses that undermined one's resistance.

Within this context, nineteenth-century sanitary reformers voiced apprehension about foul air produced by gases emanating from poorly built privies or improperly ventilated sewerage lines, or produced by the accumulation of carbon dioxide exhaled by human beings crowded into congested, poorly ventilated housing. Contingent-contagionist precepts, with their strong overlay of miasmatic concerns, were an important component in the viewpoint of both lay and physician sanitary reformers, who pioneered efforts to ameliorate public-health and related social conditions in Europe and America in the mid- and late nineteenth century. Their endeavors helped instigate major sanitary campaigns that gave rise to improved street cleaning services, the construction of extensive underground sewerage and fresh water systems for household use, and rudimentary tenement housing and workplace safety legislation. By removing sources of fecal infection and raising the living standards of millions, these measures made significant contributions to public health, even when the bacteriological explanation for their efficacy was misunderstood or not yet known.[15]

During the second half of the nineteenth century, the contagionist germ theory of disease increasingly gained favor among medical theorists. Aided by the previous decades' important technological advances in microscopy, the French chemistry professor Louis Pasteur virtually pulled the theoretical legs out from under the popular zymotic view of disease in the late 1850s. Contrary to the zymotic theory, in which infections were considered to be the product of chemical fermentations, Pasteur's experiments demonstrated that living bacterial organisms were the causal agents of infections. And his experiments in the 1860s undermined the scientific basis of the persistent belief that bacteria could, *de novo*, spontaneously generate. The spontaneous generation thesis had bolstered those contingent-contagionists who accepted the existence of bacteria but believed that such microorganisms needed miasmatic or other negative environmental conditions to kindle their existence.

In these findings, Pasteur did much to lay the groundwork for individuals such as the German physician Robert Koch, who in the 1870s and 1880s would further develop the link between germs and disease, effectively proving that infectious diseases are caused by discrete entities that attack particular human organs. In the late 1870s, Koch developed new laboratory techniques that greatly enhanced the ability of researchers to isolate, and thus identify, specific microorganisms that caused particular diseases. This accelerated the process whereby Koch and other researchers, from the late 1870s through the 1880s, discovered numerous specific bacteria—such as those causing tuberculosis, cholera, typhoid fever, and diphtheria.

The identification of specific bacteria, in turn, opened the way for researchers to figure out how these diseases are transmitted, and even to begin to make significant strides toward discovering how these diseases might be prevented or ameliorated. With Pasteur's breakthrough development of a rabies vaccine (in 1885) and Emil von Behring's development of a therapeutic serum that greatly enhanced the body's ability to ward off the effects of diphtheria (in 1890), an enthralled public greatly reinforced the prestige accorded to the past generation of bacteriological researchers, to the point that by the 1890s all but the most recalcitrant scientists were convinced of the validity of the germ theory of disease.[16]

In fact, by the early 1900s, the association of bacteriology with scientific legitimacy had begun to erode some public health reformers' self-identification with the environment-oriented sanitary reform movement. This was particularly the case among those physicians who emphasized that microbes are transmitted through personal contact, and who stressed their unique professional responsibility to understand and control such dangers.[17]

Nevertheless, even in 1907, many practicing physicians (and many nonphysician public health activists) had not yet discredited factors other than the specific bacterium. Having received their education many years earlier, these physicians were still influenced by transitional theories linking miasmatic and contagious causation. Nor did the modern era's more mechanistic view of the body prevent many physicians from partially adhering to older conceptions of the body as a system in flux, continuously interacting with external and internal stimuli. They believed that diet, mental and moral states, exercise, the degree of personal cleanliness, and inborn constitutional factors influenced the balance of each person's system and, likewise, that external factors such as air quality, housing, family relations, and the degree of environmental cleanliness were powerful factors affecting one's system as well. Clearly, there was no definitive boundary between measures considered necessary to promote personal or social felicity and measures to promote health. In short, the anxieties of physicians and lay people during the strike were reinforced by the intellectual legacy of the miasma theory, with its emphasis on foul air and filth, and the enduring emphasis on the body as a system that can be affected by deleterious social and psychological phenomena.

The newer laboratory-based bacteriological approach to medicine, with its more precise identification of the sources and modes of transmission of infectious disease, offered the physician new prospects of wealth and prestige. Nevertheless, many physicians remained uneasy about this new direction. Some were afraid that their traditional clinical bedside role, with its potential for stimulating the healing powers of individuals and their families, would be undercut by the near-formulaic protocols of disease specificity. Others distrusted new trends in public health that seemed to overemphasize the prevention of specific diseases through medical epidemiology and personal hygiene measures at the expense of programs geared toward general well-being that could make life easier for the poor (for example, by providing cleaner streets or improved ventilation in tenement housing). In short, they feared that a preoccupation with laboratory-based medical science would preclude the holistic search for community well-being that had been the basis for community sanitation and related social reform efforts during the nineteenth century. The public's panicky reactions to the odors and filth of the garbage strike would reinforce the perception of the old school that contingent-contagionism was indeed relevant to public health. Like old warhorses that bolt at the sound of a trumpet, many of these physicians were eager to offer their sometimes shrill advice to the public during the strike. The crisis atmosphere of the garbage strike provided them much public attention and respect, even as they themselves were aware that laboratory science was chipping away at the familiar moorings of their medical beliefs.[18]

Contrary to Commissioner Craven's expectations during the first day, the strike did not die a quick death. By the second day, June 26, nearly every driver on the East Side was out, and an increasing number on the West Side joined them. Craven claimed that "many of the men would come back if they were not afraid they would be attacked."[19] (This is not implausible, considering the violence that followed during the next several days.) The press reported the presence of large piles of refuse in crowded immigrant quarters "where disease is always ready to spread," tying up traffic and creating "dangerous odors [that] wafted on the heated air."[20] Hospitals complained that the "tainted atmosphere" was killing their more debilitated patients.[21] And with residents depositing their household trash in mounds on the street, it was all the more difficult for DSC street sweepers—who were already talking about joining the strikers—to gather and remove the accumulating quantities of horse manure and other detritus from the roadways.

A break in the hot weather brought some relief to residents on June 27, the third day of the strike. But by now, three-fourths of Manhattan's seven hundred fifty drivers had walked off their jobs. Tension mounted as the fear of disease spread. Mayor George B. McClellan Jr., son of the controversial Civil War general and opponent of Abraham Lincoln in the election of 1864, tried to calm civic anxieties, stating that "the accumulation of garbage . . . while unsightly and noxious to the senses, is not in a state to spread disease."[22] Nevertheless, anxious residents and DSC street sweepers attempted to set fire to the growing mass in the streets. A reporter for William Randolph Hearst's *New York American* called to mind the city's traditional torchlit political parades, observing that the streets of the Upper East Side "resembled an election night" as bonfires of burning garbage lit up the night skies for dozens of blocks from Fifty-fifth Street up to Harlem. Neighbors attempted to shovel the streets' decaying refuse onto the fires, but they barely dented the mounds, and the resulting dense black smoke itself tormented residents.[23]

The drivers made little headway with Craven, who stated to the press that the strikers "want permission to disobey the rules of the department and to boss the foremen." Employee spokesmen met with representatives of the Teamsters Union on the night of June 27 to draw up a formal list of demands. They vowed to present these as an ultimatum to Craven. If he did not relent, representatives of the department's sweepers promised to join in the strike. The major demands called for hearings for fines of any sort, the restoration of job tenure to employees who had been unfairly deprived of this benefit, and a forty-eight-hour work week with twenty-five cents per hour for overtime.[24]

The issue of fines was crucial. Drivers contended that they were often docked as much as two weeks' pay for paltry offenses. In other city departments, a complaint concerning an employee would first be brought before high departmental officials. Fines or any other disciplinary action were imposed only after a hearing had been conducted by these officials. In the DSC, however, district superintendents and over one hundred foremen had the power to impose fines summarily. One worker used an old British term connoting severity in stating that this system of fines amounted to "Jersey justice."[25] Moreover, rather than being purely a work-related disciplinary device, fines were also used as a whip to maintain a system in which politically connected officials would rule their own fiefdoms, unafraid of challenge from their intimidated workers. Craven was not strong enough to subdue this patronage-based system, which reform-minded critics had for years criticized for its corrosive effects upon efficiency and morale.[26]

Because their work was related to public health, employees could legally be forced to remain on the job, without compensation, beyond the city's norm of an eight-hour day (six days per week). Thus average workdays of nine and one-half hours were justified on the basis of a statute that was meant to apply only in public health emergencies. A Socialist Party newspaper, using a traditional analogy, compared these conditions to the slavery of the antebellum South.[27] Craven told the press that he worked the men more than eight hours solely in emergencies, and that only a few extra minutes were required on such occasions. In a departmental report, however, he stated that uncompensated overtime work was in fact a problem, but he believed that there was no viable alternative, given the department's lean appropriations and the considerable demand for its services. (Manpower resources were overtaxed particularly during the cooler months, in which DSC services were strained to the limit due to the additional bulk produced by waste ash from the burning of coal in stoves and furnaces.)[28]

The issue of employment security deepened the drivers' discontent. Departmental rules stipulated that after eighteen months of employment, workers earned a badge that entitled them to the highest wage—eight hundred dollars per year—and job security. The Craven administration had nevertheless fired numerous employees after the winter season, since fewer men were needed during the months in which waste ash was less of a factor. Craven took advantage of this situation, firing more men—including previously tenured ones—than the circumstances warranted. He soon rehired many of these same men, classifying them as temporary "extras" in order to obtain their labor at lower wages. Thus a certain amount of money could be saved for other uses in the department (including, ironically, to hire some additional workers during peak months).

Craven also maintained that DSC employees received better pay than most other unskilled laborers and consequently had no right to complain about salaries.[29] While it is true that eight hundred dollars per year was a satisfactory salary when compared to that of many unskilled laborers, it was still barely enough to provide a family a decent standard of living. The department's manipulation of tenure and imposition of heavy fines made it impossible for most drivers to attain even this level of pay. Craven's attitude ignored the views of the late George Waring, who, as commissioner during the 1890s, came to recognize that there was a relationship between salary levels and productivity. DSC employees were subject to frequent accidents, sunstroke, pneumonia, and other maladies attributable to the strenuous and unsanitary conditions under which they labored. Given these conditions, and the vigorous demands placed upon DSC employees, Waring contended that payment of less than a decent wage engendered an unproductive and disgruntled staff.[30]

Although conceding that the situation was bad, Commissioner Craven optimistically informed Mayor McClellan that his men would soon be back at work. Seemingly unconcerned, Craven had not attempted to hire large numbers of extra men, nor had he spoken to officials of the city's health department about the strike situation and its potential impact on public health.[31] Community representatives were less nonchalant. Officials of one Lower East Side neighborhood organization pleaded with the mayor to end the strike "without regard to the merits of the dispute"; and David Blaustein of the Educational Alliance, a Lower East Side settlement house, complained both to the mayor and to Thomas Darlington, the health department commissioner.[32] Hopes were raised when Dr. Darlington announced on the afternoon of June 27 that his department would immediately begin an investigation of the situation. Rumors began to circulate that Craven would soon resign.[33]

Events took a dramatic turn on June 28. A columnist for the *Tribune* reported that "a [political] bomb exploded . . . in the office of Street Cleaning Commissioner Craven when it was learned that the Mayor ordered the Health Department to clean the city of its accumulated garbage, acting over Mr. Craven's head." Mayor McClellan had been forced to order the health department "to do Craven's work" by pressure from delegations of indignant citizens and by the public's growing fear of pestilence.[34]

Darlington put his assistant sanitary superintendent, Dr. Walter Bensel, directly in charge. Craven's political star was falling fast. Bensel ignored Craven in his statement to the press, while noting that DSC Deputy Commissioner Edwards "will do everything he can to help us." Furthermore, Bensel observed that carts from the DSC stables would be deployed "regardless of any orders from the department, superintendents, or foremen. I am in full charge of this work."[35] Darlington added that "this situation has been put squarely up to the Health Department, and it is a matter that concerns the health of the city and I intend to let nothing interfere with the complete solution of the trouble."[36] High expectations rode on the health department takeover. The *American* observed that "only an official like Dr. Bensel, representing the Health Department . . . can straighten out the situation . . . and save the administration from condemnation such as no city administration ever before has been made to feel."[37] Ordinances authorized the health department to spend almost unlimited funds in public health emergencies, and it possessed a special squad of seventy policemen to enforce the sanitary code.[38] New Yorkers were heartened by these facts, particularly in light of the public's perception of the powers inherent in scientific medical expertise.

The prestige of physicians had declined during the early decades of the previous century, as statistical studies cast doubt on the efficacy of their orthodox techniques and as various medical sects competed with physicians for status as authoritative healers. Physicians did, nevertheless, garner increased prestige by midcentury through the participation of medical luminaries in the sanitary reform movement. And the subsequent work of Pasteur, Koch, and others filled a tremendous gap in biological knowledge concerning bacteria that had both impeded the advancement of medicine and detracted from the credibility of physicians. By the late nineteenth and early twentieth centuries, physicians were able to employ findings from bacteriology that significantly strengthened the public health movement—through the introduction, for example, of relatively disease-free water and milk supplies, more effective quarantine measures for people with communicable diseases, and educational efforts to promote better personal and public hygiene. While improved nutrition in reality contributed more than anything to the period's impressive reduction in disease, public health measures did in fact play an important role in raising living standards (and thus in lowering the incidence of disease), and the public gave a considerable degree of credit to such measures. Although most practicing physicians did not actively participate in the public health movement, and although many leaders within the movement actually were not physicians, the identification of an important segment of the medical profession with the public health movement promoted greater respect for the profession as a whole. In addition, the use of aseptic surgery—another innovation made possible by the new understanding of bacteria—helped save many lives. And new technological phenomena, such as the X-ray machine, held forth the promise of ever-expanding horizons for medicine. These advances were viewed with awe by a public that began to foresee a world previously unknown, one in which human mastery of disease would be significantly enhanced.[39]

The general rise of specialization within most professions also reinforced the stature of physicians. In the mid-nineteenth century, many Americans had taken as an article of faith the belief that, in their nation, social conflict could be resolved naturally and harmoniously, either through the hard work of individuals, which would bring personal advancement, or through the political leadership of broad-minded men who eschewed narrow desires and interests. By the turn of the century, this viewpoint was being severely threatened by the discord inherent in the urbanization of society.[40] Eager to have harmony restored, many people placed their faith in experts whose status was reinforced by the imprimatur of science. After all, was it not scientists who had discovered the sources of infectious disease and then taken promising steps to prevent these scourges? Had not technical expertise made possible a system of transcontinental railroads that ran as if by clockwork? And had not scientists and engineers been largely responsible for the invention and development of the electric light bulb, indoor plumbing, the automobile, and numerous other items that promised the coming of a heretofore undreamed of world of possibilities? Then surely, the logic ran, experts could make our cities function efficiently by putting to use their impressive scientific, engineering, and accounting knowledge. Good men would still be needed, but now they were to be greatly assisted or indeed embodied by the specialized, objective professional. Progressives put great faith in this combination. Indeed, many of them retained a sense of ingenuous hopefulness that seems almost incomprehensible in our own era.[41]

While they benefited from a general idolization of science and expertise, the Progressive Era physicians' seeming ability to save life and limb catapulted them into a realm of public veneration all their own. It was with this public mandate of authority that Dr. Bensel and the health department stepped into the strike on June 28. Health department officials embraced a style of pseudo-military efficiency that was gaining popularity during these years of Theodore Roosevelt's administration. "God help the man who interferes with my work," Bensel remarked, as he drafted eighty-five health department employees, summoned one hundred workers from the Otisville Sanitarium in upstate Orange County, solicited laborers from homeless shelters, and contracted with agencies that specialized in procuring strikebreakers. Bensel emphatically declared that the "situation [is] well in hand."[42]

Despite these manly assertions, many New Yorkers began to panic at the sight and smell of garbage mounds that at times reached over five feet in height. The *Tribune* stated that sanitary conditions in East Harlem's "Little Italy" were "beyond description," and the next day asserted that "the smells in districts never noted for ambrosial fragrance were stunning." The reporter deplored the piles of refuse and, reflecting an enduring preoccupation with aerial contamination, lamented that "the rain [that had] poured down in the afternoon and night soaked this mass and made it steam." The *American,* observing the same effect, caused by sunlight shining on mounds of wet garbage, reported that "clouds of deadly vapor" were rising from these piles. And the paper declared that hundreds of garbage barrels were on any given street, with millions of flies "ready to carry pestilence into the homes as soon as the garbage has rotted." The city, it added, "never before knew what it would mean if the Street Cleaning Department were crippled by a strike, but the horrible stenches carried the fear of a citywide fever into the heart of so many thousands that physicians everywhere were advising people to get their young ones out of town as soon as possible." One health department official warned that "if we don't clear the East Side of this accumulated matter, the children will die off by the thousands."[43]

With public fears of disease mounting, DSC and health department officials arranged to augment their force of strikebreakers by hiring over a thousand men from a Philadelphia labor contractor, three hundred of whom were due to arrive on June 30.[44] Meanwhile, violent disturbances broke out at the first attempt to use strikebreakers on a large scale.

Some of the worst conflicts occurred in East Harlem's Little Italy. The DSC employed many unskilled Italian American laborers. Nativist prejudice was commonly directed against this ethnic group during the era, and newspapers played to these sentiments during the strike. "Most of the drivers are Italians," observed the Pulitzer newspaper, the *Evening World,* "and whatever violence has been displayed thus far has been incited by Italians." The strike, like numerous other Progressive Era events, was suffused with ethnic overtones that sharpened the public's anxieties.[45]

For many years, New York's Italian population had been composed largely of men awaiting assignment to railroad work gangs throughout America, temporary workers earning money to provide for a higher standard of living upon re-emigration to Italy, or men working to earn passage-money for their families to join them in America. Such a population was typically too unsettled to become involved in labor unions or other collective activities for social change. By 1907, however, the Italians were becoming a more stable, family-oriented community rather than an agglomeration of disparate individuals. The social basis for greater support of ongoing union-organizing efforts was thus taking shape. This was exemplified, in effect, by the support that neighbors gave to DSC strikers in 1907.[46]

On June 28, a formidable contingent of Italian American strikers and their sympathizers overturned garbage cans throughout East Harlem and intimidated strikebreakers.[47] Forty strikebreakers were sent out to work from the area's DSC stable, only to be forced to line up against the walls of nearby buildings by men brandishing knives, clubs, and revolvers. The strikebreakers returned to the stable, refusing to go out unless a policeman accompanied each cart. Constantly expanding crowds gathered all afternoon near the stable, jeering and threatening the strikebreakers and the two hundred policemen sent in as reinforcements. Under pressure from Bensel, the police department ordered its men henceforth "to put aside all considerations of gentleness or mild treatment to cope with violence." Virtually all of the city's reserve policemen were subsequently ordered onto duty for the remainder of the strike.[48]

On the Lower East Side, wagons leaving the DSC stable, each with a police guardian, encountered a crowd of seven hundred people. Bottles and stones showered down from the rooftops. A melee ensued in which dozens of drivers were dragged from their carts and beaten. The police sustained several injuries and drew their revolvers "to fight their way out."[49] Not surprisingly, fifty men drafted from the health department refused to work as strikebreakers after this incident. Darlington promptly fired these employees, referring to them as "jellyfish . . . with no backbone. . . . a few stones and a brick or two falling from the top of a house scares them off."[50]

Still, there were glimmers of hope. In an open letter to the *Times,* the strikers stated their willingness to abide by arbitration. Moreover, Commissioner Craven, stung by his fall from ultimate power in the department, agreed to a request from Tecumseh Sherman, the state labor commissioner, to meet with a delegation of strikers on June 29.[51]

On June 29 and 30, strikebreakers were deployed more effectively, but political tensions intensified. Darlington attempted to defuse public fears by stating that there was no "immediate danger" of an epidemic.[52] Nevertheless, his concurrent refusal to rule out the possibility of widespread disease, coupled with the newspapers' airing of dire warnings from respected physicians, only served to spread the perception that pestilence was near.

The fear of disease was not, however, the sole factor undergirding the era's penchant for sanitation (and, perforce, its strong reaction to the garbage strike). To understand why the *Times* would state that "the very existence of the city" depended on the smooth operation of the DSC, we must realize that sanitation was equated not only with the struggle against disease per se, but also with civilization, morality, and an orderly way of life.[53] Cleanliness was popularly associated with wholesomeness, good character, and social order. Sanitary reformers expected that the provision of public sanitation measures would usher in "not only a healthier but a higher and more goodly civilization."[54] Filth was equated with ignorance and was viewed as a breeding ground of crime and other social perils. Accordingly, M. T. Harris, a New York rabbi concerned with urban social problems, advocated housing reform measures to help "prevent the conditions which breed uncleanliness and crime." He noted that "to keep clean requires space, light, and privacy." Without these elements, people find it difficult to maintain "pride, self-respect, and modesty. . . . [Then] moral degeneracy follows."[55]

To many mothers in the tenements of New York, therefore, the overflowing communal toilet in the hallway was part of an ensemble of overcrowding, filth, poor nutrition, and disease that symbolized the gulf between their own families' existence and society's ideal of "decency." These women often were forced by economic circumstances to take jobs outside of the home or work long hours doing sweatshop piecework inside the home. Many yearned for the time and money needed to fashion a wholesome home environment for their children— one with clean clothes, supervised play, regular meals, and other middle-class amenities.[56]

Most New Yorkers believed that cleanliness, good health, wholesomeness, and education were interactive ingredients in the formula that would allow families to rise out of the lower classes. Darlington, in urging social reform measures to alleviate the unwholesome surroundings of slum dwellers, had once observed that "sickness is the enemy of prosperity, and physical improvement means mental and moral improvement." In an era in which Darwinian concepts influenced social thought, philosophers postulated that the families that struggled successfully to remain healthy and moral would be the mainstay of civilization. In this context, a garbage strike was seen as a threat to individual families' rising expectations and to the "moral condition" of the entire social order.[57]

Many people associated disease with what a WML member referred to as the "unclean nationalities" of New York's immigrant districts, and with the intemperate or unhealthy behaviors—from drinking heavily to spitting in streetcars—that the inhabitants of these districts purportedly indulged in more often than most city residents.[58] Poverty, illness, and a lack of decency were considered to be interrelated elements of a complex whole. Given the moral component of this viewpoint, progressive reformers often frankly expressed the hope that poor people would learn to stop spitting in public (a practice associated with the spread of tuberculosis), bathe more often, wash their hands and their clothing, and refrain from the heavy consumption of alcohol. Without such individual efforts to attain decency, families would have no hope of rising above the ill health–poverty nexus. Physical and economic improvement were inexorably linked with what Rabbi Harris termed "moral cleanliness," and the well-being of society as a whole was presumed to be imperiled by the critical mass of demoralization, degradation, and disease generated within slum districts.[59]

Progressive Era reform organizations often balanced this emphasis on individual responsibility with a concern for social conditions that were not the fault of the individual—conditions that in fact hampered the moral improvement of even the most well-meaning tenement dweller. Reform-minded individuals, for example, maintained that overcrowded and ill-ventilated housing produced tenants who were more susceptible to tuberculosis, and that tuberculosis and other poverty-related illnesses, in turn, made it much more difficult to work one's way out of poverty. Many civic groups, therefore, lobbied for housing reform, improved schools, child labor laws, factory safety inspection, clean water and milk, and of course, effective street cleaning.[60]

The popular appeal of the Woman's Municipal League was rooted in its particular concern for issues with which mothers could identify. Many individuals believed that a natural continuum existed between the home and the community. That which took place in the home affected the community, while that which took place in the community affected the home and family. If a mother was concerned about the cleanliness of her home, it was just another step to appeal to her to help create more salubrious conditions in the community, that greater home in which she and her family resided.[61]

In addition to their efforts to monitor DSC activities, the WML's predominantly middle- and upper-class members organized programs to inform the public about other aspects of "municipal housekeeping." Members particularly sought to educate poor people to keep their own homes clean, and encouraged them to take an interest in the cleanliness and wholesomeness of their community. Pamphlets discussing these topics were distributed in many languages to

tenement dwellers. WML members also funded a number of community-oriented services, including the provision of ice-water fountains in slum districts
and summer recreational opportunities for young girls. And, of course, members
lobbied the city government for more effective street cleaning and other sanitary
reform measures.[62]

The ideal of municipal housekeeping struck a popular chord across class lines,
even though the poor sometimes resented middle-class society for expecting a
level of cleanliness and decorum that was difficult to achieve on a meager income.
Although many people today are uncomfortable with the thought of wealthier people instilling middle-class values among poverty-stricken individuals of
other ethnic groups—a more coercive example of which was the WML's efforts
to censor the budding movie industry—most lower-income families urgently
wanted their members to break out from the tenement environment of filth,
overcrowding, crime, and disease. And for many, "decency" signified a way out
of the slums—if not for the adults themselves, then for their children.[63]

In short, to early twentieth-century city residents, the concept of sanitation
carried a symbolic meaning that produced a special sense of urgency in the
public's perception of the garbage workers' strike. The strong emphasis of many
civic groups on personal and public cleanliness served to reinforce the more
general belief that health, morality, and an ordered way of life all depended on
proper sanitation.

Physicians' comments during the strike illustrate the compelling nature of the
crisis, as well as prevailing conceptions of disease. Germs, poor surroundings,
and the foul air arising from what one doctor termed the "malodorous decomposition" of garbage in the streets all played a role in a statement issued by the
Coroner's Physician, Dr. Timothy Lehane: "The garbage left in the streets to rot
will breed germs, which will infect the crowded tenement houses, and unless the
strike is stopped quickly, we will have a plague on our hands. Infants will become
stricken with diseases which under ordinary circumstances could be easily cured,
but with the decaying garbage lying around rotting in the streets the air in the
tenements will become so bad that it will be impossible to cope successfully with
the sickness."[64]

Clearly, the miasma theory—foul air as a key element in disease—had not died
by 1907 but had been juxtaposed with the newer germ theory. This reliance on
older beliefs to help grasp the germ theory served to heighten the fears of many
physicians and lay people.

Dr. Edward E. O'Donnell's remarks during the strike illustrate the prominent
role that numerous physicians still ascribed to emotional factors, as well as the era's
common association of poor hygiene and contamination with foreigners: "The
odor of accumulating garbage had a depressing effect upon persons and placed
them in a receptive condition for disease germs. . . . I shouldn't be surprised if

Asiatic cholera and bubonic plague should follow, for there are many foreigners in the crowded districts where the garbage situation is at its worst."[65]

Other contemporary accounts of the crisis illustrate a curious mixture of old and new medical beliefs. Dr. Walter G. Crump, a member of New York University's medical faculty, expressed surprise that thousands of people had not already been stricken by disease, and he stated that the dead dogs and cats he had seen were "no doubt killed . . . [by] the poisonous fumes from the decomposing garbage." Reflecting a tendency among health professionals to combine the older miasma theory and the newer germ theory in focusing on the infective power of street dust or house dust, Crump noted that the meat, fruit, and vegetables being exposed to "germ dust" from the filthy thoroughfares would soon become "coated with germs flying through the air." Voicing the era's faith in scientific expertise (and the prestigious ambitions of the medical profession), he declared that "no one can realize what a serious thing this is unless he understands the situation thoroughly from a medical point of view."[66]

Other physicians predicted the imminent visitation of typhus, tuberculosis, yellow fever, and serious intestinal disorders such as typhoid and the more common diarrheal ailments that were so frequently deadly to younger children during that era. Because children were playing in the rotting matter left in the streets during the strike, and because flies might be transporting this matter to food items that New Yorkers would consume, many physicians feared that the incidence of dysentery ailments would soon increase.

A health officer for the Port of New York, Dr. A. H. Doty, was one of the more optimistic of the medical commentators, observing that garbage could not produce any types of microorganisms that were not already present and that, consequently, an epidemic was unlikely. The *Tribune,* however, headlined his comments ("Expert Quiets Fears") next to another headline that proclaimed "Physicians Fearful . . . See Epidemic Arising."[67]

While New Yorkers tried to cope with the threat of disease during the strike, labor violence continued to wrack the community. On June 29, numerous fights, brick-throwing incidents, and other assorted confrontations, often with accompanying arrests, once again kept potential strikebreakers away. "Upper Little Italy," observed the *American,* "was crowded with excited men. . . . Residents intermingled freely with the striking drivers and there was a strong undercurrent of brewing trouble from the start."[68] The *Evening World* expanded on the story, noting that the "strikers began to make trouble. . . . Great throngs of Italians mingled with the striking drivers of the same nationality, and the strikebreakers were soon trembling with apprehension. Details of police moved through the crowds with clubs swinging." Once acquainted with the possibility of striker violence, two out of every three strikebreakers chose not to remain on the job; and with violence hampering efforts to dispatch those strikebreakers and regular workers who did remain, only one-third of the usual number of carts were deployed in Manhattan on June 29.[69]

Nevertheless, the police force was strengthening its presence. By Sunday, June 30, five hundred policemen had been deployed on the Lower East Side alone. The authorities let it be known that rioting strikers would be summarily consigned to the workhouse upon arraignment. Tenement dwellers were forbidden to go onto their rooftops, and saloons were closed. Police began using military convoy formations to guard the carts, with at least one policeman per vehicle. On Fourteenth Street, which funneled into the dock area where drivers dumped their loads, additional policemen were placed twenty-five paces apart along the entire length of the street. Health department officials wanted it "clearly demonstrated . . . to the people of the East Side themselves, that the Department could and would do the work, and that it could be carried on in a decent and orderly manner."[70] Approximately one-quarter of the usual number of drivers reported to work that day, and the heavy police presence did help keep striker disturbances to a minimum.[71]

Meanwhile, Mayor McClellan felt the political heat. With the WML leading the way, the Streets Conference Committee publicly disclosed the contents of an appeal that it planned to present to the mayor. Its petition called for emergency action, without regard for expense, to clean the streets immediately. Pressing for a reorganization of the DSC, the committee strongly implied that Commissioner Craven should be fired. With concern over the possibility of an epidemic running high, the presence of the New York Academy of Medicine on the Streets Conference Committee lent extra weight to its recommendations.[72] Various East Side organizations also called upon the mayor. McClellan was shaken by the description of conditions on the Lower East Side related to him by Joseph Barondess, a garment industry labor leader and spokesman for the Federation of Jewish Societies. Barondess seemed to sum up the feelings of many New Yorkers when he urged the mayor to allow arbitration of the strike. "I grant that the strikers are wrong," he stated, "and I do not appear for them. I am here because of the great danger of an epidemic. There is sickness on the East Side now, and it is spreading. There will be deaths tomorrow." To add to the administration's woes, the three hundred strikebreakers expected from Philadelphia failed to appear.[73]

The meeting on June 29 between the strikers and Craven bore no fruit. Craven commented afterwards that the system of fines was proper, adding that "[if an employee] goes into a saloon . . . he knows what to expect."[74] The drivers then met on June 30 with Teamsters representatives. Together, they called on the Brooklyn drivers to join the strike on July 1 and agreed to bypass Craven and meet with the mayor himself; if unsuccessful there, they would bring the Manhattan sweepers into the strike. During the drivers' meeting, amidst bitter denunciations of Craven, George W. Prescott, second vice-president of the United Teamsters of

America, pointed to an encouraging political factor. "That little boy down at City Hall, Mr. McClellan, the Mayor," he observed, "may need us at the next mayoralty election. So may some of his followers and district leaders, and I'll find out who is back of this stand against our just demands."[75]

Meanwhile, the Central Federated Union (CFU), the core organization of American Federation of Labor (AFL) affiliates in New York City, decided to support the drivers and the fledgling Teamsters local.[76] The CFU's executive board appointed a committee to call on Mayor McClellan to demand Craven's dismissal. If unsuccessful, they publicly vowed to appeal to the governor of New York, Charles Evans Hughes, to "impeach" the mayor.[77]

July 1 began inauspiciously. According to the *Tribune*, "A sullen air of menace pervaded the Lower East Side. . . . The tempers of drivers were growing ugly, and the police, worn out by more than twenty-four hours of continuous work . . . were near the end of their powers of endurance. . . . 'The men can't stand much more,' said Police Inspector Burns. 'We are none of us getting any sleep. We are few of us getting any food. There may be serious trouble, if conditions remain unchanged.'"[78]

A fair amount of garbage was collected that morning. But by the afternoon, violence erupted uptown. The *American* reported that "Italian bombs," made from the fireworks used in Italian festivals, were pitched from rooftops in East Harlem, while a "mob" of several hundred people was dispersed by police who "cracked many heads."[79] Meanwhile, a crowd composed predominantly of African Americans attacked police-escorted strikebreakers in Harlem. (In addition to large numbers of Italian American drivers, the DSC in 1907 normally employed members of numerous ethnic groups, including African Americans.) Police were "forced to use their clubs regardless of sex," as African American women purposefully clung to policemen, giving male rioters the opportunity to attack them. Police reserves were called in to clear the area, which was put under curfew for three hours. The garbage workers' strike had added fuel to an already tense atmosphere in the Little Africa section of Harlem, where several racial disturbances had recently occurred.[80]

Earlier that day, DSC officials were dismayed when half of the Brooklyn drivers walked off the job and the Manhattan street sweepers announced that they would join the strike the following day. In addition, contrary to the city's request, the superintendent of the parks department, a Tammany man, refused to force any of his men to work extra hours for the DSC. To top things off, the Tammany-dominated board of aldermen passed a resolution urging Mayor McClellan and Commissioner Craven to meet with the strikers. Alderman Kenneally, the resolution's sponsor, blasted the DSC, citing "unjust fines" as the main problem. Alderman "Little Tim" Sullivan, weary of having to vie with expert administrators such as Craven for influence within city departments in his area of town, criticized the commissioner and longingly recalled the days when the DSC was more thoroughly under Tammany control.[81]

Tammany Hall generally portrayed itself as the friend of the working man, and it depended on working-class votes. The organization provided informal social welfare services in return for these votes—the dispersal of holiday food or coal baskets, the provision of jobs with the city or with contractors tied to the organization, and the general availability of a personal connection in high places. Two years prior to the strike, Mayor McClellan had been subtly threatened with the loss of the Italian vote if he refused to back a pay increase for DSC employees. George Prescott's statement during the 1907 strike ("That little boy . . . may need us at the next mayoralty election") further illustrates the reliance of the city's Democratic candidates upon the unskilled labor/immigrant constituency. While McClellan had been Tammany's mayoral candidate, he was actually often at odds with the leader of that organization, Charles Francis Murphy. Nevertheless, criticisms of the DSC offered by the board of aldermen made it more likely that the mayor would seek a rapid settlement in which at least some of the strikers' demands would be accommodated.[82]

The turning point of the strike took place later in the day on July 1. Through the efforts of the CFU and the New York State Department of Labor, workers' representatives met with the mayor. McClellan was conciliatory. Although insisting that he would hear grievances only after a return to work, he promised that such a hearing would be a fair one. To show good faith, the mayor offered additional pay for the extra hours that would be required during the arduous cleanup following the strike. In a slap at Commissioner Craven, McClellan also remarked that the drivers should have approached the mayor's office in the first place, before going out on strike.[83]

The strikers' lawyer, Frank A. Acer, and state labor department officials advised the drivers that the mayor would be fair with them, whereupon the men announced that they were willing to return to work. They would "give [the mayor] a chance to show if he means business."[84]

Jubilation greeted the announcement of the strike's termination. Shouts were heard for blocks on the Lower East Side, as women waved petticoats and bandanas from tenement windows and male strikers on the roofs threw their bricks up in the air in glee. At a mass meeting of the men that night, Acer told them that "you have won."[85]

Within two days, the streets were relatively clean once again. On July 8, the politically isolated and physically ailing Craven saved face by resigning for health reasons. "To do something with this work of the cleaning of the city's streets has been the ambition of my life," he remarked, "and when I undertook the work I felt that I was going to be able to accomplish something. But I can't do it."[86] Bensel, on loan from the health department, took over the reins of the DSC for the next four months. The mayor and board of aldermen acquiesced to Bensel's recommendations during these months, adjusting themselves to the formidable combination of civic reform opinion backed by the authority of medical expertise (as well as by the threatened resumption of strike action by the men).[87] During his term in office, Bensel established a more just disciplinary system and scrapped the old system of fines. Foremen and district superintendents were now held more accountable for their actions. He also promoted the rationalization of employees' wages so that drivers would not be deprived of their duly authorized earnings, and he established fairer standards pertaining to work hours and mandatory overtime.

Bensel's brief command was one of the brighter spots in the circuitous path that the DSC took toward a more modern form of organization. Subsequent Progressive Era DSC commissioners varied in their degree of adherence to Bensel's relatively fair labor standards. Although employees were granted some significant perquisites by the end of the era (for example, pensions and medical benefits), DSC labor-management relations remained a source of friction throughout the period. The eight-hour day and fair disciplinary procedures were not firmly rooted until the 1930s, under the mayoral administration of Fiorello LaGuardia, who, de facto, recognized an employees' union.[88]

Strikes—or any social action for that matter—do not take place in a vacuum. During the Progressive Era, the radical rhetoric of labor agitators, the growth of the Socialist Party, the violence that sometimes accompanied strikes (from both labor and management), and the sheer frequency of serious strikes caused alarm at the mention of any such event. Moreover, to threaten the cleanliness of people's surroundings was to menace public health and civilization as a whole, and the connotations attached to odors were graver than those that we apprehend in the present day. Concerns about health and decency, therefore, added to the base of public fear generated by the threat of any serious strike during the Progressive Era. In short, New Yorkers were likely to perceive a garbage workers' strike as possessing the potential for disaster.[89]

The heated public reaction that accompanies a garbage workers' strike is, however, a fickle political variable. Anger and fear stemming from concerns about disease and social order can augur either well or poorly for strikers. A telling comparison may be drawn with another New York City garbage workers' strike, which occurred in 1911. As in 1907, the public was very concerned about disease and disorder, but this time its apprehension translated into support for a ruthless suppression of the strike. As a result, city officials promptly fired the strikers and replaced them, without any discussion of concessions.[90]

One key factor that helped tip the scales in 1907 was that the workers were dealing, in an era of heightened sensitivity to malfeasance, with a department already charged with corruption and incompetence by a united front of twenty-five civic groups.[91] These civic groups were products of an age in which a reform zeitgeist produced a somewhat more receptive environment for union activity than in previous years. Although affluent reformers often felt threatened by labor unions in general, the sympathy of prominent civic group members for lower-class victims of *specific* injustices often furnished a crucial measure of community pressure for the fair settlement of labor disputes. In short, employers could not count on elite hostility toward workers during labor disputes. In 1907, the fumbling administration of Commissioner Craven swung the civic groups over to an emphasis on the department's wrongdoing during the strike. By 1911, these conditions had changed. No longer under attack for corruption, the department had learned to cooperate with the WML and other civic groups. In most New Yorkers' eyes, the onus in the 1911 strike was on the strikers.[92]

In 1907 the press, reflecting community sympathies, was divided over the strike. Most papers were critical of the strikers, but some focused their wrath even more upon the DSC commissioner or the mayor.[93] In 1911, however, the press unanimously condemned the violent strikers, focusing on the need to crush them quickly. The Tammany "Tiger" was of course mindful of its labor constituency in 1907. And even more important, it smelled the scent of dying political meat, and accordingly nipped at the DSC. In 1911, with newspapers and reform groups backing the DSC, Tammany would not tread that path.[94]

The CFU usually ignored the plight of unskilled workers, as it did during the strike of 1911. In 1907, however, it sensed the political momentum of the strikers and joined the bandwagon.[95] The ambivalence of the press during 1907 and the support of the CFU and Tammany for the workers helped to tip the political scales in the direction of a just settlement. Yet, these participants' inclinations were to a significant extent conditioned by the ongoing outcry of civic groups against DSC malfeasance—a key element absent in 1911.

The outrage of the civic groups in 1907 can be more fully comprehended when set against the backdrop of the investigation into DSC corruption in 1906, which in turn followed upon the New York State utilities and insurance scandals of 1905. More generally, the pervasive disgust over corruption can be seen as a palpable representation of the desire of Progressive Era citizenry to tame or reconcile the powerful political and economic forces that were emerging with industrialization and urbanization. Within this context, the garbage workers' strike was part of a long-term process in which society fitfully adapted to the demands of modern interest groups (such as labor representatives or civic reformers) and to citizen demands for adequate public services.[96]

Melvyn Dubofsky has observed that "in those cases where public employees, rightly or wrongly, legally or illegally, strike . . . power as always will be the final arbiter."[97] In 1907, the combination of a vulnerable DSC commissioner, public health anxieties, and the political calculations of a city administration that did not want to be in the untenable position of causing death and disease spelled a significant (yet limited) victory for the drivers.

Concrete episodes such as the garbage workers' strike of 1907 reveal the attitudes and social and political forces of the Progressive Era in tangible form: the importance of sanitation in people's lives, and its relationship to notions of decency and civilization; the nature of early twentieth-century conceptions of disease, with their overlay of beliefs that antedated the rise of modern scientific medicine; the presence of immigrant groups in a land that was in need of their labor yet fearful of the social changes taking place all around, changes that were visibly symbolized by the immigrant; the role of civic reform groups, composed of people who also feared the nation's changes, yet acted directly to help shape the direction of those changes; the nature of Tammany Hall, an organization that held the allegiance of hundreds of thousands of New Yorkers; the use of corruption as a political issue; and the rise of professional expertise and its use as a political weapon. The interplay of these factors transformed a garbage strike into a major crisis in which elements emblematic of many Progressive Era concerns played a crucial role.

CHAPTER 2

George E. Waring Jr. and the Civic Promise

Between 1895 and 1898 the DSC had gained national attention for its success in cleaning the city's streets. The department's fame was linked with the name of its commissioner during those years, George E. Waring Jr., who instituted changes in refuse collection and disposal practices, personnel procedures, and labor relations that significantly improved the DSC's performance. Waring emphasized the importance of educating the community in public sanitation issues; and his promotion of the idea that clean streets could be provided for all areas of the city helped garner the citizen support needed to gain greater appropriations for his measures. This support was forthcoming, in part, because his approach epitomized the increasingly popular notion that both personal and civic responsibility are necessary in addressing persistent social problems.

As commissioner, Waring highlighted issues to the general public that many reformers grappled with for the remainder of the Progressive Era. Because he kindled the effective performance of the DSC—an accomplishment previously considered infeasible—many people nationwide viewed him as a symbolic embodiment of their hopes for municipal reform. They believed that his accomplishments belied the doubts of those who had abandoned the prospect that cities could effectively clean their streets. And if this could be done, they reasoned, then cities could provide other services effectively as well (for example, housing inspection and child recreation), if public agencies were adequately funded and their employment decisions were based upon questions of efficiency rather than political patronage.

Mayor William Strong, who appointed Waring to head the DSC, had been elected in November 1894 on a reform "fusion" ticket backed by the Republican Party, independents, and Democrats who were unhappy with Tammany Hall's domination of their party in New York City. The Tammany Hall organization had grown very powerful in the late 1880s through its control of city government offices. Among other uses, such power placed the awarding of city franchises and contracts in the hands of men who owed their jobs to Tammany's chief, who in the 1890s was Richard Croker. Croker often arranged for Tammany subchieftains ("sachems") to be hired as contractors or subcontractors for public works. Sachems also were privy to inside information about the siting of public projects, which allowed them time to make prescient real estate investments. In exchange for favorable treatment, many business people would make Croker a stockholder in their enterprises and feed him speculative tips. Firms that refused to go along with Tammany's plans were harassed by biased enforcement of municipal ordinances.[1]

The Tammany political machine garnered votes in part through the legwork of thousands of city employees, who not only owed their jobs to the organization but also contributed a regular part of their salary to it. And thousands of these employees' relatives and friends went to the polls to help repay the favor of city employment. Improprieties at polling places were not uncommon, although Tammany also attracted the genuine support of many voters of Irish or eastern and southern European background because of cultural affinity, or because of the informal welfare services previously noted. Moreover, the democratic ideal was often an abstraction to individuals who hailed from authoritarian lands in southern and eastern Europe. A politics that lacked a vision of the broad public good but that was based on personal relationships and the provision of rudimentary personal services (in return for the vote) seemed reasonable.[2]

While many business people were happy to profit from Tammany's activities, the bulk of New York's middle class was only dimly aware of the extent of local political corruption until State Senator Clarence Lexow's dramatic investigation of 1894. The Lexow Commission uncovered evidence that New York City policemen were required to purchase job security and promotions from Tammany district leaders. To afford these arrangements, many policemen would extort money from houses of prostitution, gambling establishments, and even shoeshine boys dependent on sidewalk permits. The nexus between the police, Tammany, and vice shocked the sensibilities of many New Yorkers, including a good number who had theretofore faithfully voted for the political machine.[3]

In late 1894, Strong rode to victory on the strength of the ensuing public outrage. Campaign material of the prestigious Committee of Seventy, which led the fusion movement for Strong's election, advocated the nonpolitical management of the police department, promising efficiency and economy in government while also espousing the provision of more municipal parks, public baths for poor neighborhoods, and cleaner streets. The committee blasted Tammany incumbents for the DSC's "failure to keep the streets of New York City in a clean and healthful condition," noting that "the air we breathe in our houses and our place of business is supplied from the streets and . . . whatever deleterious particles in the form of infectious dust gain access to our dwellings stay there for protracted periods." For many voters, the memory of the cholera scare of 1892 reinforced their attention all the more on the foulness of the city's streets.[4]

Reformers had unsuccessfully agitated for effective street cleaning and improved collection and disposal of household refuse throughout the nineteenth century. The tempo of these demands had increased by midcentury as the city's population burgeoned and the public health movement gained momentum. Unfortunately, upon taking office, Strong lacked a coherent vision of how he could attain all of the somewhat conflicting goals of his platform, but he did promise Waring that there would be no political interference with his management of the DSC.[5]

Waring (b. 1833) had gained national fame as a civil engineer in supervising the construction of a sewerage system for Memphis in the wake of the devastating yellow fever epidemic of 1878. Thereafter he prospered as the head of an engineering firm specializing in the installation of municipal sewerage systems and as the patent holder of certain sewerage system designs. He contributed numerous articles in popular and professional journals on a variety of sanitary reform issues, offering advice on topics ranging from sewerage to municipal street cleaning to personal hygiene, and he was popularly considered the leading sanitarian of the late nineteenth century.

Waring did, however, garner criticism from within the civil engineering profession during this period. Most seriously, some engineers charged that his desire for self-promotion and profitable sewerage contracts skewed his professional judgment, particularly in influencing some municipal officials to adopt his sewerage designs when it was actually relatively inefficient and costly to do so for their types of cities. There seems to be some truth to these accusations, though it must also be emphasized, as did some professional colleagues at the time, that Waring's aggressive salesmanship was undergirded by his sincere and passionate beliefs about the benefits of proper sanitation, which had been reinforced by the near-death of one of his children from typhoid fever.[6]

While today we have come to expect professionals to be narrowly focused on their own fields, many engineers—including Waring as well as some of his critics—maintained wide-ranging interests in social and political issues, and were instrumental in defining a new agenda for urban government from the mid-nineteenth through the early twentieth century. Often informed by a classical education that encouraged broad concerns, these engineers played a prominent role in the drive for sanitary reform, which was a major component of the public health movement and of urban social reform in general.

In this, they frequently worked in tandem with other socially conscious professionals from the fields of medicine, landscape architecture, and the social sciences, as well as enlightened business people and citizen lobby group representatives (who by the 1890s often were women from the settlement house movement or from organizations such as the WML). The engineers' professional experience was particularly useful in educating public opinion and lobbying public officials about the need to upgrade services for street cleaning and refuse disposal, and to construct and maintain municipal sewerage and water systems, public parks, massive street-paving projects, and other public works. Although there were sometimes disagreements among the engineers and the other key groups of the urban reform culture, they all agreed that sanitary reform projects would help stymie disease, raise the level of human comfort, and in turn encourage the aspirations and moral development of urban residents (which they believed to be of special concern in poorer neighborhoods). The historian Stanley K. Schultz has observed that these activists effectively advanced a new concept in American governance, in their conviction that the public should "through its tax dollars and its political support for public works projects, take charge of its own destiny in building a safer, saner, and more sanitary urban environment"—with the corollary recognition that such new responsibilities would require the permanent expansion of the scope of municipal government.[7]

In the years prior to the Strong administration, the DSC had been a rich source of patronage within municipal government, as Tammany Hall politicians awarded jobs in return for votes or political favors. Consequently, job security was precarious, because employees were subject to removal at any time to make room for someone else at the discretion of political leaders. On the other hand, as long as an employee was politically protected, there was no incentive to work hard.[8] Waring's predecessor as DSC commissioner, William S. Andrews, had been a politically minded administrator who at times personally profited by bestowing DSC contracts to associates such as George Washington Plunkitt. (Plunkitt later gained historical fame when his classic Tammany views on politics were published, including his observation that his own epitaph might read "He seen his opportunities, and he took 'em.") But this type of practice was at odds with Andrews's sincere desire to do a good job. Early in his term, shortly after firing a clerical worker for loafing on the job, the commissioner was informed by a political authority that the clerk "is my man; you must take him back." Andrews did so and thereafter took a back seat in managing certain aspects of DSC administration. Such stories were commonplace within other city departments as well. As other urban reformers were asserting generally concerning government services, Waring argued that New York could not be cleaned effectively while most workers were hired and fired according to considerations of political rather than occupational merit.[9]

To manage a city department by nonpartisan standards was a long-standing dream of many members of Waring's generation, who had come to maturity during or shortly after the Civil War. They shared certain values shaped by a tradition concerning civic virtues that extended back to the nation's founding and beyond, values that historians have termed "republican" because proponents commonly sought to identify those conditions that would allow representative democracy to remain viable.

Fearing the potential threat to freedom posed by powerful individual or group interests, reform-minded people viewed parties as necessary evils on the national scene but feared that these organizations often stimulated unnecessary factional discord, especially on the local level. Believing that greed was part of human nature, they argued for limitations on government powers in order to protect individuals from those who might use its machinery to advance their personal or group interests at the expense of the community. In this view, community harmony and unity could be realized if citizens recognized their duty to discipline their individual interests for the overall public good. Likewise, it was the duty of those blessed with wealth and education—the "best men"—to take part in public affairs. Unable to be bought, and remaining above the grasping needs and interests of the potential wreckers of the polity, they had a "disinterested" sense of civic morality that would help bring the community into the natural harmony that was the promise of rational government.[10]

Given these shared values, we can understand the fear with which these "mugwumps"—the term that was often used to identify the nonpartisan reformers preceding the Progressive Era—viewed the power of late nineteenth-century political machines. These men were frightened by what they considered to be an alliance of moneyed interests, political favoritism, and the strange new ethnic groups that the political bosses represented. And many middle-class Americans believed that monopolistic corporations were an important element within this collection of potential community menaces, fearing their capacity to gain power over individuals and less formidable groups.

The social conditions and complex interests spawned by industrialization and urbanization could not, however, be easily fitted into the traditional political formulas of small-town American life. As the mugwumps adjusted to the realities of the modern era, many retained their essential wish to foster civic harmony but adjusted their conceptions about the role of government. Thus Progressive Era reformers hoping to restrain the power of interest groups still upheld the ideal that individuals supporting these groups should curb their desires for the sake of the broader good, but at the same time reformers increasingly recognized the need to come to terms with these interest groups.

In effect, the progressives began to understand that tirades against corruption and simplistic appeals to the community interest did not constitute a sufficient approach to politics. Their frantic declarations of concern about corruption were in part a way of expressing the anger engendered by a variety of vexing social problems that were difficult to identify and comprehend, problems that required people to think beyond formulaic notions—often a painful process. Corruption was dramatic, with more easily recognizable heroes and villains than were furnished by issues of urban poverty and other complex social problems. It is to the credit of the progressives, however, that they began to fashion something more than a superficial approach to corruption. Many increasingly recognized that social problems predisposed their less affluent fellow citizens to support the corrupt politicians who provided at least a primitive form of social welfare. These reformers sought to identify strategies to address these social problems, recognizing that honest government in and of itself was not an adequate solution.

The Progressive Era thus witnessed the blossoming of what some called reform "with a heart." Activists hoped that expert-led management in city departments, the influence of informed civic pressure groups, and investigative reports conducted by a more open and accountable government would produce a relatively rational system in which the various interests of a modern urban society could be addressed without sacrificing the broader needs of the whole. To cope with the new problems posed by urbanization, industrialization, and massive immigration, the progressives made adjustments to the traditional emphasis on individual responsibility and small government—while still retaining the belief that individuals are morally responsible to make the most of what they do have.[11]

The common association of filth and foul air with disease helped motivate late nineteenth and early twentieth-century public health activists to seek measures that they hoped would provide greater levels of sanitation and comfort, and therefore healthier lives, to poverty-stricken urban residents. Like many other public health advocates who grew to maturity prior to the widespread acceptance of the germ theory in the 1880s, Waring had been influenced by notions about miasmatic disease and related contingent-contagionist concepts, which maintained that unsanitary conditions increased the chances of disease propagation and increased people's susceptibility to disease. The contingent-contagionist viewpoint was evident, for example, in a paper that he had presented to the American Public Health Association in 1876 concerning street and house drainage. In this, he asserted that "the causes of grave infection are precisely the same in the city that they are in the country, and they grow in both cases from improper protection against the emanations from the organic filth which is a necessary product of all human life." Because of lurking dangers such as unhealthy sewer gas, which might back up into households in areas that had installed sewerage systems, "improper methods for the public and private disposal of the wastes of the body and of the household" constituted a danger that needed to be addressed.[12]

In referring to an analogous form of foul air, arising from soil contaminated by improper drainage, Waring warned about "the debilitating effect of the exhalations [which give rise to] . . . headache, neuralgia, loss of appetite, intermittent fever, etc. . . . The low condition and consequent susceptibility to infection which the malaria [bad air] of damp soil produces doubtless aggravate very seriously the dangers arising from . . . infection, when a robust and vigorous person would withstand it." To public health advocates such as Waring, proper sewerage, well-ventilated housing, and clean streets exemplified the wholesome living conditions that were prerequisite to the maintenance of personal health.[13]

Since Progressive Era reformers often equated wholesome living conditions with good health, it is not surprising that they believed that matters related to order and morality were important factors in maintaining health and general well-being. In this view, proper sanitation was a key in determining whether a person could attain a wholesome way of life; disease, immorality, and disorder were perceived to be parts of an ensemble that loomed whenever public sanitation was seriously deficient in urban areas.

In an article written in 1899 concerning the contributions of engineers and architects to public sanitation, William Paul Gerhard, a prominent sanitary engineer who had worked with Waring on sewerage projects, observed that "civilization and sanitation are so closely allied that one cannot exist without the other." "Health and cleanly living" were two sides of the same coin, and without clean streets and other marks of proper civic sanitation, the moral tone of the community was considered to be in jeopardy. J. C. Pumpelly, an official of the City Improvement Society, remarked in 1894 that "the condition of the streets of a city are an index of its civilization, and their condition affects not only its economic but its intellectual and moral status as well." These examples can help us to understand the gravity of Waring's characterization of the ambiance of filthy streets in New York's slum districts prior to his administration as "squalid and hopeless." People commonly assumed that the depressed atmosphere engendered by dirty streets bred crime and other antisocial behaviors, as well as disease. Citizens of the 1890s were well aware of the significance of the pairing of words in the phrase "filth and squalor."[14]

The potent meaning ascribed to sanitation undergirded the common perception that clean streets and moral tone were linked. Sanitation was a conceptual handle that helped many individuals to identify and comprehend impediments to well-being that were rooted in the social structure of society. The meaning ascribed to sanitation thus helped push public opinion toward greater cognizance of the role of the social and physical environment in fostering poverty and other perplexing social problems that intersected with individual behaviors. Health and morality, already linked in the predominant viewpoint of the preceding decades of the nineteenth century, were still linked within the progressive mind of the later part of the century, but the relative position of health and morality within the equation had changed. Earlier in the nineteenth century, public opinion generally held that a lack of moral character was responsible for poverty and much disease. Although they often remained ambivalent, Progressive Era reformers commonly stood this formula on its head, in considering poverty to be the cause of much moral degradation and disease.[15]

In this view, appropriate sanitary measures heightened the possibility of individual improvement. Community spirit and individual good health and joy in life were more likely to flourish when a city maintained well-kept, healthful streets. After Waring had achieved a measure of success as DSC commissioner, he commented that "the trophies of [clean streets] . . . are all about us—in clean pavements, clean feet, uncontaminated air, a look of health on the faces of the people, and streets full of healthy children at play."[16]

Relatedly, a tenement dweller exposed to clean streets would be more likely to acquire habits of personal cleanliness, a livelier personal outlook, and greater civic spirit. The end result would not only be less littering on the streets but also the cultivation of more concern among the poor for complex civic issues that affect the broader community (including, of course, the issue of public sanitation). As DSC commissioner, Waring acted to attain the sanitary conditions that were considered prerequisite to this vision. And with a flair for public relations, he strengthened people's awareness of the meaning and importance of sanitation—which, in turn, helped him to earn increased public support in his drive to clean New York's streets.[17]

Waring took office on January 15, 1895, in the middle of a snowy winter. Without snow plows propelled by motor vehicles, the pre-automotive DSC mainly relied on its workers to shovel, by hand, as much snow as they could. Extra men and carts were often hired for temporary snow duty. Waring's predecessor had typically cleared only the major commercial thoroughfares and wealthier residential areas such as Murray Hill or Upper Fifth Avenue. The new commissioner publicly lobbied Mayor Strong, through a letter published in the city's newspapers, to fund snow clearing in all of the crowded areas of the city, and especially in the worst slum district, the Lower East Side. He described conditions there:

> The uncleaned streets are in a horrible condition of filth. It is bad enough in the better quarters, where the people have the comfort of well-warmed houses and of abundant clothing, and where the ordinary wastes of daily life can readily be removed. When we go into the tenement-house districts, the conditions are really appalling. The population is dense; the home is often bare of comfort, clothing for a dry change is often wanting, and on a melting day the people live and move in the midst of slush and dirt and great discomfort. The general wretchedness of hundreds of thousands . . . can be hardly imagined. . . . Delancey Street could be kept as dry and clean as Broadway is today, and the health and happiness of the people would be vastly increased. But it would cost tremendously; it would perhaps cost for the tenement house district half as much as the whiskey and beer that the present state of misery, due to snow, leads the people to buy.[18]

It was in the wake of this public letter that Waring applied to the New York City Board of Estimate, whose approval was required for municipal budget items, for an extra $50,000 appropriation to hire greater numbers of temporary laborers and carts during the remainder of the snow season. A little over a month into his term, Waring had already spent $180,000 for snow removal, while his predecessor had spent only $59,000 during the entire previous winter on this item. But Waring had removed as many loads of snow as had the department during the entire five-year period prior to his administration, and he had cleared many streets that had never before seen the civic snow shovel. In effect, he presented the board of estimate with a fait accompli. He had overspent his budget but had shown much better results than any prior efforts. He gave the board and the city at large a taste of what the streets—including those in areas such as the Lower East Side—could be like when cleaned properly, and he declared that with greater funding, he would be able to clear the snow in virtually all of the densely inhabited sections of town. Despite some groaning, the desire for clean streets won out and the board relented.[19]

With the arrival of warmer weather in the spring of 1895, Waring used the same tactic of cleaning the streets (now of non-snow filth) more thoroughly than his predecessors and then requesting funds for a fait accompli. He was generally successful in attaining funds throughout his term, if only because most people demanded clean streets and believed that he was in fact delivering that commodity.[20]

Tammany politicians often complained that Waring was profligate with public funds. In doing so, they used a political tactic that the mugwumps themselves had employed to vilify Tammany leaders during prior administrations. But the commissioner and his defenders countered that the money was now well spent. They asserted that the public mainly resented larger appropriations and the corollary of higher property tax rates when, as had been the case in Tammany administrations, the money was spent on street cleaning but there was little to show for it.[21]

Letters to Mayor Strong illustrate that many New Yorkers recognized the importance of street cleaning and other aspects of public sanitation, and they confirm the board of estimate's sense that the collective political will existed to tackle the street cleaning problem. In 1895, for example, Louis H. Rullmann of 337 East Forty-third Street wrote the mayor a follow-up letter regarding complaints that he had registered just prior to Waring's term in office. He had described a set of nuisances in his "thickly populated neighborhood" as "making life almost unbearable at times." Smoke from nearby factories, the "drunken revels" of derelicts carousing in a neighboring stable yard, and the "offensive vapor" from the nearby gashouse were bad enough, but the "rancid and fetid fatty odors" from neighborhood slaughterhouses often forced his family to give up in disgust as they tried to eat their dinners. Butcher's shavings and sawdust were routinely deposited on the sidewalk at the foot of a stairway down the block, and in the absence of public toilets, some New Yorkers used this as a pissoir. Rullman noted that "the germinating properties of the [sawdust and meat residue] when soaked with urine is a well established physiological fact." In his letter, he gratefully acknowledged Waring's attention to this nuisance, and asked the city to forbid slaughtering houses in "populous neighborhoods."[22]

Considered dangerous to health and unaesthetic, foul odors reinforced Rullmann's assertions. With the smell of rotting garbage evoking such perturbed responses during the era, one can imagine the distress of citizens prior to Waring's tenure in those sections of the city that were rarely swept. Streets there were often covered with a layer several inches thick of items such as discarded paper, rags, decaying food scraps, manure, mud, and ashes (from coal furnaces and stoves).

Odors were also a major consideration in testimony taken during hearings held early in 1895, regarding the DSC's policy of using garbage as fill material to add more land onto Rikers Island. Residents of nearby sections of the Bronx claimed that the resulting fumes wafting in from the island had caused the deaths of several children. A physician, James P. Daly, confirmed that "there was more sickness created by the miasmatic poisons emanating from this nuisance than was ever known in the District before." Gastroenteritis was considered to be the main threat, although he suspected the poisons were responsible as well for the recent increase in diphtheria and scarlet fever cases. Daly stated that the microbes breeding in the garbage on Rikers Island were becoming "as fat as the proverbial alderman."[23]

Mayor Strong personally attended these hearings. One witness gave the mayor an earful on the subject of the relative importance of money compared to garbage removal: "Suppose you, sir, had lost your boy last summer by reason of this stench? What is the use of talking money? If we are going to ruin a whole section of our City, it is time to call a halt when men talk about saving money." Another witness concurred, and challenged the mayor: "If it takes money to give us relief, spend the money like a man; have the courage to do it." The mayor probably recalled these statements a few days later when, as a member of the board of estimate, he voted to appropriate the crucial funds for snow-clearing that Waring had requested.[24]

Vociferous objections to the dump at Rikers Island paralleled criticisms from residents of shore communities in the Rockaways and New Jersey about another DSC disposal practice. People complained that their beaches were intermittently deluged with New York's detritus, as a result of the city's traditional practice of dumping much of its garbage into the ocean.

To resolve both the Rikers Island and shore predicaments, and to make refuse disposal more economical over the long term, Waring implemented an innovative disposal system based on the reutilization of refuse (that is, recycling, in current-day language). Under his plan, residents were required to separate their household refuse into three categories: "garbage," which consisted of organic waste; ashes; and "rubbish," which consisted of items such as paper, rags, glass, and other non-organic household objects. ("Refuse" and "trash" were all-encompassing terms denoting waste products in any of these categories, although the latter term was used less often.) Separation of these materials made each more utilizable, thus increasing the likelihood of productive (or even revenue-producing) reuse.

By the end of Waring's term in office, these measures were largely in place. Garbage was sent to a large "reduction" plant on Barren Island, where through various cooking, pressing, and skimming processes, grease and fertilizer were extracted and then sold, respectively, to soap manufacturers and southern cotton plantations. The separation of refuse also made it easier to employ the long-standing practice of sorting out rubbish articles for resale. Whatever rubbish that remained was then burned at municipal incinerators or mixed with ash. And with ash now free of decomposing organic matter, the DSC could use this less odoriferous material to resume fill operations at Rikers Island and other properties in low-lying areas throughout the metropolitan region. (Now the location of the main city jail, Rikers Island was expanded to four hundred acres from its original eighty-seven acres by the time dumping ceased there in 1938.)

A fire at the Barren Island reduction plant, a decline in the market for by-products of the reduction process, and perhaps most important, neighborhood protests about the odors emanating from both the Barren Island facility and a new reduction plant on Staten Island forced the city to resort to ocean dumping once again at the end of World War I. As this suggests, even though Waring had made significant strides in turning New York away from primitive refuse disposal methods and toward a sophisticated system based on recycling, refuse disposal remained controversial during the Progressive Era. Residents near Rikers Island, for example, continued to complain of odors from fill operations, even though the situation had improved somewhat. In part, the problem there was due to the admixture of street sweepings with the ash that was used as fill. This difficulty was seriously compounded following Mayor Strong's term in office, when city administrations all too often failed to resolutely enforce household refuse-separation ordinances. This allowed some garbage, that most pungent of all categories of the city's solid wastes, back into the ash fill.[25]

Waring boasted of the improvements he effected in the disposal and collection of household wastes, and in street sweeping as well. He pointed to a substantial drop in the incidence of disease and death during each year of his term, claiming that his efforts played a significant role in this achievement. The president of the city's health department concurred that cleaner streets—along with better milk inspection and improved tenement sanitation—had largely been responsible for the reduction in deaths, especially those resulting from the sometimes fatal childhood diarrheal ailments.[26]

Waring was happy to take credit for his role in improving public health. In some ways he personified the transition from a more staid and cautious mugwump emphasis on individualism—with its wariness of government action that had been reinforced in observing the corruption of late nineteenth-century politics—to a more activist progressivism, which included a greater emphasis on the social-environmental causes of poverty and disease. In discussing declining disease and death rates, Waring extolled the role of clean streets, but he cautioned that "whatever the favoring causes may have been, there are to be remembered, on the other hand, the poverty, overcrowding, and defective nutrition that have been so marked in these dull [economic] times, and have had so depressing an influence on the public health."[27]

Yet, while sanitarians such as Waring favored environment-oriented solutions for urban woes, they also continued to believe that individuals were ultimately responsible for improving their lives and that, in the aggregate, individual behaviors largely determined the character of the streets and of society as a whole. Waring believed that the very existence of clean streets, now a reality for the first time in many neighborhoods, and the enthusiastic model set by the DSC's auxiliary children's clubs (juvenile street cleaning leagues), had helped promote an enhanced cleanliness ethic in private homes as well as in public locations. Accordingly, many New Yorkers had grown increasingly aware that littering was an impolite and unhealthy habit, and had intensified their efforts to maintain clean homes.[28]

Waring came to realize, however, that raising community awareness could hardly generate clean streets if the DSC work force was dispirited. Waring ran a tight ship. He believed in firm but fair discipline, a characteristic that may have grown out of his military experience during the Civil War. (Reflecting the rank he had attained in the Union Army during that conflict, he was forever afterward known as Colonel Waring.) He ran the department on a merit basis, retaining Tammany appointees without prejudice if they performed their jobs well; at the end of his term, 60 percent of his workers were holdovers from the previous administration. Waring also broke the color barrier, in hiring the first African American DSC foreman and in abandoning the department's custom in which blacks were hardly ever hired on as sweepers. "It does not make the slightest difference to me," Waring exclaimed to reporters, "whether a man is green, blue, black, or white. . . . What I wish is good men, and that is all I care for."[29]

Waring refused to permit the customary practice of assessing contributions from his men to Tammany's coffers. He insisted that "one could not serve two masters successfully." This attitude also exemplified his feelings toward labor unions, though he was not simply opposed to the rights of workers. Rather, he grappled with an age-old paradox. He hoped to be fair and attain high worker morale while he also hoped to retain the prerogative to make key policy decisions.

Waring belonged to a generation of reformers who, to a significant degree, still assumed that an educated elite of broad outlook would (or should) guide society's institutions. Although they believed that progress and American democracy embodied the promise that the pool of people capable of this leadership role would expand to include a broader section of the population, it was actually difficult in many cases for elites to come to terms with the assertive representatives of interest groups spawned by industrialization and urbanization, particularly when these groups challenged elites' prerogatives. This was a key concern of many progressives, one that Waring faced in defining his department's relationship with its laborers.[30]

During the first year of Waring's term, there was grumbling among DSC employees, especially when he proposed pay cuts to assist the city in its drive to economize as much as possible while improving services. On this score, the colonel was politically vulnerable, coming under fire from Tammany Hall.[31] Aside from these political considerations, Waring recognized that employee morale was eroding and that this could negatively affect his plans to raise the department's efficiency.

Accordingly, he studied methods of labor relations and instituted an innovative arbitration plan in 1896. Under its provisions, workers elected their own men to the Committee of Forty-One (one representative for each DSC district), which met regularly to air employee grievances. The committee heard worker complaints—for example, if a driver received what he believed to be an unjust disciplinary fine. Waring was gratified that the system also helped bring to his attention complaints about abusive officers and foremen and suggestions from workers to improve administrative procedures and provide more effective services. The committee itself settled two-thirds of its cases. Unresolved grievances were then considered by the DSC's joint labor-management Board of Conference, which consisted of equal numbers of representatives from the Committee of Forty-One and Waring's office. If the board could not agree on a particular case, it was sent to the colonel himself. This occurred only once, with Waring deciding in favor of labor in that instance.[32]

Recognizing that the issue of proposed wage reductions was a chronic irritant, Waring dropped the idea. To justify what some critics considered high wages for unskilled work, he publicly stated that his employees were "no longer common laborers; [rather,] they have become efficient members of an organization as important to our welfare as the police and firemen."[33]

Waring often extolled his men in such idealistic terms to the public, asserting, for example, that his force was "made up of well trained and disciplined men, the representative soldiers of cleanliness and health, soldiers of the public, self-respecting and life-saving. These men are fighting daily battles with dirt, and are defending the health of the whole people." He believed that the labor arbitration system, the merit basis for employment, and other facets of his administration promoted self-respect among the men as well as a spirit of mutual trust between employees and himself. He maintained that the latter was the "highest possible reward" for his work with the DSC.[34]

In part to boost worker morale early in Waring's tenure, he directed DSC street sweepers to wear white thick-woven cotton (duck-cloth) uniforms and pith helmets. He hoped to encourage his workers, as well as the public, to feel pride in this distinctive look and to associate it with the efficiency and respect often accorded the military and health professions. Although the public at first mockingly dubbed the newly uniformed sweepers the "white wings," as the department began to show positive results many New Yorkers began to express this moniker with a certain sense of pride in the employees' seemingly angelic mission. Waring also hoped that the white uniforms would help foremen to spot loafers from afar, and he encouraged ordinary citizens to let DSC officials know if employees neglected their duties.[35]

When Tammany officials regained control of the DSC in 1898, they abolished the labor arbitration system and reverted to a more authoritarian form of labor relations. The workers' urge to organize on their own behalf was forced into sub rosa union activities, instead of being channeled into what had been, in effect, a rare instance of a good-faith company union. Tammany politicians wanted neither a Committee of Forty-One nor a Teamsters local that could undermine the workers' dependence on political connections and the traditional system of hierarchical relations to which their administrators were accustomed. Within this framework of labor relations, employee grievances festered—sometimes more and sometimes less, depending on the commissioner—and broke out into two bitter strikes during the course of the Progressive Era (see chapter 1).[36]

To further reinforce worker morale and public support for the department, Waring instituted an annual employee parade in 1896. Tammany aldermen opposed the parade, voting down a proposal for an official viewing stand; they claimed that people would ridicule the DSC men, who were typically considered low-status workers, if they ventured to march down prestigious Fifth Avenue. Against this background, the success of the parade was all the more surprising to both the press and the politicians. Crowds packed Fifth Avenue from Fifty-ninth Street down to Twenty-sixth. Some of the spectators were proud friends or relatives of the employees who, the *Times* remarked, "had never seen Fifth Avenue before."[37]

Waring's showmanship was a key to his political persona, and the "Wagner of the Street cleaning brigade," as a *Herald* reporter called him, played up the parade to the hilt. The fourteen hundred sweepers, dressed in their distinctive white uniforms, marched military-style down the avenue, while approximately a thousand other employees marched or rode in six hundred freshly painted garbage and ash carts, whose drivers vied for a prize for the best decorated vehicle.

Bands and mounted police accompanied the parade. A contingent of juvenile league boys marched with the men, while a group of juvenile league girls rode in carts, shouting "Rah! Rah! Rah! We are the aids of the DSC," to the applause of the crowd. Waring himself rode mounted on a fine brown filly. Spectators greeted him like "an uncrowned king." This was New York's day to show its appreciation for a service that had long been denied to its citizens. "After this," noted one spectator, "he can have all the money he wants." Indeed, aldermen watching from the (unofficial) reviewing stand were the figurative subjects of a wry comment from the *Herald* reporter, who declared that "Waring . . . saw his enemies broken under the wheels of the newly painted ash carts."[38]

Following this event, political opponents had to strain to find grounds upon which to attack Waring and the DSC. Some mocked the colonel's aristocratic lifestyle, pointing to his pleasurable jaunts on "the finest pair of horses in the Park." Waring's detractors also accused him of traveling to Europe at the city's expense, failing to mention that he made a detailed study of innovative street cleaning methods while there. As the mayoral election campaign heated up in the fall of 1897, the Tammany candidate for district attorney, Asa Bird Gardiner, in one of the campaign's famous "To Hell with Reform" speeches, charged that DSC officials had stolen more than a million dollars per year from the department's coffers during Waring's tenure.[39]

Nevertheless, Tammany leaders soon restrained Gardiner from uttering further remarks of this kind about Waring's DSC. Though many Tammany men were angered by the loss of hundreds of DSC patronage jobs under Waring's administration, other Tammany leaders were intimidated by the libel suit Waring initiated after reading Gardiner's remarks, and more important, they recognized the popularity (and perhaps the importance) of Waring's reforms. After all, as more of the immigrants that Tammany claimed to represent acquired an education and moved up the economic ladder, many underwent a change in their level of aspirations. Able now to look beyond the next day's meal, they increasingly related to many of the same civic issues as did the more affluent constituencies of the reformers. With Waring's DSC now cleaning 144 miles of streets daily compared to only 28 miles under the previous administration, Tammany needed to respond to higher expectations for systematic city services if it wished to secure and maintain power. Although Tammany candidates won most Progressive Era mayoral elections after Strong left office, reform candidates attracted enough support among the poor to attain the mayoralty again in 1901 (Seth Low) and 1913 (John Purroy Mitchel). Indeed, competition from candidates such as these forced Tammany to recognize the concerns of some of the members from within its own ranks who were thinking seriously about social reform issues.[40]

In doing so, by degrees, the Tammany organization underwent a maturation process in which its leaders aligned themselves closer to reformers' concepts of proper governance. Tammany did not simply consist of unthinking corruption-robots; there were those within the organization who had broad concerns. Indeed, by the end of the Progressive Era, when Tammany figures such as Al Smith and Robert F. Wagner gained national stature, the Democratic Party was in the process of superseding the increasingly conservative Republican Party as the major political advocate of progressive ideals (or "liberal" ideals, the term more often used by the 1930s). Leaders such as Smith and Wagner were harbingers of an evolving progressive (liberal) synthesis that would become a core element of the New Deal political coalition, which supported the use of government to raise living standards but involved itself less often than the earlier version of progressivism had in issues pertaining to personal morality. In part inhibited from tackling such issues because of the divisiveness of prohibition and immigration-restriction legislation during the late 1910s and 1920s, these reformers also tended to assume that behavioral problems in slum districts would largely clear up as a matter of course when those in need could more readily attain decent living standards.[41]

As a result of changes within Tammany, by the early years of the new century, the city's Democratic organization began to field candidates, at least for higher offices, who were substantially independent from the organization's control, men who offered programs that could compete with those of middle- and upper-class reformers in their depth of vision and in their acceptance of rationalized administrative controls over street cleaning, public health, mass transit, and other complex fields of operation. After Tammany suffered defeat in the mayoral election of 1901, those who saw the political wisdom and even the intrinsic value of a more mature policy began to turn the tide within the party. Thereafter, corruption was still present, but less often on a scale that would affect the day-to-day operations of city departments. Indeed, with reformers concurrently moving away from the small government ideal, a larger consensus concerning political goals became possible.[42]

This process unfolded gradually, gaining appreciable momentum during the latter part of the era. But even in 1897, Tammany leaders did not wish to run against Waring's programs. In fact, they had hoped—until his lawsuit ruled this option out—to retain the colonel as DSC commissioner if their organization's mayoral candidate was elected that year.[43]

Strong himself did not seek another term in 1897, and the reform mayoral candidate, Seth Low, lost to Tammany's Robert Van Wyck. Because of his identification as the reform candidate, Low suffered by association with the mostly unpopular Strong administration. On the whole, Strong was too weak a leader and was not creative enough to reconcile the tensions caused by competing pressures for more municipal services on the one hand and economy in government on the other hand. Acrimony also arose between Democratic and Republican elements of his coalition over political appointments. And the cultural distance

between reformers and foreign-born citizens made it difficult for city administrators to communicate with and understand the problems of these New Yorkers. This cultural distance also produced disaffection over some of the Strong
administration's moral reform policies—particularly concerning the enforcement
of blue laws that restricted the sale of alcohol on Sundays.[44]

Soon after Waring left office, President William McKinley appointed him to
head a fact-finding mission to report on sanitary engineering deficiencies in
Havana in the wake of the Spanish-American War. While in Cuba in October
1898, the colonel contracted yellow fever, and he died soon after returning to
New York City.[45]

Sanitary reform groups throughout the United States were by this time often
successfully pressing for the reform of their own municipalities' street cleaning
and refuse collection and disposal services, pointing to Waring's nationally renowned department as a model. Even before the colonel's death, Richard Watson Gilder, a housing reform activist, had exalted Waring's achievements: "You
[Waring] have done something not only for the solution of one of the greatest
of civic problems in America, but in this success, you have helped to [obtain] the
final solution of all our other problems of government. . . . If we clean the streets
of the Republic, we can accomplish other cleanings that have in the past seemed
hopeless of accomplishment."[46]

With Waring's untimely death while working in the cause of sanitary reform,
many civic activists invested his administration with a significance that grew to
near-legendary proportions. Over five thousand people, including five hundred
juvenile league members, attended a commemorative ceremony at Cooper Union
Hall following his death. In paying tribute, Felix Adler, founder of the Ethical
Culture Society, extolled Waring's legacy in municipal labor relations, proclaiming
that "he had sought to give dignity to the men in his department. . . . He was the
advance guard of a new race of civic servants." And a spokesman read a letter from
Governor-elect Theodore Roosevelt (who had been police commissioner in the
Strong administration): "The City of New York owes [Waring] a great debt and
no less a debt is owed him by the friends of good government in all cities of the
Union." (The two charismatic figures of the Strong administration, Waring and
Roosevelt, had both gone to Cuba on matters related to the Spanish-American
War, but they were of course affected far differently by their respective journeys.
Roosevelt returned as a war hero, donning the hero's mantle that propelled him
eventually into the White House. It is interesting to speculate on Waring's future
had he not been felled by yellow fever. He had recently been named president of
the City Club and was slated to be the independent reform candidate for state
engineer and surveyor during the election of November 1898; he was also mentioned as a possible future candidate for mayor of New York City.)[47]

The Reverend Dr. William S. Rainsford also eulogized Waring in a memorial

religious service held at St. George's Episcopal Church. Rainsford was a prominent minister and a supporter of what came to be known as the Social Gospel
movement, which promoted a greater concern within organized religion for
social justice on earth. In his sermon, he lamented the city's myopic refusal to
retain Waring's services after 1897 and predicted that "the time will surely come
when we shall be able to teach our children that the free man is best served by
the free servant. And the free servant of a free people shall go forth to perform
for the State duties second to none. When the day comes, and God speed the
day, George Waring will not be forgotten."[48]

To Waring's eulogists, the commissioner's work signified a successful break
with a pattern of governance in which politics was often perceived to be a road
to personal financial advancement more than an instrument for promoting the
public good. During the election campaign of 1897, Seth Low had spoken in stark
terms about the era's political culture: "We are battling here for the right of local
self-government of the city of New York. . . . What was it that made it possible
for the United Colonies to throw off the yoke of England and begin to govern
themselves? Simply that they had a local self-government that trained them in the
art of government. Now if our own cities have no capacity to govern themselves
and have to be governed by the man who controls one machine or the other, do
you not see that the very fabric of our Republic is in danger?"[49]

To an extent, such sentiments were the product of sour grapes, of frustration
with the fact that a considerable part of the population did not vote the way that
reformers would have preferred. But Low also spoke for many who shared a traditional concern that powerful interests might subvert democratic processes. For
the ethical New York business people who had been squeezed out of contracts; for
the citizens whose complaints went unheard because they did not have connections; for the honest job-seekers who had no chance of employment with the city
even though well qualified; for the voters concerned with reports of fraudulent
repeater votes; and for people who were angry because patronage-driven departments provided deficient street cleaning and other services, these sentiments rang
true. In response to these concerns, reformers offered a paradigm of protest and
action—an alternative to the avenues of cynicism and distrust that would only
have further eroded the vitality of democratic government.[50]

However functional the machine may have been in procuring occasional assistance for struggling immigrants, city departments filled with political hacks
could not effectively provide widespread systematic services. Modern street cleaning, for example, demanded rationalized personnel and accounting procedures,
ongoing scrutiny by analysts expert in their knowledge, and an appreciation of
the input of civic groups—all elements of sound administration that Waring
helped develop during his term in office.[51]

Prior to the 1890s, American urban reformers had been frustrated and seemingly stuck in a dilemma. They were indignant about corruption and were aware of the inadequacy of the political machines' welfare functions, but they spoke mainly on a theoretical plane. They studied the experiences of Western Europe in implementing municipal services on a rationalized basis, but most American urban reformers lacked solid first-hand practical experience in governing. And righteous indignation would certainly not clean the streets.

Many reformers viewed Waring as having provided substance to their doctrines. The colonel was not, of course, the only American to effect changes in municipal practice during the 1890s. Nevertheless, his achievements within a large and notoriously troublesome department were quite impressive; and his talent for self-promotion, honed during his years as a nationally successful entrepreneur, reinforced his renown. American reformers, hungry for signs that their vision could succeed, drank in Waring's articles and interviews during his stint with the DSC, as well as other writers' laudatory accounts of his work. Waring's sudden death reinforced his status as a model figure that reformers pointed to throughout the Progressive Era to show that their yearnings could be substantiated.[52]

New York reformers preceded Tammany in initiating many social programs—for example, in providing municipal baths, playgrounds, improved tenement housing codes, and the effective administration of public health and street cleaning services. And even many of the moral concerns raised by reformers should not be dismissed as irrelevant to the well-being of urban residents. When sanitary reformers such as Waring stressed the need to teach immigrants an appreciation of personal cleanliness, they were, indisputably, attempting to foster particular values. In order to function, all societies must set some behavioral standards. If there is little sense of personal accountability to the standards of a society, then there is little to prevent that society from slipping into chaos except for the enforcement of legal statutes, which in itself would prove inadequate unless pursued in an authoritarian manner. A more substantive issue concerns the types of standards that a society accepts as valid. Do these standards, for example, encourage the expression of diverse ideas? Do they encourage political debate and activism (even while at the same time valuing stability)? Are standards so rigid that they preclude even the consideration of the values of groups outside of the mainstream? And does the society recognize when there is no consensus on certain values, and thus rein in overzealous pressures to conform? These questions notwithstanding, it is important in the case of the progressives to realize that they were at least trying to take into account the role of the social and physical environment in fostering immorality, rather than simply assigning personal blame.[53]

We can better understand the reformers' concerns for individual values and behaviors by examining the work of Waring's juvenile street cleaning leagues, which will be discussed in greater detail in chapter 4. Mainly formed among children of the poorer districts, these after-school clubs became quite popular, tapping the natural idealism and camaraderie of the young, who, for example, would compete to pick up the greatest number of littered banana peels and candy wrappers in their neighborhoods. The praise of the community at large—apparent in newspaper articles and in the reception afforded league members in the annual DSC parade—reinforced the kids in their activities, as did the feeling of authority gained in conducting meetings and earning badges and certificates.[54]

The juvenile league program in one sense was an attempt to direct tenement children toward a certain set of attitudes and behaviors. "It is desirable . . . ," wrote David Willard, a DSC official who helped Waring guide the leagues, "that an interest in the rules of the Sanitary Code be awakened in the minds of at least the ignorant foreign population crowded into the East Side districts. To use for this end the influence of the children who are recognized by their parents as superior to them in education and intelligence, is not a new idea."[55]

Waring contended that the juvenile leagues would be effective in promoting cleanliness within homes as well as in the streets. He maintained that this would lower the death rate and reinforce feelings of self-respect and civic pride. These feelings would, in turn, help raise the personal aspirations of household members and engender a sense of responsibility to the community. Intrinsic to these beliefs was Waring's assumption that he was raising moral tone and promoting public health at the same time. In the holistic medical approach common to the times, parks and playgrounds, less-crowded housing, clean clothes, and clean streets were part of an environmental ensemble that could help uplift the health, aspirations, and character of people struggling to succeed. Inextricably woven into the progressive belief in environmental benefits was the parallel assumption that these benefits would be of no avail without the personal striving of individuals toward "cleanly living."[56]

Waring's work with the juvenile leagues was grounded in the concept that governmental and personal efforts were both important components in the amelioration of oppressive social conditions, a concept that informed the general approach that Progressive Era reformers took to community problems. In a meeting of league members, Waring accordingly expressed gratitude that his efforts to clean the streets were increasingly being matched by the reciprocal efforts of league members and other New Yorkers.

A letter that a league member wrote to Waring illustrates the sense of responsibility that reformers hoped young people would acquire (and would, in turn, help spread to other New Yorkers):

> There was a barrel full of paper in East Broadway and when the cartman emptied the barrel a lot of small pieces of paper fell all over the sidewalk. The housekeeper [the wife of the building superintendent] took the barrel in and did not even try

to pick them up. I went up and asked her to pick them up and she refused. Then I asked her to loan me a broom and I would sweep. She consented and I swept. She was baking in her stove so I put the paper in the fire. While doing this she asked me who I was, and I told her I belonged to a club which is interested in having clean streets. She asked me if I had a badge and I told her we could try to keep the streets clean without a badge and she said we were right.[57]

Waring did not believe that he was imposing a harsh set of standards in his work with the community, certainly not a set of standards that inhibited free will or individuality. Rather than attempting in this instance to inhibit such qualities, the young man and, indirectly, his adult sponsors were, in effect, beckoning the housekeeper to join in developing a more pleasant community in which a thoughtful *assertion* in public affairs, as exemplified by the actions of the juvenile league letter writer, would become more commonplace. The Progressive Era concepts of individual fulfillment and of individual responsibility to others signified two interrelated aspects of a civic ideal.

This sense of community responsibility was considered a two-way street. Waring offered the benefits of street cleaning to some long-neglected neighborhoods and asked citizens to make a personal effort to keep the city clean in return. The colonel thus attempted to instill moral standards, but as part of a mutually beneficial relationship in which the improved DSC would help provide an environment wherein the poor could have a more positive stake in society and in their own lives. In effect, the goal was one of empowerment (in today's terminology), which was exemplified as well by Waring's pleas to juvenile league members to participate in municipal affairs as thinking individuals when they grew to adulthood.[58]

Of course, while Waring helped provide more effective public services, other elements of the far from monolithic reform community emphasized a more coercive agenda—for example, in working to restrict Sunday tavern sales—or an intrusive agenda with moral overtones, as when the efficiency-minded administration of Mayor John Purroy Mitchel questioned street sweepers, in 1915, in order to determine their personal buying habits. The heavy-handed imposition of a majority's (or a vocal minority's) moral predilections upon others constitutes a classic conflict that free societies will always have to confront. While reformers viewed the poor as a potential threat to social order, at the same time they hoped that reform programs would make it easier for individuals and families to move up to a life of greater independence, self-realization, and civic involvement. Although conflicts occurred between reformers and the poor, it would be myopic to dismiss the Progressive Era as repressive because it included *some* repressive features. Rather, as one social commentator has remarked, it is important to study the "tension between traditional values and innovative policy, between a liberal disposition and the fragility of the social fabric"—a tension much in evidence during the Progressive Era, when reformers struggled to reconcile an evolving liberalism with the conservative features of American political culture.[59]

Edmund Burke observed that a certain continuity of values during changing times is a necessary prerequisite for the long-term acceptance of many of the changes engendered during such periods.[60] In this view, continuity does not necessitate a static society in which the ruling class keeps all contending forces in check. It does imply, however, that stability is a legitimate value and that successful democratic societies tend to cherish this value. During the Progressive Era, social stability was often an elusive commodity. Yet that stability which did exist was enhanced by an imperfect yet significant give and take between segments of society—a give and take that helped advance social/sanitary reform policies and that was rooted in values and aspirations shared by many people across class lines.

The Progressive Era was a time of both promise and foreboding. To the younger reformers then emerging, Waring became a symbol, an embodiment of their hopes. In his approach to the new urbanized society, he was at times highly critical of aspects of the period, but he was not ruled by fear. In the persona that he projected to the public, he faced the new society optimistically and ready for the challenge. His faith in the future, which embodied the hopeful side of a populace that was at the same time fearful of social change, helped make him one of the most celebrated urban reformers of his time. Raised like many of the era's reformers in a rural and far different world from the urban one in which he would live, Waring retained characteristics of an earlier time while adapting to the new. His labor arbitration board exemplifies this duality, in that he sought harmony but implicitly recognized that that was only possible now if the contending interests inherent in an urban society were equitably addressed.[61]

In hindsight, Waring may have been naïve at times. He did not realize, for instance, that in the absence of labor unions, DSC workers would be vulnerable, once he left office, to the rule of arbitrary administrators who would not act in good faith. In a similar vein, critics have asserted that the progressive presidents Theodore Roosevelt and Woodrow Wilson were naïve in fighting to establish federal regulatory agencies, noting that these presidents' cherished agencies would later be staffed with appointees who would contravene their very intent. To a certain extent, this type of criticism blames progressives for the nonprogressive acts of their political opponents, who more justly deserve the bulk of historical criticism. The Progressive Era experience demonstrated that, under pressure from government, elite interests would cooperate to reform their practices and help address interrelated social problems. But this type of modus vivendi did not endure when public pressure—which had fueled governmental pressure—waned during periods since the Progressive Era.[62]

Post-hoc alternative scenarios, suggesting that the progressives might have embarked upon various more preferable courses of action, are difficult to conceive once we take into account the historical exigencies of the situations at issue. Of course, constructive judgments of the progressives' shortsightedness or naïveté should be welcomed, and in fact the effort to incorporate criticism and the willingness to self-evaluate are distinguishing characteristics of the progressive spirit, a spirit that extended down to a significant number of citizens in the generations that followed. Rather than judging the progressives simply on the basis of their particular attitudes and policies, it is advisable to recognize that, more than most generations, they grappled with their anxieties about urban problems by facing complexity, as they sought to formulate humane plans of action that could transcend the simpler approaches of the past. And although some progressives in time became static figures, many hoped that future generations would continue to modify and build upon their work.[63]

Garbage opposite 35 Rutgers Street, on the Lower East Side, during the garbage work-ers' strike of 1907. *Annual Report of the Board of Health of the Department of Health of the City of New York for the Year Ending December 31, 1907.* Courtesy of the New York Academy of Medicine Library.

IN POSSESSION.

On the front page of the *Herald* newspaper, the famed cartoonist William A. Rogers's familiar King Garbage image reinforced the common perception that garbage and dis-ease ruled the streets during the 1907 strike. *New York Herald,* June 29, 1907.

William A. Rogers depicted Commissioner George Waring persevering even though the Tammany tiger has set upon him the dogs of envy, spite, lies, and slander. *Harper's Weekly,* September 14, 1895. Courtesy of A. A. Lemieux Library, Seattle University.

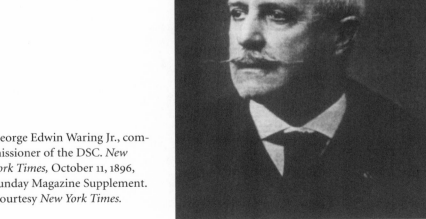

George Edwin Waring Jr., commissioner of the DSC. *New York Times,* October 11, 1896, Sunday Magazine Supplement. Courtesy *New York Times.*

Dressed in the white duck-cloth uniforms that earned them the nickname "white wings" (or "white angels"), street sweepers reduced the tons of horse manure and other detritus on the city's streets. *McClure's Magazine,* September 1897. Reprinted with permission of Manuscripts, Special Collections, University Archives (MS-CUA), University of Washington Libraries, UW23090.

Waring, pictured in the center on his brown filly, initiated an annual parade of DSC workers to reinforce employee esprit de corps and promote citizen awareness of civic sanitation issues. *Harper's Weekly,* June 26, 1896. Courtesy of A. A. Lemieux Library, Seattle University.

Waring's recycling measures sharply reduced the dumping of garbage at sea during his term in office. *Scribner's Magazine*, October 1903. Reprinted with permission of Manuscripts, Special Collections, University Archives (MSCUA), University of Washington Libraries, UW23095.

The *Tammany Times* reprised a newspaper cartoon from the *Telegram*, picturing Waring as a clownish braggart who plays fast and loose with "other people's money," and whose medallion reads "The pen is mightier than the broom." *Tammany Times*, August 31, 1895.

Tammany street cleaning before Waring's days, in front of 9 Varick Place, ca. 1893. Courtesy of the Museum of the City of New York, Jacob A. Riis Collection (#338).

Varick Place after Waring was appointed street cleaning commissioner. Courtesy of the Museum of the City of New York, Jacob A. Riis Collection (#LS-31).

Hester Street, Lower East Side, 1903. Concerns about disarray and lack of sanitation on pushcart streets fueled conflict over street use during the Progressive Era. The desire for unimpeded traffic flow increasingly trumped the needs of more traditional activities. Courtesy National Archives, photo no. 196-GS-369.

"Abe Livinsky's Dry Goods Wagon Is a Money Maker." *Hardware Age,* June 11, 1914. Courtesy of the Carnegie Library of Pittsburgh.

The Woman's Municipal League provided a drinking fountain for the Jacob Riis Settlement House, offering relief for children at play. Woman's Municipal League, *Bulletin*, September 1910. General Research Division, New York Public Library, Astor, Lenox, and Tilden Foundations.

The Little Women Civic League, a juvenile street cleaning league of Public School No. 4, Manhattan, 1910. *American City,* November 1910. Courtesy University of Washington Libraries.

Sophie Loebinger sponsored the Junior Park Protective League, in the neighborhood of St. Nicholas Park in Harlem. *New York Times*, May 4, 1913. Courtesy *New York Times*.

CHAPTER 3

Political and Moral Choices
in Pushcart Policy

When people think of the New York pushcart peddler of the early 1900s, they often visualize a scene in which a rough-hewn Old World vendor sells his wares to teeming crowds from a quaint wooden cart. If we look beyond this nostalgic image to explore the ways of the pushcart peddler, a much more significant figure emerges. An examination of conflict concerning the litter generated by the carts and the placement of carts on the city's streets can help sharpen our comprehension of urban social reformers' attitudes toward health and sanitation, poverty, and social disorder. Relatedly, controversy over proposals to reform pushcart policies spotlights the existence of a number of significant urban groups, with differing interests, that clashed over these policies. And a tentative convergence of opinions on pushcart issues by the end of the Progressive Era illuminates attitudinal changes within both the reform community and Tammany Hall, changes that reflected the general direction of urban social reform in the later years of the Progressive Era.

New York had a venerable peddler tradition, in which itinerant vendors supplemented public farmers' and wholesalers' markets. In accordance with European custom, eighteenth- and early nineteenth-century peddlers roamed the streets selling foodstuffs and household goods from hand-held baskets, horse-drawn wagons, and two-wheeled carts that they pushed through the streets (pushcarts). By the late nineteenth century, the burgeoning population of immigrants from southern and eastern Europe created a demand for inexpensive goods that increasingly was met by peddlers who stationed pushcarts in single locations for entire days at a time. While peripatetic peddlers remained a feature of the city throughout the Progressive Era, the use of stationary pushcarts would be the predominant mode. By the early years of the twentieth century, between four thousand and six thousand of these vendors lined the city's streets, mostly on the Lower East Side.[1]

Several ethnic groups were active in the trade. Jews, who sold a wide variety of food products and household goods, became the major force in pushcart peddling on the Lower East Side, but Italians with fruit and vegetable carts were also quite important in the area. Many Greeks worked fruit and candy carts on the Lower East Side as well, and both Greek and Italian peddlers predominated in Greenwich Village and farther down Fourteenth Street into the West Side. Jews and Italians established themselves in Harlem, as did African Americans (although the latter were not present in large numbers until the Great Migration from the South during World War I). Pushcart markets also spread to Jewish and Italian areas of Brooklyn, while a mostly Jewish contingent worked the pushcarts of "Paddy's Market," held on Saturday evenings in the Irish and African American working-class neighborhood known as Hell's Kitchen, on the West Side of midtown Manhattan. Second- and third-generation Irish Americans worked pushcarts selling inexpensive lunches to people working in the Wall Street financial district at the southern tip of Manhattan.[2]

Although men operated most of the pushcarts, women participated to a significant extent. Some were single women and widows supporting themselves and their families but most were at the carts to relieve their husbands or fathers for a few hours of what was a very long workday, which often lasted from early morning until well into the evening.[3]

The presence of so many Jewish immigrants in the densely populated Lower East Side was a major factor in the growth of the pushcart markets. A high proportion of Jews were from the Russian Empire, where discriminatory laws had largely prevented them from owning farmland and restricted them to a few crafts or to minor businesses such as peddling. It thus seemed natural for many to gravitate to this business in America.[4]

Repression in Eastern Europe and an elaborate code of rituals had, in addition, reinforced the strength of the Jewish family and its socializing function. This socialization often encouraged in young Jews a yearning for education and a belief that some sacrifice of short-term gratification is required in order to maintain hope of achieving an adequate standard of living for one's family and a peaceful and orderly community. Relatedly, Jewish religious tradition maintained that humans possess the potential to affect their own surroundings and the world at large, and this tradition encouraged a high rate of Jewish literacy—a relatively unusual trait in the underdeveloped areas of late nineteenth-century eastern Europe.[5] Having developed these underlying cultural characteristics in the face of hundreds of years of oppression by a society that did not wish them to develop their economic or intellectual abilities, and now presented with the relatively open opportunities offered by the American city, Jews responded with a vigorous work ethic. Seeking economic fulfillment and greater status, many immigrants were attracted by the opportunity to become an entrepreneur, albeit a petty one, by putting five dollars down to rent a cart and purchase some stock.[6]

While pushcart peddling was not considered a high-status occupation, as a business it did confer higher status than unskilled labor jobs or manual trades, and the work was far less monotonous than toiling in sweatshops. New York Jews seeking the higher-status occupations that had been largely closed to them in eastern Europe even had their own peddler version of the American rags-to-riches Horatio Alger myth. It told of wealthy German Jews, particularly department store owners such as Benjamin Bloomingdale and Adam Gimbel, who had emigrated to the United States in the mid-nineteenth century and had begun their careers peddling wares from packs on their backs in rural America.[7] Many immigrants perceived the pushcart to be a first rung on the ladder to entrepreneurial success and wealth.

The pushcart granted a degree of independence that was highly prized, not only for reasons that any American in the Jeffersonian tradition could understand but also because peddling allowed Jews to refrain from work on Saturdays, the Sabbath, a day on which most gentile employers demanded work as usual. And the relative autonomy of peddling allowed one to avoid the anti-Semitic bosses who were all too common in this era.[8] Newly arrived immigrants often used pushcart peddling as a transitional job until they learned the English language and the general lay of the land. One could peddle by day and then go to school at night, learning English and, if ambitious, bookkeeping or other skills that could help foster a future career. Although an Adam Gimbel was rare, the numerous successes of a more moderate nature validated the image of the pushcart as a potential vehicle to higher entrepreneurial ventures. In addition, individuals in tailoring, carpentry, and other trades sometimes temporarily operated carts during seasonal layoffs or strikes.[9]

Most peddlers worked hard, hoping that the pushcart would eventually lead to more rewarding occupations or to a material foundation from which their children could attain a higher degree of success. There were others, however, who considered peddling to be a more or less permanent occupation in which an individual could grow old and work with less fervor than a proto–Adam Gimbel. Such a man earned a bare living but could take time while at work to engage in conversation, *schmoozing* with his cronies. He retained much of the prized independence of a merchant, as well as the rewards of the traditional family economy in which his wife or children tended the cart while he took breaks. This arrangement sustained a communion of interests among both parents and children that helped preserve a family-centered existence in the topsy-turvy New World.[10]

Some people peddled not because of positive choice but because they were too old or too ill to learn a trade or hustle themselves into higher realms of entrepreneurship. Many pushcart peddlers were men who had been disabled or were what we would today term "burnt out" by work in New York's garment industry or other trades.[11] These men, as well as the young and fit who found the economic opportunities or social horizons afforded by peddling to be less than golden, often grew frustrated by their lot. A Rumanian immigrant complained: "This was the boasted American freedom and opportunity—the freedom for respectable citizens to sell cabbages from hideous carts, the opportunity to live in those monstrous dirty caves that shut out the sunshine." Abraham Cahan, an important Progressive Era commentator on the Jewish immigrant experience, wrote of a fictional yet true-to-life character, David Levinsky, who as a young man brooded under such conditions: "My push-cart bored me. I was hungry for intellectual interest, for novel sensations. I was restless." Such an individual would have recognized himself in a contemporary article in the *Tribune:* "Sometimes . . . among the younger [pushcart peddlers] . . . one sees faces of those who chafe fiercely upon the work that fate has thrust upon them. At least one strapping, handsome young fellow, late a cavalryman in the Czar's army, is peddling today with a volcano in his heart; and there are doubtless many like him."[12]

At times, the crowds that the peddlers catered to in the poorer areas of the Lower East Side were immense. Especially on Thursdays and early Fridays, when Jewish women shopped for the Friday night Sabbath meal, corners in the Hester Street area were packed with hundreds of people, "pushing to and fro," haggling over prices both on the sidewalks and in the streets. Over the steady din rose the clamor of quarreling voices and the piercing whistles of horse-drawn-wagon drivers trying to avoid running into carts or pedestrians. Above the crowds stood the five-story tenement buildings packed with families and boarders that patronized the carts lining the streets. In some areas, a person could walk out into the street, look down the block, and view a scene crowded with people and with pushcarts lined lengthwise along the curbs, one after the other far into the distance, with a canyon of tenement houses enclosing the whole ensemble.[13] Alluding to gutters heaped with trash from the carts, one reporter spoke of the omnipresent paper and nutshells among the refuse, on top of which "the poultrymen contribute feathers, the fruit and vegetable men a variety of decayed stuff, and someone always has an old hat to top off an east side rubbish heap." Amidst this scene, children played on the sidewalks and in the streets, often the only recreation spaces available. At night, the streets took on an air of the exotic from the glow of peddlers' acetylene torches lining the curbs.[14]

Approximately 70 percent of New York's pushcart peddlers sold food items, especially fruit and vegetables, though the pushcart markets in the Jewish areas of the Lower East Side were known for a variety of other goods as well. A partial list of both edible and nonedible items sold by Jewish peddlers would include hot corn, fish (especially for the Sabbath meal), poultry, meat, cheese (not on the same cart with meat), pickles, bread, cake, candy, cookies, candles, wallpaper, oil cloth, furniture, glassware, utensils, crockery, books, jewelry, stockings, furs, shoes, and many other types of clothing.[15] Through wholesale purchases of factory seconds and surplus or damaged food items, peddlers were able to sell to the poor at inexpensive prices. A housewife could buy a dozen rotting pears for a penny and salvage the edible portions, or a nice pair of shoes for one dollar and twenty-five cents. A full wedding outfit could be purchased for ten dollars. Many peddlers were able to avoid attending the wholesale food markets in the middle of the night by pooling their money and authorizing a fellow peddler to buy from the wholesalers and deliver the goods to their respective carts.[16]

A prospective peddler could buy a pushcart outright for five to ten dollars, but most chose to rent them for ten to twenty-five cents per day. Vegetable peddlers often finished work by late afternoon, but fruit and dry goods vendors frequently stayed on the street until 11 P.M., with family members commonly taking the peddler's place for a few hours. With an investment of five dollars, the peddler would net an average of twelve to fifteen dollars per week. Though those making below the average amount were poor indeed, most earned enough to suffice in an era in which seven hundred fifty dollars per year could provide a tolerable living for a family of five.[17]

It was not an easy life. The pushcart peddler spent much of the time in a standing position and endured exposure to rain, bitter cold, and summer heat, fending off children intent on stealing pieces of fruit, and enduring constant quarrels with customers—about prices or related matters—which all too often yielded the "dull hurt" of rebuff or the insults of a boorish customer. The self-respect and status of the peddlers eroded when they experienced the mockery of gangs of malicious boys, who would pelt pushcart men with rotten fruit and even occasionally physically assault Italian or Jewish peddlers who wandered into unfriendly ethnic enclaves. A journalist, Marion Winthrop, complained about the "teasing little hoodlums driving delivery carts who are unmercifully beating their horses . . . [and] deliberately charging into foot passengers and push carts." Educated lads who had left Russia hoping to obtain a finer existence, or pious men of learning, more comfortable with Talmudic argument than price-haggling, were often less than enamored with the peddler lifestyle.[18]

Many peddlers were polite and kindly, but others, perhaps influenced by a brutalizing environment, were distrustful, rude, and sometimes foul-mouthed—even occasionally toward female browsers who refused to buy. One observer commented that the scramble to buy produce from the wholesalers was hardly conducive to goodwill, noting that "men and women [at the wholesalers] forget their sex, forget almost that they are human, in their passion of . . . buying cheap." If the peddler was a sensitive soul, his self-esteem might suffer as he found himself adopting some of the common tricks of the trade to survive. To enhance sales, for instance, Abraham Cahan's David Levinsky character crumpled up pieces of perfectly good clothing, wet them a bit, and then shouted that he was only selling them "so cheap" because they were slightly damaged. Some peddlers, although certainly not a majority, would also short-weight their customers.[19]

Peddlers endured other perils as well. On occasion they were hauled into court when neighborhood retail store merchants gathered enough political strength to prompt a sweep by the police.[20] The same held true when other interests complained loudly enough. In 1906, for example, staff at a school in East Harlem objected to the noisy haggling and crying of wares from the nearby pushcarts. The peddlers claimed the right to remain in place, but the police invoked a usually unenforced ordinance that prescribed a maximum standing time of thirty minutes per cart. A small riot ensued when the authorities attempted to make arrests. Peddlers threw their produce and garbage at the police. One woman smashed a policeman's helmet and tore the buttons off his uniform. The police ordered an obliging street sweeper to hose down the crowd and called in reserve officers to arrest the vendors. The malfeasants were let off lightly in court, incurring a reprimand from the judge (except for the female helmet-attacker, who was fined three dollars, more than an average day's pay).[21]

Fundamentally, the status of the pushcart peddlers was degraded by the insecurity of their legal standing and by their ensuing vulnerability to extortion and arbitrary arrest. Peddlers were arrested for obstructing traffic; violating sanitary regulations; standing too close to a corner; standing on a restricted street; failing to obtain a peddler's license; breaking the thirty-minute rule; and breaking Sunday blue laws that prohibited numerous types of commerce.[22] Ordinances affecting peddlers were often either unenforced or enforced capriciously; local custom, corruption, and political favoritism precluded neutral and consistent enforcement.

The balance of social and political forces within a neighborhood effectively determined whether a street would be open to stationary pushcarts.[23] Peddlers might establish themselves on a street for months, or even years, but then find themselves abruptly ejected without warning. Many middle- and upper-class New Yorkers objected to the presence of the carts in their neighborhoods because they associated them with filth and poverty and the social disorder believed to be concomitant to these conditions. The ethnic character of the pushcart trade only reinforced these perceptions in many people. Commenting on a visit to a Lower East Side pushcart area in 1895, for example, a reporter for the *Tribune* voiced an overwrought apprehension that wherever he looked "there [was] a variety of unsavoriness, of unique ugliness, and typical mongrel humanity of the lower order."[24]

As we shall see, pressure from sanitary reformers and the DSC added to the chorus of voices speaking against unrestricted peddling. Nevertheless, it was the pressure from store owners that typically tilted the political balance against the presence of pushcarts in individual neighborhoods during the era. Ironically, most shopkeepers on pushcart streets actually wanted the carts to remain, as the presence of numerous peddlers attracted droves of pedestrians in the mood to buy (and the peddlers' "rent" money for street space fattened these shopkeepers' wallets as well). But some store owners carrying products such as groceries, which were in direct competition with pushcart wares, typically complained to city officials about the carts, as did store owners on nearby streets that the pushcarts did not actually occupy. These merchants believed that the pushcarts undermined their attempts to establish a middle-class shopping ambiance in their districts. They also believed that the peddlers' low prices siphoned away customers and that the attendant street congestion impeded vehicular access to their stores.[25]

The store owners' assertion of a right to freer vehicular access exemplified a type of outlook concerning the proper use of urban streets that had only begun to gain widespread adherence since the mid-nineteenth century. The preindustrial city had been a compact entity, in which walking was the common mode of transportation. People often gathered in streets to socialize, watch their children at play, and shop for food and other items that peddlers would bring in baskets, pushcarts, or slow-moving horse-drawn wagons. With the exception of the most prominent thoroughfares, vehicular traffic did not dominate the life of the streets. Likewise, cities typically did not enforce ordinances that forbade sidewalk or street encroachments (such as pushcarts) from impeding vehicular traffic, deferring instead to a Jacksonian type of decentralized neighborhood autonomy that for the most part characterized nineteenth-century urban governance.

By the late nineteenth century, however, improved technology made efficient streetcar lines to locations outside of the bounds of the old city feasible, while industrial production and greater prosperity significantly increased the number of heavy commercial wagons and other horse-drawn vehicles plying the streets of the older city districts. For many people the value of the urban street as an artery for vehicular traffic began to trump the value accorded to the street's other uses.

At the same time, late nineteenth- and early twentieth-century reformers and many city officials sought to establish centralized decision-making processes for city governance, in order to improve and more effectively maintain a variety of city services. Centralized decision making tended to strengthen the trend toward vehicular dominance of street usage, although in Progressive Era New York the power wielded by prominent store owners within local neighborhoods often reinforced this trend as well.

After the turn of the century, the advent of the automobile merely reinforced the triumph of the vehicle in street usage, as single-occupancy ridership became more and more of a mass phenomenon. Despite the fact that many people in city neighborhoods objected to increased vehicular traffic, most opinion makers identified urban commercial development and suburban residential development with progress and prosperity. Rather than remaining gathering places where peddling and other premodern uses were accepted, more and more streets became thoroughfares dedicated to vehicular use.

The virtually privileged position of vehicular traffic in urban decision making from the late nineteenth century to the present has prompted many of today's citizens to realize that much has been lost in our rush toward modernity. While city neighborhoods possessing a preindustrial urban village character have not all been equally affected by the modern reign of traffic, a largely unquestioning attitude among much of the population concerning the role of traffic and the streets has helped produce, in many neighborhoods, a profound deterioration in the quality of urban life. While early twentieth-century pushcart controversies entailed more than simply a conflict between peddlers and ambitious store owners, that conflict can be seen as an early salvo in a broader struggle over the appropriate use of urban streets and the appropriate ambiance of city life.[26]

On those Progressive Era streets where New York pushcarts were generally accepted, a lack of definite, legally sanctioned street space allowed store owners to extort bribe money from peddlers, who would pay as much as ten dollars or more per month if they wanted to retain a choice position outside the busiest stores. If a peddler failed to pay, store owners would seek an obliging policeman to arrest him on whatever grounds seemed appropriate. Magistrates were usually not harsh, fining violators one or two dollars.[27]

A corrupt political system sanctioned these arrangements. In addition to payments to merchants for the use of the curb in front of stores, the pushcart peddler often paid bribes of ten to twenty-five cents per day to a "collector." This collector, who sometimes was a street sweeper for the DSC, acted as an instrument of an association of neighborhood pushcart peddlers, sometimes referred to as "de organization," which had ties with the local ward political machine. Acting in tandem, "de organization" and the neighborhood political "man of influence" (often a saloonkeeper) allowed peddlers to locate on choice streets, providing them "protection" in return for their contributions. The "rake-off" of dimes and quarters from hundreds of peddlers would be divided up between the collector; his cronies in the peddlers' organization; the cop on the beat and the district police captain; local political figures; and occasionally a person higher up on the political ladder, such as an alderman, who could restrain municipal attempts to overhaul the system. If peddlers did not cooperate, policemen would dump their stock on the street and force them to leave the area, or threaten to arrest them, or occasionally even point a gun at a peddler's chest to silence objections. No payment was required under this system if a peddler engaged in active political work for the ward boss. Fear muted opposition to these arrangements, and many vendors figured that under this system they were at least allowed to peddle in profitable locations.[28]

Nevertheless, the effect of such a system was to lower the self-esteem and status of the pushcart peddlers in the city as a whole. Their vulnerability and lack of legal standing left them isolated and further reinforced the perception of many New Yorkers—of which the peddlers were painfully aware—that pushcarts were a public nuisance. Numerous policemen were unhappy with the system themselves and would have preferred definite, evenly enforced rules by which peddlers could honestly earn a living.[29]

A different sort of threat to pushcart peddlers stemmed from the good intentions of public-spirited Progressive Era reformers. Many of New York's progressives maintained that the carts posed a threat to immigrants and to the city at large. The settlement house pioneer Lillian Wald asserted that "the [Lower] East Side needs no reform more urgently than the liberation of its streets for their legitimate purposes." For the "health, comfort and safety" of the neighborhood's inhabitants, pushcart reform was imperative. Only then could "the decencies of life be maintained."[30] Wald was appointed to a special Mayor's Push-Cart Commission convened in 1906 to study the issue. Its report summarized complaints against the carts:

> Congestion of traffic in many streets, both for teams [horse wagons] and for foot passengers, the effect of which is to seriously delay merchants in the delivery of goods, increasing the cost of their business and interfering materially with their rights as citizens; an increased difficulty in cleaning the streets . . . ; an increase in the danger from fire by impeding fire engines and delaying their prompt arrival at fires, thus seriously endangering the lives of tenement dwellers; danger from improper food supplies because of dirt and germs; an improper and unfair competition with shopkeepers; persecution and blackmailing of the peddlers by policemen and shopkeepers; . . . discomfort . . . through additional odors and noise in neighborhoods where conditions are now almost unbearable; the use of space now needed by children for opportunities for play; and finally the attraction to this City of immigrants by reason of the ease and facility with which a livelihood is obtained in this occupation.[31]

Many New Yorkers feared that garbage left in the streets by the peddlers and their customers would create an unhealthy environment for nearby tenement dwellers.[32] A *Times* reporter investigating conditions on the Lower East Side in 1910 observed that

> many streets in the tenement sections, where danger to health is most pressing, are filthy. On Suffolk, between Rivington and Stanton, were fifty fruit and vegetable peddlers. Under each cart was a pile of cast-off wares, in a state of decomposition. The street was an inch deep in mud, mingled with banana peels,

corn cobs, paper, peeling melon rinds, all swarming with flies. Here was seen a lone sweeper, but his one broom against all that filth was like Hercules trying to clean the Augean stable with a coffee spoon.

In Attorney Street were four overturned garbage cans . . . and around them children were playing. The gutter was one-half foot deep with dirt. There were also decomposing fruits and vegetables . . . papers, ashes, and three dead kittens. . . . Thirty pushcarts each had a refuse pile beneath it.[33]

Social reformers, public health officials, and DSC administrators contended that street garbage, much of which originated from the pushcarts, was ground into bacteria-laden dirt and dust that, when churned up, was transmitted through the air onto the peddlers' edible items. The threatened atmospheric contamination of food produced emotional reactions in many New Yorkers in part because of the lingering influence of the old miasma theory of disease causation.[34] But a number of other factors reinforced the public's sensitivity to this threat as well. A widespread public health campaign against pulmonary tuberculosis (TB) during the first decade of the century significantly raised awareness of the lethal effects of this disease and of the need for measures aimed at its prevention. The TB campaign's emphasis on impure milk as a source of infection heightened concern in general about the contamination of food supplies, as did the publication, in 1906, of Upton Sinclair's best-selling novel *The Jungle,* which detailed the filthy conditions found within the nation's meat-packing industry. Anxiety that TB germs would be transmitted by way of airborne dust strengthened the perceived interconnectedness of impure air and disease—a perception that was reinforced as well by the common belief that flies could readily transport germ-laden dust (and the related fear that dust might contain fly excreta).[35]

Public health activists often warned of the dangerous nexus of bad air and food. Ellen Swallow Richards, a prolific author who pioneered instruction at the Massachusetts Institute of Technology in sanitary chemistry and helped found the home economics educational movement, was one of the many non-physician professionals prominent in the public health field at the turn of the century.[36] In *Sanitation in Daily Life,* Richards drew on the classic Hippocratic prerequisites to good health in asserting that "the sanitation of the house . . . consists in keeping the air fairly clean, the water supply safe and the food good." Of these elements, "modern sanitarians are inclined to believe that . . . vitiation of the air is by far the most important." Richards emphasized that a variety of air contaminants could either directly produce infections in human beings or weaken the body's resistance to disease. And she warned that "dried sputum, excrement, decayed food or refuse may be lifted by the wind and scattered over . . . several miles . . . into markets to fall on fruit and meats."[37]

Not surprisingly then, public health activists shuddered to think of the effect of airborne elements that settled upon pushcart food items. The commissioner of the New York City Department of Health, Thomas Darlington, placed the issue in stark relief at a conference concerning pushcart reform in 1904. Darlington asked why "the death rate is higher than it was this time last year. Where is it higher? Is it up on Fifth Avenue or the upper West Side? Not at all. The increase is to be found right here in the push cart district, and I believe it is due to the exposure of foodstuffs to the dust of the streets."[38]

The commissioner's professional judgment resonated with the concerns of a letter writer who complained to the *Times* that unwholesome fruit sold from the carts "was exposed for hours in the dust-laden air, accumulating and propagating disease germs." In addition, the writer feared that the carts were "spreading if not creating disease" through the immense amount of litter that they produced.[39]

Many New Yorkers considered the odors produced by the congregation of numerous stationary carts both unhealthy and offensive. In 1911, Morris D. Waldman of the United Hebrew Charities of New York, an immigrant-aid organization, emphasized the need to prevent the "filth and evil-smelling odors dangerous to the public health" that emanated from the carts. Likewise, earlier in the era one of the branches of Waring's juvenile street cleaning leagues had submitted a petition to the mayor to limit the pushcarts to restricted market sites, stating that "the health of the people of the east side is greatly endangered by the odor coming from said push carts."[40]

Others expressed anxiety that the carts might spread disease through the unsanitary handling of food or the sale of rotten food. A neighborhood group protesting what they termed a pushcart "invasion" of the Yorkville district on the Upper East Side presented testimony from a Mrs. J., who had seen some dill fall from a cart "into the street into a heap of horse manure. . . . The push cart dealer immediately gathered up the dill and placed it back on the cart." Another complainant, Mrs. R., observed "an Italian fruit vendor take out a filthy handkerchief from his pocket and wipe his apples with it after first expectorating on the handkerchief in order to moisten it."[41] Such conditions seemed appalling to public health activists who were by the early 1900s increasingly concerned with personal hygiene issues. A physician writing for the *Journal of the American Medical Association* advocated regulations that would restrain food handlers "from introducing their fingers into any of the body cavities. . . . I have noticed that food handlers in the dairy lunches, for instance, are very prone to introduce their fingers into their noses and into their ears and into their mouths and then handle food with the same unwashed fingers. The possibility of disease transmission in such instance is very great, and the habit is repulsive and repugnant."[42]

Earlier in the era, a *Times* reporter, probably animated by anxiety about social disorder as well as the decomposition of food on the Lower East Side, wrote of a "slatternly young [pushcart] woman who had a scarcity of clothing" selling cheese upon which "it did not require a microscope to detect the mites[,] . . . for they were large and lively." The ethnocentric journalist stated that he had "received such a shock from the powerful odor thrown out that [I] almost had a spasm. Phew! how that cheese did smell. Yet the long-whiskered descendants of Abraham . . . put their fingers in it and then suck them with great and evident relish." Nearby he observed carts selling meat and poultry marked by "a huge swarm of great blue flies [which] buzzed about and laid their eggs on the meat, which was already alive with the larvae of insects." And blending concern about food decomposition with apprehension over fraudulent sales, the *Tribune* in 1905 reported that a policeman assigned to enforce litter ordinances had observed Anna Wolpert, a fish peddler under the Williamsburg Bridge, "painting the gills of the fish she had for sale. The fish were beginning to be tainted and the gills had turned white. She put rouge on each gill, thus restoring them to their normal appearance."[43]

In reality, public health investigations typically found that the fruit and vegetables sold from pushcarts were relatively free from serious decomposition. Fish, meat, and dairy products were more problematic because of a lack of refrigeration and plumbing facilities. Many middle-class customers, however, stigmatized pushcart products in general. In part, they were alarmed by the prospect of food contamination deriving from street dirt and dust, flies, unsanitary handling, and decomposition. But intertwined with these health concerns was the common inclination to negatively stereotype immigrants, which, along with related anxieties about social disorder, reinforced a tendency to associate the neighborhoods of the poor with foulness in general.[44]

The pushcart issue proved to be politically unmanageable early in the Progressive Era, when George Waring attempted to implement one of Mayor Strong's campaign promises. As a candidate, Strong had emphasized the widespread consternation over dirty streets, and had pledged to address the Committee of Seventy's concern that "the practice of licensed venders of fruit and vegetables throwing refuse into the streets" greatly aggravated the litter problem. Once in office, Waring advocated the demolition of an entire square block of the Lower East Side in order to establish a regulated pushcart marketplace that would both accommodate a large number of peddlers and be accessible to neighborhood residents. Pushcarts would be banned from Lower East Side streets and "segregated" into the market; there they would occupy stands under open-sided sheds protecting both peddlers and shoppers from the sun and inclement weather. Street cleaning services would be much easier to provide on pushcart-free streets. Subsequent reformers throughout the Progressive Era advocated variations of this plan, with the number of segregated market sites and the proximity of those sites to the peddlers' customer base being key variables. An exception to this typical pushcart market plan was the proposal recommended by the Mayor's Push-Cart Commission, which considered the issue in 1906. The commissioners envisioned a system for the Lower East Side in which only one cart would stand on each corner, thereby allowing a total of only four peddlers per block. All Lower East Side streets would be open to the pushcarts, with the better locations auctioned off by the city once a year. As we shall see, however, attempts to significantly alter pushcart procedures found little success until the early 1920s.[45]

While Waring pushed for his expensive ($1,000,000) plan, Police Commissioner Theodore Roosevelt acted on Waring's complaints about street congestion. He ordered his men to enforce the existing, but rarely enforced, maximum standing time ordinance, which at that time prohibited carts from standing more than ten minutes in any one location. Peddlers objected strongly when these provisions were enforced. Headlines in the February 21, 1896, issue of the *Jewish Gazette,* a Yiddish-language newspaper, told of a "Police Pogrom" on Hester Street. The paper reported that "panic struck" the peddlers as they fled in the face of policemen brandishing clubs. "The ordinance to rob a person of his only market, and not allow poor people to earn an honest dollar is . . . issued by . . . Colonel Waring." Waring agreed to meet with peddler representatives, a committee of aldermen, and an officer of the Reverend Charles H. Parkhurst's Society for the Prevention of Crime to discuss a fairer and more rational solution. (Parkhurst gained fame during the 1890s primarily through his vigorous denunciations of the collusion between Tammany politicians and vice figures, but he also maintained a sympathetic interest in the plight of the pushcart vendor, believing in this case that the ten-minute rule was far too harsh a measure.)[46]

The result was a set of licensing procedures that would allow more standing time but decrease the number of peddlers on the streets. The regulations stipulated that pushcarts could now remain in one place for a maximum of thirty minutes, though an official license would be required—available for the relatively high price of fifteen dollars per year.[47]

The peddlers were far from thrilled with the new regulations. And they were wary of Waring's segregated market plan, which foundered due to fiscal restraints and the resistance of peddlers and of some city officials who doubted that the proposed marketplace would satisfy consumers who lived several blocks distant from the site.[48] And in the absence of an alternative plan that could satisfy Lower East Side customers, local police and courts ultimately failed to enforce the new ordinances. Like subsequent attempts to restrict the total number of pushcarts on the streets, this plan was, in the words of one later Progressive Era reformer, "unsuited to the time, contrary to the popular will and repugnant to the common sense of the authorities. . . . General convenience and the 'higher law' of statute-killing public opinion . . . customarily prevail." In order to clean popular pushcart streets now, Waring recurrently cleared peddlers off of them, sometimes for hours at a time, a strategy that occasionally produced harsh encounters and resentment.[49]

The failure of the reform mayoral candidate Seth Low to win election in 1897 signified, in part, the feeling among many voters that Strong's reform administration had not adequately delivered on campaign promises to provide improved public services, including an equitable settlement of the pushcart issue. Progressive Era reformers sometimes failed to gain consensus across class and ethnic lines in seeking measures, such as pushcart reform, that they hoped would protect urban residents from factors that could weaken their character or health. Relatedly, a tendency toward paternalism and ethnocentrism among many Progressive Era reformers, when combined with their belief in the scientific nature of their investigative findings, occasionally made them overconfident about their ability to divine the needs of the poor. Consequently, they sometimes failed to take fully into account the more immediate needs of those in distress. While many people on the Lower East Side were pleased with the clean streets that Waring provided, the administration's approach to the pushcart question won few friends there, even though Waring and the mayor had honestly sought a just solution. Generally, the goal of protecting residents from degrading influences in the urban environment helped make the middle class more aware of the need for social policies that could foster greater hope in the lives of the poor. But without an adequate consensus among the general population on specific issues, the reformers' protective impulses could conflict with the cultural norms of residents of impoverished immigrant districts—as seen, for example, in Theodore Roosevelt's divisive attempts to enforce the Sunday closing of taverns during Strong's administration—or could, as the pushcart issue demonstrates, even conflict with the material needs of these residents.[50]

By the turn of the century, Tammany was already beginning to evolve in new directions, as its immigrant constituencies became more acculturated and increasingly demanded the types of programs that middle-class reformers (or politically competitive Socialist Party candidates) were offering for consideration. Nevertheless, between 1898 and 1902, the Tammany-backed administration of Strong's successor, Robert Van Wyck, revived a pattern of pushcart-related corruption in which bribe money secured favorable positions for peddlers on the streets. Fees for licenses were lowered to four dollars, but they were restricted to a relatively small number of peddlers who were politically connected with an alderman or some other city official whose word brought quick action from the licensing bureau. Other peddlers had to rent licenses underground from people who illegally obtained numerous licenses, or they would sell their wares without a license, hoping that they could reach an accommodation with policemen that they might encounter. For many of the less established, poorer peddlers, rental of a license on the black market actually seemed more affordable than paying a four-dollar annual fee, especially if a peddler worked only intermittently. Of course, those peddlers who were caught working unlicensed or illegally licensed were relatively easy to threaten if they objected to the entrenched system of bribery involving policemen, ward politicians, and storekeepers.[51]

Under the Van Wyck administration, the problems of congested and filthy streets only grew worse as the number of peddlers increased and as DSC services deteriorated under patronage-oriented management. Reform elements began campaigning far ahead of the 1901 mayoral election, capitalizing as in 1894 on public disgust with a system in which policemen were enriched by bribes from widespread gambling and prostitution networks (as well as the extortion money gained from pushcart peddlers).[52] Reformers portrayed the deterioration of the DSC as a sign of the general decline of city services under Tammany rule. In successfully battling for Seth Low's election as mayor in 1901, they blasted the Van Wyck administration, claiming that it fostered corruption and lacked vision. And they portrayed themselves as superior to Tammany not only concerning moral issues (such as corruption) but concerning social policy issues as well.[53]

Accordingly, the reform-minded Citizens' Union accused the Van Wyck administration of neglecting schools, playgrounds, tenement code enforcement, and street cleaning. The political machine had, in its view, "bullied the push cart peddlers into paying for protection" and had left "the streets foul, unclean and dangerous to the health. . . . In its contempt for the comfort and safety of the people of the east side, Tammany Hall shows . . . its absolute corruption and the falseness of its claim that it is the 'poor man's friend.' Streets [are] covered with dust, waste paper, horse refuse, and decaying swill from which a sickening, disease breeding vapor rises through the streets, floats into every window . . . and raises the death rate. . . . This is friendship for the east side!"[54]

During the long election campaign, several reform groups established a newspaper, the *New York Vigilant*, that they hoped would strengthen their candidates' appeal to the working class by claiming the high ground of social reform. According to the *Vigilant*, people struggling to make a living would take pride in clean streets if given the opportunity. More effective street cleaning and other municipal services would acquaint them with the notion that life could offer more than a grim struggle for survival. With the resulting growth in civic pride and duty, working-class New Yorkers would then join in civic campaigns to root out violations of the housing and sanitary codes, helping to "clean out every dark yard, court, and other nesting place for tuberculosis germs." They would even cooperate in supporting a ban on pushcarts from the streets, where "green groceries and fruit [are] exposed to the street sweepings and dust." Under a reform administration, the legitimate role of the pushcart peddler in meeting the consumer needs of tenement dwellers would be fulfilled by creating an adequate number of segregated marketplaces.[55]

While voters favoring pushcart reform and improved street cleaning helped elect Seth Low in 1901, many peddlers and their customers were displeased by the manner in which the new administration actually handled the pushcart issue. Mayor Low's chief of staff, James B. Reynolds (a former University Settlement official), instituted pushcart policies that he believed would serve the public interest until the ideal solution of conveniently located, segregated markets became a reality. He hoped to foster more effective street cleaning and a freer flow of vehicular traffic, allay the complaints of store owners about peddler competition, and remove the circumstances that allowed policemen and store owners to demand payoffs for the privilege of locating pushcarts in prime spots. To reach these goals, Reynolds began prodding the police during the early months of Low's term in office to enforce the thirty-minute standing time and a proviso that forbade the placement of pushcarts on both sides of a street, while also cracking down on peddlers who did not possess a city license. And in 1903, during the waning months of the Low administration, Reynolds sought to reduce the number of peddlers by enforcing a rarely used ordinance that forbade licenses to people who had resided in the city for less than a year and to immigrants who had not applied for citizenship.[56]

Under Reynolds's measures, peddlers found that they could not attract their usual number of customers, mostly because they were unable to remain in any one location for a long enough period of time. In February 1902, only one month into Low's term, a force of five hundred peddlers marched on city hall to protest his administration's policies and to demand a meeting with the mayor. Low spoke with their representatives, who reminded the mayor that he had promised to treat them fairly in his campaign. Nevertheless, the mayor did not force Reynolds to retract his regulations.[57]

A politician on the Lower East Side, Bennie Myers, explained to the *Tribune* that the regulations were being unevenly enforced in that area of the city. In sections where the local police captain enjoyed a good working relationship with the reform administration, the thirty-minute rule was duly enforced, but in Tammany-dominated sections only a few blocks away where the police captain was "less admired by the powers that be," enforcement was spotty.[58]

As in the Waring years, peddlers felt let down. Although many had been unhappy with the previous (Tammany–Van Wyck) administration's approach, in the words of the *Tribune,* "the poor pushcart pedler [*sic*] can understand a shakedown, but when he is driven from pillar to post, when his money is refused and his offers of garden truck [fresh fruit and vegetables] . . . are spurned, the pushcart man is moved to cry out: 'What is this reform, that it is?'" In this vein, one peddler complained that he had to waste his time now, going to city hall to obtain a license: "Things ain't what they used to be; a while ago all we had to do to keep on the good side of the cops was to tip them a quarter or else take them in for a glass of whisky. . . . Now they're after us." Not surprisingly then, Reynolds's pushcart policy—and, as we shall see, the measures that the DSC commissioner, John McGaw Woodbury, took to segregate fish peddlers during Low's administration—alienated many peddlers and Lower East Side residents, who subsequently helped defeat Mayor Low's bid for reelection in November 1903. Years later, the *Times* paraphrased the remarks of a University Settlement official who recalled that the pushcart peddlers had campaigned against Low in 1903, believing "that the Mayor was a man who liked to put all poor men in jail."[59]

Reynolds thought that the ultimate solution lay in a plan similar to Waring's, in which pushcarts would be placed in several large market squares, as close to the location of their customary trade as possible. Because the prospect of such uncertain change produced anxiety among the peddlers, and because of the expense involved in clearing away existing blocks of buildings to make way for the markets, Reynolds could not achieve this solution within the two-year span of the Low administration.[60]

Although attempts to address the pushcart issue did not succeed during the Progressive Era, there were grounds for potential concord between reformers and pushcart peddlers. The latter's concerns about extortion, favoritism, and grueling competition, as well as their desire for respectability, attracted many peddlers to the prospect of a municipal system of segregated markets—provided that they would be assigned an adequate number of spaces, located within walking distance of most customers.[61]

At mass meetings of peddler associations and at hearings held by civic groups and the city government, pushcarters complained of being "constantly abused," and of not knowing when they woke up each morning whether more money would be squeezed from them that day for "protection." They worried that they might lose a good location because of favoritism shown by the neighborhood "man of influence," or be arrested or subjected to rough usage by an unfriendly policeman. And they feared that the carts might be expelled altogether from more areas of the city where the balance of neighborhood political forces had changed.[62]

Sigismund Schwartz, president of the largest peddler trade group, the United Citizens Peddlers' Association (UCPA), testified at the Mayor's Push-Cart Commission hearings of 1906 that "wherever we go now, we feel the hand of the law. If we leave one street and go to another we are hounded out of that. Our men have been pounded and arrested, and there has been much suffering." Such complaints had long been made. Thirteen years earlier, in 1893, two hundred fifty pushcart peddlers had petitioned the mayor for help, calling the corrupted policemen extorting money from them "blue-coated blood suckers."[63]

Lambert J. Marcucci, an editor of one of the city's Italian-language newspapers, represented the Italian Push-Cart Peddlers' Association at the commission hearings. His sympathies for the peddlers and their customers were apparent in his answer to those New Yorkers who complained that the pushcarts created traffic congestion. In effect, he highlighted the social strains produced by the middle and upper classes' new conception of the proper functions of urban streets, suggesting that the commission look at the traffic issue "in its true and very democratic light: the million people who daily buy fruit from the push-carts cannot afford to cry their complaints from an automobile, because they are working people." This friend of the pushcart peddlers recommended that the city authorize between twenty and forty district pushcart markets, which would be convenient to neighborhood residents. Such a plan, he believed, would provide "full justice for all."[64]

Many UCPA peddlers were not averse to the idea that regulated markets should be reserved only for those who actually owned their carts, since this would reduce the competition (by disallowing those who rented carts). Observing that a significant number of pushcart peddlers wanted to restrict entry into the fold, a *Tribune* report in 1905 noted that "the competition has become fierce on the East Side, and those who are 'in' do not want any more admitted to the fraternity." UCPA leaders criticized recent immigrant ("greenhorn") vendors, as well as stable owners and others who rented numerous carts to the newcomers. It was the greenhorn, one UCPA official asserted, who was "responsible for blocking the streets and he is the one who refuses to go into [segregated] markets. You can't get markets too soon for us old pushcart men."[65]

To even out the playing field for unmarried peddlers who could not put family members to work at their carts, UCPA leaders also intermittently sought to forbid non-widowed females and anyone under twenty years of age from working at the carts. Yet such proposals met resistance within the UCPA itself, in part because many peddlers had wives and children who helped operate their carts, but also because such proposals went against the expanding notion of rights that was a hallmark of the era, not least among immigrants who had fled czarist Russia. One peddler commented that "if it is necessary that a woman should marry and that her husband die before she can conduct a pushcart, I want to say that the inference kind of scares me."[66]

Exclusionary proposals also met with opposition from the less well established peddlers, who did not typically belong to associations but actually constituted a majority within the trade, a majority that was not easily ignored. One senior peddler declared his sympathy for them, stating that it was not ethical to deprive unlicensed peddlers of the means to make a living. "What shall we do," he asked, "with our . . . brothers who have no licenses? Throw them into the river?" With pushcart association members divided over such issues, pressure from below usually prompted the organized peddlers to advocate segregated markets that could accommodate all who wished to peddle rather than only those who owned their carts.[67]

Rational reform was stymied in part because the system of extortion that marked the status quo was quite profitable to many policemen, politicians, store owners, and stable owners. The latter reaped handsome profits by renting carts and illegal licenses. They were quick to notice that peddlers would be assigned regular positions in many market proposals, which would make it easier for the city to rationalize licensing procedures, and that stalls eventually would be provided in most proposals too, obviating the need for rented carts. Opponents of serious reform also enjoyed the backing of that minority of well-connected peddlers who, in effect, owned the choicest locations on the streets. Many other peddlers, aware that prior reform attempts had been disappointing, were fearful of any change in the status quo. Stable owners and their allies happily inflamed these peddlers' fears when the movement for pushcart reform intermittently gained steam during the era.[68]

Not surprisingly, the reaction to the presence of pushcarts could be vociferous when they began to appear in neighborhoods in which significant numbers of middle-class people lived. In 1916, for example, the Yorkville Citizens Committee submitted a "brief" to the city's board of aldermen asserting that the carts should be banned from their section of the Upper East Side. Since many members of the committee were Jewish (although the Irish president of the local Tammany Hall Club was also a member), the condemnation of the carts was influenced more by class hostility than by ethnic hostility per se.

The values displayed by the Yorkville committee were a subset within a provincial viewpoint commonly held during the Progressive Era, a viewpoint that looked askance at anyone differing from the accepted middle-class boundaries of respectability. Such boundaries were narrower than they are today, in part because of the greater threat of economic insecurity. In an era in which social safety net measures and the regulation of downward swings in the business cycle were at primitive stages of development, most Americans felt they had only a tenuous hold on their personal economic status. This condition produced psychological insecurity, particularly for those struggling to attain or maintain a foothold in the lower-middle class.

Many compensated for this insecurity by adopting stringent middle-class standards (a phenomenon that tended to hamper efforts to organize unions or social justice–oriented political movements that were grounded in a sense of solidarity with the working class). By wearing a starched collar with a neat hat and tie, a man could believe that he was maintaining himself above the abyss of poverty's chaos that swirled below, frighteningly close, never far from sight practically any-where one ventured in the city. And many tended to accept no less from others hoping to come aboard into the club of middle-class acceptance. Jews aspiring to middle-class status often hoped to reassure themselves by adopting the same stringent standards. But they experienced additional tension, as their yearning to feel secure in a middle-class American identity at times conflicted with their desire to maintain at least some of their centuries-old traditions. The bearded pushcart man speaking with a heavy accent aroused fears in many Americanizing Jews that gentiles would use the peddlers' characteristics as a basis for mocking Jews in general, which in turn would make the balancing act of the American-izing Jews even more difficult to maintain.[69]

Stating that pushcarts had been largely responsible for the "disgraceful con-ditions [of the Lower East Side] . . . from every point of view whether that of esthetics, health, safety or morality," the members of the Yorkville Citizens Com-mittee asserted their intention to learn from that section's failure to restrict the carts. Otherwise, they believed that the carts' presence would create "such chaotic conditions that their parallel can be found only in the bazaars of filthy backward towns of Persia or unpaved barbarous ghettos of Russian Poland. . . . [This] horde of people, few or none of whom are citizens . . . [bring] into the market unin-spected, inferior goods."[70]

The committee felt that the peddlers had brought with them from the Lower East Side an undesirable element that had resulted in a spate of robberies in the Yorkville area. Moreover, "Young girls of the ages of thirteen to fifteen are in the habit of following the different push cart peddlers and crowding around his cart. . . . We fear that the disappearance of many young girls from our district is due to the tempting of this undesirable element which has no social responsibil-ity." The committee added that "the presence of push carts in the district encour-ages cocaine traffic which of late has spread in the Yorkville section." Committee members summed up their case by stating that the peddler "invasion threatens to destroy the character of the streets of Yorkville and convert them into avenues of chaos, dirt and immorality."[71]

Numerous progressive reformers were concerned about the social effects of the pushcarts and probably would have sympathized with the Yorkville com-mittee. Reformers often emphasized that a negative social and physical envi-ronment increased the odds that people would adopt disorderly, immoral, and unhealthy lifestyles. The prevalence of alcohol abuse or of unhygienic, slothful, and criminal habits was considered to be a gauge that measured the extent to which the ensemble of behaviors and environmental conditions connoted by the word "squalor" existed in individuals' lives. The opposite status, "decency," signified the set of attitudes, behaviors, and environmental conditions that re-formers aimed to promote in the lives of the poor—through social programs, education, and, at times, coercive measures. Dirt, a key ingredient in the squalor ensemble, held a multilayered symbolic meaning. Its absence was considered a fundamental prerequisite if the poor were to attain the concomitant conditions of respectability, comfort, and health. Given decent conditions, a greater number of individuals would live healthy, orderly, relatively satisfied lives, which in turn would strengthen their ability to rise on the economic ladder and assume positive, assertive roles in civic life. In this context, we can better understand the anxieties of middle-class reformers who, when venturing downtown, observed the near-chaotic, claustrophobic, and filthy scene of a street lined by pushcarts with tenement canyons looming above. The filth, noise, and congestion of the unregulated pushcart streets seemed to pose a threat not only to the health and stability of individuals but also to the broader societal stability that was rooted in the aggregate condition of tens of thousands of individuals.[72]

The fact that Lower East Side residents possessed a culture that was, at least superficially, alien to most middle- and upper-class reformers merely compounded the sense of strangeness and danger, and the sense that without reform the social conditions causing disease and despair would be practically insuperable for most of the area's residents. While a sense of responsibility to alleviate suffering motivated most social reformers, they were also propelled by the fear that without the existence of hope in the lives of impoverished individuals, the resulting disorder of their lives would spread, drawing more and more people into indecent lifestyles that would, in turn, spawn disease, crime, and other symptoms of social disorder—and possibly even political unrest.

Reformer complaints that the mass aggregation of carts created filthy street conditions were not without merit, particularly within the context of an era in which sanitary reform retained a powerful meaning. This was after all a period in which contagious disease still took a heavy toll, especially among the poor. The historian Simon Schama has observed the tendency of some historians to portray sanitary reformers and like-minded individuals as products of a neurotically fearful and selfish middle class that trumpeted behavioral standards to the lower classes primarily to allow people of higher income to feel more secure in their own lifestyles and status. Schama asserts that this historiographical tendency results from an obsession with the concept of control. Thus, in discussing scholarly attitudes toward public health reformers in early modern times, he observes that some historians have projected overly complex motives onto historical figures who "by the standards of the day . . . [held] perfectly rational preoccupations with the relationship between bad air, foul water and death."[73]

It is important to recognize as well that the sanitary/social reform stance often stimulated measures to improve the living conditions of the poor, measures that were intertwined with the reformers' messages about morals and conduct. Many progressives thus sought to cultivate among the poor a strong work ethic, thrift, sobriety, cleanliness, and a general deferral of short-term gratification in the interest of long-term benefits, believing that these values could be reinforced by providing a more positive environment—through cleaner streets, wholesome recreational facilities for children, minimum wage laws, and other social reform measures.

As we have noted, moral-behavioral expectations were part and parcel of a commonly held perspective on sanitation and health, in which negative external conditions—including diverse factors ranging from garbage-borne bacteria to the perils menacing children playing in the streets—threatened individual morality and physical well-being. This perspective meshed well with the enduring concept of the body as a system interacting with the physical, social, and psychological environment. The late nineteenth-century physician and public health advocate John Shaw Billings expressed an essential aspect of this traditional concept of the body and, in effect, demonstrated how this concept could reinforce social reform when he stated that "no sharp dividing line can be drawn between comfort and health." Certainly sanitary-cum-moral precepts sometimes carried an unfortunate freight of ethnocentrism and condescension. But in many instances these precepts forwarded valid prescriptions for personal development; and they tended to expand the awareness of sanitary reformers beyond more simplistic notions of individual responsibility and, indeed, beyond a concern for sanitary sewerage systems and cleaner streets toward the even broader set of issues that engaged many of the era's social reform progressives.[74]

For example, Charles F. Wingate, a sanitary engineer, observed in the *Vigilant* that "sanitary science is the science of prevention. It destroys disease by removing damp, dirt, and darkness and by securing pure air and pure water, which, two thousand years ago, the Greek Hippocrates proclaimed the essentials of health. As a sanitary engineer, I naturally ascribe special weight to the influence of the environment upon moral and physical development. Experienced workers among the poor . . . [recognize] the impossibility of elevating the masses without first improving their surroundings. A sense of despair is created by the moral and physical degradation . . . traceable to the 'homes' of the poor."[75]

Wingate advocated housing reforms, more parks and playgrounds, and other amenities that would provide some of the comforts that the middle class relied upon in maintaining hopefulness and health. He seconded the opinion of the Social Gospel minister William S. Rainsford, who stated that without such social reforms the poor would be stuck in an environment in which they are "from babyhood, pressed down toward vice." Likewise, a physician who did clinical work for Jewish benevolent societies in the Lower East Side, Maurice Fishberg, asserted that while "healthy, sober, and cleanly . . . personal habits" were keys to health, at the same time "poverty, overwork, ill-ventilated sweatshops, overcrowding in the tenements, [and] lack of fresh air and sunshine" hindered the ability to maintain vitality.[76]

We see a similar appreciation of the tandem roles of the environment and individual character in a report written by Frank H. McLean for the University Settlement. In 1897, he accompanied DSC personnel for several weeks on their rounds in the settlement neighborhood. In his report, he recounted the role of personal habits in perpetuating filthy street conditions, observing that many immigrants had "peculiar traditions and instincts regarding personal conduct and surroundings."[77]

Nevertheless he reassured his readers that "it is not malevolence which induces the residents of some tenements to throw filth of unspeakable sorts from their windows upon the streets ... [or] put human excrement into garbage cans." Like many other sanitary/social reformers, McLean recognized that while it was important to encourage changes in the impoverished immigrant's way of life, exhortations concerning cleanliness, industriousness, and the virtues of civic involvement could hardly make a meaningful impression without the reform of environmental conditions. Thus one University Settlement official commented that without the reform of external conditions—for example, through the institution of wage and hours laws, improved housing and educational opportunities, and more effective street cleaning services—the preaching of civic ideals would be "about as useless as to preach ethical ideals to a starving man."[78]

In short, the meaning ascribed to sanitation and the corollary perception of a connection between dirt, disease, despair, and disorder usually reinforced a stronger awareness of the role of the environment in maintaining squalor more than it encouraged bigotry and defensive reactions. And it reinforced the belief that the quest for economic and social justice was inseparable from a parallel emphasis on individual values.[79] In this context, given the progressives' view that pushcarts produced congested, dirty streets that in turn hindered immigrants who were striving to maintain decency, pushcart reform seemed imperative.

Actually, Progressive Era concerns about health and negative urban environmental conditions had a double-edged effect on reformers' attitudes toward the pushcart issue, prompting their attempts on the one hand to restrict the carts, while on the other hand compelling them to grapple with whether this was in fact fair, given the need for inexpensive consumer items in the poorer districts. Waring had expressed this ambivalence in 1895, commenting that "no one, probably, would dispute the proposition that the push-carts ... constitute something akin to a nuisance. On the other hand, there is no doubt that the push-cart ... is a convenience and sometimes ... an economy to the public. ... These carts are so useful in the densely populated tenement house districts that they ought not to be dispensed with if there is any way to overcome the very serious objections to them."[80]

The typical reformer shared the opinion of most middle- and upper-class New Yorkers that the quality of urban life depended to a significant degree on the state of health and the behaviors of tenement residents who, unfortunately, were all too likely to be unhealthy and disorderly. Yet the reformers were relatively less likely to allow their fears of disorder and their ethnic prejudices to overwhelm their reason when considering the pushcart problem and other public health and social issues.

Reason certainly did not figure prominently in the opinions of the *Tribune* reporter who, in observing people on the streets of the Lower East Side, related an "astonishing disregard . . . of the commonest rules of civic health and cleanliness . . . largely due to the ignorant, the slovenly, the lawless push cart peddler. These unclean men . . . were born abroad amid dirty surroundings. Since coming here they have rubbed shoulders with the native born American, but have gained from him little of his innate love for cleanliness."[81]

A *Times* reporter, likewise, did not see beyond his fears and prejudices in discussing the pushcarts and the refuse-strewn streets in a Jewish neighborhood on the Lower East Side: "A writer might go on for a week reciting the abominations of these people. This neighborhood . . . [is] perhaps the filthiest place on the Western Continent. It is impossible for the Christian to live there, because he will be driven out . . . by the dirt and the stench. Cleanliness is an unknown quantity to these people. They cannot be lifted up to a higher plane because they do not want to be."[82]

In grappling with the pushcart issue, reformers advocating segregated market areas that would be accessible to tenement neighborhoods had to contend not only with the desires of the peddlers and their impoverished customers but also with angry New Yorkers such as the two reporters featured above and the members of the aforementioned Yorkville Citizens Committee. Many people, in fact, would have been happy to see the pushcarts off the streets altogether rather than quibble about whether this or that reform would meet the reasonable needs of the peddlers and their customers. Reformers also had to take into account the complaints of DSC officials who, hoping to preclude the necessity of cleaning up after any carts whatsoever, at times advocated draconian abolition of the carts rather than the reformers' proposed solutions.[83]

In fact Progressive Era reformers generally had to contend with powerful forces that were not "progressive." It is true that, more than in most eras, new ideas about social justice flowered into greater public consciousness, and the overall temper of the times favored a stretching of the reform agenda and a wider recognition of the role that the physical and social environment plays in conditioning values and behaviors. But many citizens were hostile to such trends. A simplistic concern for individual values prompted them instead simply to blame the poor for their lowly conditions. For people with this viewpoint, there were few ideological barriers preventing a fear of disorder or ethnic stereotyping from dictating their response to the pushcart issue or to other social problems. This more conservative segment of the population was often responsible for limiting the social reform gains of the Progressive Era. And, as the historian Fred Viehe has posited, it may be more accurate to label many ostensible "progressives" of the era "almost progressives," who, depending on the specific issue at hand, fluctuated between more traditional and reform viewpoints.[84] In part because of this, the progressive community in New York was unable to unite in a determined and consistent effort to push their fellow citizens to invest in a system in which peddlers and their customers would obtain truly adequate new market facilities.

Progressives typically shared with conservatives a moralistic belief that personal values were a key element in both individual and community advancement. As we have seen, the congestion and filthy streets associated with the pushcarts aroused fears in the minds of reformers that such conditions would foster moral and social disorder and related public health problems. Yet the reformers' emphasis on the environment's role in social pathology and their equation of good health with social well-being helped them to discipline their minds, to see more than their fears and prejudices. Many were thus able to go beyond simplistic solutions and offer social reform, in addition to individual moral reform, as a response to their concerns. In their approach to the pushcart issue, they were therefore more likely than more conservative New Yorkers to balance their fears with at least some recognition of how crucial accessible and inexpensive food was for the poor.[85]

A dawning consciousness of the need to respect the cultural preferences of immigrant groups also helped reformers to accept that the peddlers fulfilled a legitimate function. Again, the ethnocentrism of the progressives should be understood relative to the context of the times, in which it was venturesome for old-stock Americans to depart from a quasi-tribal "Anglo-Saxon" consciousness. Prejudices ingrained during childhood competed for the moral allegiance of many progressives, making their pluralistic notions tentative at best. Yet until World War I and the subsequent Red Scare turned many people sour, urban progressives often aimed to instill in immigrants only those values and behaviors that they believed would be minimally necessary for individuals to attain upward mobility and for the broader community to retain democratic political practices. While the reformers' definition of a minimum core of values and behaviors sometimes resulted in oppressive measures, the ideal at least permitted some appreciation of the validity of immigrant culture.[86]

We can see this ethical stretching in the proceedings of the Mayor's Push-Cart Commission of 1906. The commission included the top officials of the health department and the DSC, and individuals considered sensitive to the needs of the Jewish and Italian communities—Lillian Wald; Gregory Weinstein, president of the reform-oriented East Side Civic Club; and a priest, the Reverend Bernardino

Palizzo. The commission chairman, Lawrence Veiller, had been instrumental in the adoption of significant reforms in the city's tenement housing code five years earlier. In their report, the commissioners emphasized that

> in seeking a solution of this problem, we have constantly had in mind . . . that the city is a cosmopolitan one, the home of representatives of nearly every nation . . . and that the customs and habits of many of its inhabitants are not the customs and habits of others; that practices which would not be tolerated in one part of the city are necessary and desirable in other parts. Many of the attempts . . . to solve the so-called 'push-cart problem,' and also other social problems have failed because of the failure to recognize this fundamental fact: that laws which are good for one part of the city may not only be valueless but even work great hardship in other sections.[87]

Although the commission heard the testimony of pushcart peddlers and ethnic group representatives interested in their welfare, Veiller found it difficult at times to abide by his own commission's warning against ethnocentrism. He became testy, for example, when ethnic representatives insisted that the requirement that peddlers be American citizens (a requirement actually enforced only sporadically) should be dropped. Yet Lillian Wald countered that the suffering of the new immigrant should be considered: "Is not the point this, that if the privilege be accorded to anybody, that those comparatively most helpless are entitled to most consideration?" Wald won over the commission, which recommended dropping the citizenship requirement.[88]

An earlier confrontation over municipal policy, in 1904, can help us to understand the views of various factions concerning the pushcart issue—including the views of those wishing to harshly suppress the carts, those hoping for reasonable reform, the peddlers and their customers, and the local ward politicians dependent on tenement district voters.

DSC officials believed that the pushcarts' addition of large volumes of trash onto city streets constituted a "menace to health" and greatly increased the department's operating expenses. The litter produced by the peddlers and their customers purportedly served as an inappropriate model for newer immigrants. In addition, lines of carts blocking the curbs hampered street sweeping and the collection of household trash cans, which also increased the department's operating expenses.[89] In the spring of 1904, under newly elected Mayor McClellan, John McGaw Woodbury, who had been retained by the new administration as DSC commissioner, announced plans to segregate all pushcart peddlers who sold fresh foods on the Lower East Side into a market area under the approach to the recently constructed Williamsburg Bridge (which crossed the East River to Brooklyn). Although carts selling other items could remain on the streets, the banning of fresh food sales would greatly reduce the number of remaining carts and the volume of litter. Woodbury hoped that the segregation of Lower East Side pushcart peddlers would force the board of aldermen, of which he was profoundly contemptuous (having reportedly referred to it as "an illiterate body of rum soakers"), to segregate the peddlers in special marketplaces in other neighborhoods as well. But it was probably unwise to apply his model initially in the neighborhood with the city's largest population of pushcart peddlers and customers.[90]

During the previous year, under Mayor Low, Woodbury had segregated at the bridge location those Lower East Side pushcart peddlers who sold fish. The commissioner had met with a sizable gathering of worried fish peddlers, mostly immigrants from Russia, shortly after announcing plans for the fish market. They asserted that the bridge market was too far from most of their customers, and contained too few spaces. But rather than allaying their fears, Woodbury lashed out at those in the audience who had expressed their concerns: "You have had [the city government's] sympathy and you have had [its] protection. I have washed your streets for you, and in return you have littered those streets with fish refuse and made them so foul so as to affect the health of the people in the tenements. I know the conditions under which the people of the poorer class live in Russia. I know that no government official . . . in that country would ever call you together as I have done to talk with you. When you come to this country you become members of the body politic and yet from the very freedom you have you want to transgress our laws, but you will not be allowed to do so."[91]

A reporter for the *Forward,* a prominent Yiddish-language daily newspaper, complained that Woodbury's policy would put most of the fish peddlers out of business: "If Woodbury should insist on his order, hundreds of fish peddlers will die of hunger. This is a terrible blow to hundreds of poor families. It is the obligation of the East Side to take up the injustice of her poor peddlers, protecting them with their support."[92]

Yet because the number of peddlers who only sold fish was not great, they lacked the political strength to force Woodbury to rescind his plans. But a year later, in 1904, Woodbury exceeded his grasp, in attempting to place peddlers of *all* fresh foods under the bridge. When he tried to force the issue that summer, an ensuing one-day strike of peddlers and of the fruit wholesalers who supplied the entire city, and concurrent lobbying by peddler representatives, prompted Mayor McClellan to order the DSC to ease up. But Woodbury then insisted on a rigid enforcement of the thirty-minute rule to pressure the peddlers to sell under the bridge. This prompted the arrest of many peddlers selling on the streets that summer.[93]

Although many peddlers did hope that the city would eventually create an extensive system of markets, they were aghast at the idea of being placed under the bridge until the day that city officials would actually institute such a system. Peddler representatives continued to assert that the bridge market was too far from their customers—one peddler thus referred to the space as "Starvation Alley"—and that it had enough spaces for only one-third of the Lower East Side's food peddlers.[94]

Woodbury's plans also were not comprehensive enough to satisfy those reformers interested in the pushcart issue who were attempting to understand the needs of peddlers and tenement residents. Gregory Weinstein publicly blasted the DSC commissioner for forcing poorly located market accommodations upon Lower East Side peddlers and their customers, charging that the commissioner was arbitrarily deciding "the fate of these . . . human beings." Weinstein agreed with other reformers that "pushcarters . . . constitute a positive nuisance to all pedestrians . . . [and] their presence on crowded and narrow streets makes street cleaning very difficult." But having grappled with the viewpoint of each side, he asked: "Is it fair to corral [the peddlers] . . . in a faraway section of the city where making a living is out of the question? Can a woman who lives near Canal and Chrystie Streets be justly expected to walk for her provisions to Delancey and Ridge Streets?" Asserting that the city administration should solve the problem in a way that would be fair to the peddlers and to the public, Weinstein advocated "plenty of convenient market places." He believed that enforcement of Woodbury's policy would undermine the possibility of instituting more equitable reforms because the peddlers' just complaints would "win for them the sympathy of the politicians," who—owing to their lack of concern for the broader welfare of the community—would simply force a return to the status quo ante.[95]

He was right. In late September, barely two months after its inception, the Woodbury plan collapsed. The board of aldermen voted to drop all maximum standing time requirements, ostensibly to allow for more convenient shopping during the Jewish high holidays. Pressure from peddlers and Lower East Side consumers had induced what the *Tribune* had recently referred to as "loud cries of oppression . . . from the smaller politicians in the districts where the pushcart men live." It was understood that there would now be no return to the rigors of the Woodbury system. Although the McClellan administration continued to have conflicts with Tammany Hall on a number of issues, the mayor no longer had the stomach to challenge a return to the unreformed pushcart arrangements of the past.[96]

During the two-month period in which Woodbury's strictures had been enforced, the *Times* printed several letters to the editor, both pro and con. "M.R.B." claimed to speak for thousands of his Lower East Side neighbors in commenting on the changed ambiance of the area during the one-day strike in which the carts had vacated the streets: "The effect was . . . delightfully soothing and agreeable to . . . the senses. . . . Seeing, hearing, smelling, and feeling were all jubilant with wonder, surprise and hope. In the name of all that is good and true and lovely—yes, in the name of decency and safety—keep away the dirty pushcarts and dirty basket peddlers from our streets and sidewalks." Later in the era, another letter writer, angrier in tone, implored civic clubs to "demand that our narrow streets . . . be ridden, once and forever, of these abominable, filth-accumulating, health destroying and dangerous nuisances, the push cart peddlers."[97]

"D.S.M.," on the other hand, expressed sympathy for the pushcart peddlers and their customers, maintaining that "the much-abused pushcart men . . . [are] an immense convenience to multitudes of small purchasers, with little to spend." Sounding the populist note common to the era, D.S.M. theorized that the Woodbury campaign had been spurred by "the storekeepers [who] dislike the competition of the small vendor. . . . This war upon the small purveyor to the small housekeeper . . . seems only a further phase of the growing disposition to crush out individual effort and industry in the interest of the strong and the prosperous." Similarly, "Jeanne C." declared that the pushcarts "are a boon to the majority of employees downtown, whose luncheon consists chiefly in just the fruit they buy from these peddlers. I am a girl stenographer in the Wall St. District, but I should be sorry if to please a number of cranky people I 'and the likes of me' were deprived of part of our daily luncheon. And why sneer at 'penny wares'? There must also be such. Everybody cannot afford to pay a quarter for a peach at some exclusive fruit store."[98]

With tens of thousands of people living on the Lower East Side who were poorer than Jeanne C., the reform community was divided over Woodbury's policies, and high-ranking politicians found it difficult to deny the wishes of lesser politicos who were closer to the grass roots and more responsive to the cries of oppression.[99]

Although important politicians with ties to Tammany Hall did assist the pushcarters in overcoming Woodbury's strictures, and in more normal periods looked the other way when their underlings helped individual peddlers out of unusually difficult altercations with the law, they were not thrilled with the prospect of public battles over the broad issue of pushcart reform. For one thing, there was pressure from DSC and health department commissioners to abate the street filth problem in the pushcart districts. Dirty streets were also a political liability. Many city residents—not just the middle and upper classes—wanted clean streets.[100]

In effect, Tammany politicians wanted to have their cake and eat it too. They claimed to be for public health and clean streets but wanted to give peddlers and their customers free rein where pushcarts were established. And they needed to satisfy two different types of store owner, one of which wanted to keep peddlers on the streets while the other wanted to ban the carts from the streets or at the very least significantly reduce their presence. Many of the latter group of merchants owned large stores and were key supporters of Tammany. At the same time, though, Tammany leaders needed to consider all those people who extorted money to "protect" the peddlers; these folks earned lots of nickels, dimes, and quarters, a portion of which found its way to Tammany.[101]

It was difficult to maintain a balance of these political elements. How could a politician, for example, judiciously weigh the pressures from within city government against the demands of peddlers, or the popular pressure for clean streets and public health against the consumer's need for inexpensive food? At which streets would one draw the boundaries demarcating peddler districts from peddler-free districts? Which business interests should one satisfy, the pro-peddler or anti-peddler? Hoping that the pushcart problem would remain below the political surface, Tammany administrations tinkered piecemeal with the problem by responding cautiously and indefinitely to conflicts that arose within individual neighborhoods. Any serious consideration of rational, systemic change threatened to upset the existing equilibrium. This was especially difficult to contemplate for Tammany members, who, rooted in an American political tradition that was in many ways still Jacksonian in its mind set, were reluctant to take on the role of directing government regulatory enforcement rather than simply distributing government munificence.[102]

Under Tammany rule, because of the cozy ties between established business interests and the political machine, pushcarts were banned from most districts of the city. Lower-level ward-based Tammany politicians nevertheless maintained close contact with voters of the less affluent districts. In those areas with sufficiently strong consumer demand for pushcart wares, such as the Lower East Side, this helped provide the peddlers with enough political clout to remain a fixture throughout the era. Local politicos thus at times served as a check on some ill-conceived plans of reformers and city administrators.[103]

The overall effect, however, was a lack of system, a political free-for-all in which pushcart policy was decided along what one aldermanic committee report called "the lines of least resistance." By 1912, most pushcarts were crammed onto the Lower East Side, having been forbidden in almost all of the neighborhoods of Manhattan where they had once been established. While this helped meet the needs of Lower East Side residents, the hybrid system of extortion, favoritism, and insecure legal standing created discontent not only among reformers but also among the peddlers themselves. And, particularly when crammed into already crowded areas, the carts contributed significantly to the problem of chronically filthy streets.[104]

In short, a number of factors inherent in the political culture of New York City—factors present more or less in many American cities of that era—thwarted attempts to systematically address the pushcart problem. A cultural gap between reformers and peddler representatives undermined mutual understanding; corrupt public officials and store owners had a stake in the status quo; the city lacked the funds to build adequate markets; competing retailers, DSC officials, and many conservative New Yorkers opposed reasonable compromise; mayors reared in a predominantly Jacksonian political culture were caught in the cross fire of competing interests and did not have the political nerve to tackle such a contested issue; rifts existed within the peddlers' ranks; and at the most basic level there was a conflict between two public goods—between the desire on the one hand to provide inexpensive food for the poor and, on the other hand, to achieve greater public health and well-being through more sanitary and orderly surroundings.[105]

The latter part of the Progressive Era nevertheless witnessed a growing convergence of attitudes toward the pushcart dilemma which in turn made it easier to arrive at a compromise solution. Some of the factors that underlay this convergence also contributed to the general upsurge of interest in urban social reform issues and to the coalescence of varied groups around such issues during the latter years of the era—years in which the social reform agenda reached its zenith.

Concern for public health was one consideration that impelled middle-class reformers toward a greater awareness of the pushcart's importance in meeting the nutritional needs of the poor, particularly as inflationary food prices made news during the 1910s. Settlement workers' daily contact with real people suffering in tenement districts reinforced a greater consciousness of the needs of the poor, a consciousness that the settlement workers helped spread within the broader middle class through journalistic accounts. This increased level of awareness was apparent in attitudes toward a number of poverty-related issues.[106]

To promote reform measures that would lower food prices for the poor, James William Sullivan, a labor investigator for the American Federation of Labor (AFL) and the National Civic Federation who had also worked for the Citizens' Union, studied New York City's market conditions between 1909 and 1913. Sullivan's desire to alleviate the conditions of the poor underlay his recognition of the peddlers' value. He found that officials concerned with solving the pushcart problem generally had not fully taken into account the needs of the food-consuming public, and thus had tended to favor "regulations . . . which ignore the right of consumers, as well as a pressing need of the masses." Sullivan favored regulations that would ensure adequate sanitary inspection, litter control, and the mitigation of traffic obstructions, but he believed that these aims could be accomplished while also granting relatively free rein to the peddlers.[107]

In language that combined radical rhetoric with a Wilsonian emphasis on freeing the energies of the small businessman, Sullivan asserted that established food retailers who feared competition, as well as politicians and storekeepers who thrived on the peddlers' payoffs, were the main obstacles to an open system that would lower food prices. He pointed to the peddler-friendly regulations of England, which produced "the cheapest of all systems, efficient, natural, democratic, and rightfully communistic. It often gives the masses double rations." In an era in which as many as one-third of the residents of large cities in the United States were underfed, Sullivan blasted New York's system for tolerating the pushcarts only in a few sections of town while banning them elsewhere. The exclusion of the carts amounted to a "storekeeper's tax on the poor . . . [a] tax on human force through insufficient feeding." "In the name of humanity," he asked, "why not let the peddlers push their carts wherever they can find customers?" Echoing Sullivan's concerns, an article in the Social Gospel–oriented magazine, *Outlook,* informed its mostly middle-class readers that cutting off the supply of pushcart foods "would inflict cruel hardship on great numbers of people—to say nothing of the peddlers themselves."[108]

Political competition between the city's reform and political machine elements also contributed in some ways to the momentum of urban social reform. While reformers sometimes did not fully understand and empathize with the more immediate needs and desires of the poor, the urban political machine on the other hand often failed to plan adequately for complex long-term social problems that required sophisticated research, efficient ongoing administration, and the input of interested civic groups. In the crucible of Progressive Era political competition, both reform and machine elements began to change some negative traits in response to criticisms by the other, not simply to compete for votes (which was an important reason) but also because some of their opponents' charges began to make sense to them.

Reformers, for example, had complained that the littering attendant to the pushcarts undermined public health. Now, however, these reformers were less able, within their own consciences, to complain about this type of danger without also considering another public health problem, poor nutrition, which was normally hidden from the view of the middle class. At the same time, the social and political agenda of reform groups forced Tammany to compete for votes by offering a more issues-oriented politics that included promises for the provision of systematic social services or government-mandated health and safety regulations that many reformers had been touting. In order to maintain successful services within Tammany administrations, personnel and accounting procedures were professionalized at least to the extent that agencies could function fairly smoothly, and administrators allowed professional expertise and reformer input to significantly affect governmental policies and procedures. Tammany Hall was consequently better prepared to help systematize pushcart policy by the end of the Progressive Era.[109]

Criticism from political competitors on the left, particularly from Socialist party activists and from followers of the then quasi-populistic William Randolph Hearst, also pushed reformers toward a greater awareness of the needs of the poor. At the same time, competition from the left pushed the machine toward recognition of the need to sponsor effective street cleaning services and other systematic social reforms that went beyond the inadequate approach of providing occasional coal baskets and other personal favors.[110]

The search for solutions to the pushcart dilemma (and to other vexing urban problems) was also buttressed by the fact that both middle-class and working-class New Yorkers, native and foreign-born, to a significant degree held many values in common concerning order and cleanliness, at least as ideals.

In 1911, the DSC commissioner, William Edwards, asked the editor of the Yiddish-language newspaper, the *Warheit,* for his help in gaining the cooperation of Lower East Side residents during the traditional spring cleaning of homes before the celebration of Passover. Edwards wanted to encourage people to bundle up their trash properly so that it would not break open on the sidewalks before the DSC could pick it up outside their buildings. In response, the *Warheit* ran an editorial that, after detailing Edwards's request, asserted that the request was "for the good and welfare of the Jews" and that "the existing uncleanliness in the Jewish districts . . . is not because the Street Cleaning Commissioner is neglecting his duty. We, only, are to blame for the conditions as they exist and we, Jews, must remedy these conditions ourselves. Ashes, garbage, and rubbish are strewn about. . . . It is a disgrace to all Jews to have their neighbors say that they cannot pass through the Jewish districts because they are in fear of having their garments soiled by the accumulation of rubbish in the streets, a great deal of which is thrown from the windows of our homes."[111]

Evidently the editor of this left-centrist newspaper did not feel that asking and expecting people to adopt cleanly habits was degrading or that this deflected from true reform. Rather, he seems to have believed that such expectations could help empower the immigrants and aid them in achieving their aspirations.

Many of his readers agreed, although often with an ambivalence born from a recognition of how difficult it was to obtain a modicum of cleanliness on a low budget. We can see this ambivalence in the works of Anzia Yezierska, a Jewish immigrant whose short stories illuminated life in the early twentieth-century city. In "Soap and Water and the Immigrant," the young woman narrator aspires to obtain a solid education and career but suffers setbacks due to the unfair judgments "of the well-fed, well-dressed world—the frigid whitewashed wall of cleanliness." In her shabby clothes, she feels condemned out of hand by the "agents of clean society." These "agents" fail to recognize the expense of new clothing and that the poor usually do not have bathtubs in their homes or are often too exhausted from unceasing work to maintain sparkling hygiene. The narrator becomes embittered, noting that she "had suffered the cruelty of their cleanliness and the tyranny of their culture to the breaking point." Yet part of her anger stems from the fact that the agents of cleanliness "did not see how I longed for beauty and cleanliness." Finally, her soul revives (as well as her hope for America) as she finds a friend "from the clean world," one who is equal to her in sensitivity and intelligence, with whom she can share her feelings and find support in evaluating adaptive strategies for bounding back and getting ahead.[112]

Most immigrants tried hard to keep their homes and persons as neat and clean as budget and time constraints allowed. They sought the comforts that running water could bring and saw cleanliness as a palpable symbol of having risen above their harsh surroundings. These immigrants, and even more so their children, usually attained a higher level of social mobility than could have been expected in their countries of origin. America certainly did not greet these newcomers with an open, unprejudiced invitation into realms of power and prestige, and at times the price of assimilation was a painful disavowal of customs. But in considering this country's impediments to social mobility and status, many immigrants made mental comparisons to the impediments in places such as economically depressed Sicily or pogrom-plagued Russia. In that context, the adoption of modern hygienic values seemed *relatively* feasible, especially when representatives of the dominant culture—for example, settlement workers, or a friend such as the one that Yezierska's narrator met, or even more abstract factors such as the passage of social reform legislation—provided a sense that at least some Americans were rooting for the immigrants' success.[113]

A sense of some common ground, then, helped sustain many New Yorkers, of varied backgrounds, in their search for solutions to vexing urban problems like that of the pushcarts.

As historians such as David Hammack have pointed out, independent working-class and ethnic interest groups had a powerful influence on Progressive Era urban policy decision making and on the attitudes of both reformers and members of urban political machines. The influence of such groups helped impel New York toward political compromise on the pushcart issue by the end of the era. James Sullivan's work for the AFL, for example, helped shape his stance toward the pushcart issue. And the peddlers themselves followed the Progressive Era inclination to organize. Their representatives provided significant input into the policy-making process. The rise of Jews of eastern European origin to positions of wealth also helped individuals and groups from the Jewish community to gain influence within the middle- to upper-class reform echelons of New York. This, in turn, reinforced a greater sensitivity within these circles toward the peddlers and their customers.[114]

The effect of independent political factions and of working-class, trade, and ethnic interest groups on the pushcart issue belies the traditional conception of Progressive Era politics as a two-way Manichaean struggle between machine and reform elements. In this vein, the historian Jon Teaford has also suggested that the exigencies of city departments—as exemplified in this study by the DSC's concerns about the pushcarts—were so formidable that reformers and politicians of all stripes had to take government administrators' concerns into account when formulating their own positions on policy questions.[115]

By the tail end of the Progressive Era the complex convergence of attitudes about the pushcart problem produced a consensus, albeit a shaky one, which led to the establishment in 1920 of a system that allowed the carts to stand on a generous number of designated streets in the more impoverished areas of the city. Reformer concerns were taken into account through tightened inspection of pushcart food products; improved enforcement of litter laws by regulatory police; attempts to eliminate favoritism and extortion in the assignment of peddler locations; and the supervision of traffic problems by a Department of Markets officer on the scene daily. The system was an improvement, though in practice corruption to some extent stymied its effectiveness.[116]

Several factors undermined the viability of this system by the late 1930s. The number of incoming immigrants had been greatly reduced during the 1920s with the passage of restrictive federal legislation. This reduced the population in neighborhoods such as the Lower East Side, which in turn reduced the demand for pushcart peddlers' wares. The volume of demand was further undercut by the rise of what are now known as supermarkets, which, by cutting out various middlemen in the wholesale food distribution process, were usually able to charge prices that could match those of the peddlers. More crucial politically, neighborhood business organizations seeking to eliminate what they believed to be unfair competition and to create a more middle-class ambiance in their shopping districts were able to organize themselves to gain greater power during the 1920s and 1930s than they had possessed during the Progressive Era. Moreover, during the 1930s, the city received infusions of Works Progress Administration (WPA) funds that could be used for the construction of indoor market buildings.[117]

Mayor Fiorello LaGuardia provided the final impetus in the effort to restrict most pushcart peddlers to enclosed, rented marketplaces, a process that was nearly complete by the early 1940s. LaGuardia was a son of immigrant parentage and was proud of this heritage. But in a world with narrowly defined boundaries of middle-class respectability, this very pride reinforced the mayor's discomfort with the image of immigrant life that pushcart peddlers projected to the public. In effect, he believed it insulting to immigrants that they continued to be associated with a symbol of low-class existence, the pushcart. He also felt that it was cruel that peddlers and their customers had to stand outside in cold and inclement weather, something that middle-class New Yorkers did not have to do when shopping. It is interesting that, in contemplating Waring's plan to build sheltered pushcart markets over forty years earlier, a reformer had similarly bemoaned the discomfort of both the peddlers and "the poor mothers who buy [when standing] in the slushy streets. The purveyors of canvas-back ducks, English pheasants, or venison are well cared for, as are the customers for such luxuries. Why then, should the buyer of a potato or an onion be pushed into the streets?"[118]

It is equally noteworthy that the late Progressive Era street-oriented resolution of the pushcart problem was reversed by a reform mayor who had previously instituted impressive and humane measures in several fields. Because of these measures and his ethnic background, LaGuardia possessed enough support from immigrant and second-generation voters to put into effect a pushcart policy that would have been a more risky political proposition for a reformer who sprang from old-stock America.

CHAPTER 4

Making Citizens with the Juvenile Street Cleaning Leagues

Tens of thousands of children joined the New York City juvenile street cleaning leagues during the Progressive Era. The DSC hoped that the juvenile league experience would raise children's consciousness of the harm done by behaviors that undermined civic sanitation, that the kids would experience the pride gained in helping to create a cleaner city, and that they would spread their new values to families and friends. More broadly, social reformers believed that supervised children's clubs, playground activities, public-school evening recreation centers, and related programs—often organized by women's groups, school districts, churches, and settlement houses—would remove young people from the dangerous temptations of the streets, expose them to broader horizons, promote self-esteem, combat feelings of hopelessness, and build habits of social cooperation that would broaden in time into a public-spirited civic ethic.[1]

Approximately three hundred of New York City's children were killed each year in street accidents during the Progressive Era. Not surprisingly, a researcher for the city's board of education warned that "street confusions . . . [create in the child] an unstable nervous system and an unstable character." The writer felt sorry for the children of the tenement districts, holding that "a game in the streets is a most pathetic thing"; the youngsters there experienced a stunted version of childhood, as the need to constantly dodge trucks, carts, and people distracted them from play. Moreover, the streets were "intolerably hot" in the summer, causing dust clouds "which analysis has proved to be ninety-five per cent manure . . . [that can lodge in] the eyes and lungs of the children." A settlement worker likewise commented that the streets were "dirty and always dangerous. No well-to-do parent would allow their boys and girls to dodge the heavy trucks as the children of the tenements must do in their play." Another settlement worker lamented the slum child's lack of wholesome opportunities for recreation and social contact, noting that "the foul mud of the gutter is his toy."[2]

Not simply concerned about issues of health and safety per se, the researcher at the board of education feared that the child's moral outlook was warped by the "evil influences" of an unsupervised environment in which, on any given day, he or she might observe a fight, an arrest, drunkenness, gambling, and other marks of the "profanity and obscenity . . . native to the streets." On a recent walk through a tenement district, he had observed several youths throwing objects at wagon drivers and fruit stand merchants; six boys grabbing pears from a push-cart; "a grocery man chasing a boy for [stealing] sweet potatoes from the front of his store; and a boy run [head-on] into a bicyclist."[3]

The restless children passing time on the streets of slum districts were indeed a common symbol of moral and social instability during the Progressive Era. With the rate of juvenile delinquency rising significantly in poorer neighborhoods, many immigrant parents as well as reformers feared for the well-being of the children of these districts. Commentators related that many young street gang members were inclined toward thievery and strong drink; shot craps and idled in alleyways, poolrooms, and on street corners; wreaked mischief upon pushcart peddlers, shopkeepers, and homeless inebriates; took part in street fights between rival gangs; and lived by the rule that "might generally makes right in personal disputes." Children in street gangs were considered to be likely future members of "the low criminal classes and . . . the unstable body of unskilled labor which contributes so largely to . . . prisons and poorhouses." A favorite enterprise of the more roguish childhood street gangs was the "grifting" expedition, in which some members of the group faked a fight in a park or on a streetcar; this allowed other members to pick the wallets of distracted onlookers.[4]

One settlement worker, Frederick King, spoke of a prospect that was frightening not only to middle-class reformers but also to many immigrant parents when he contended that the practically autonomous street culture of the gangs provided adolescents of both genders a permissive sphere for sexual exploration. In this milieu the more timid young people were negatively influenced by the sight of "those who are inclined toward vulgar and improper relations [who] take ad-vantage of such a condition of affairs. . . . The streets . . . have destroyed many a girl's or boy's character."[5]

Although girl gangs were not nearly as common as boy gangs, many people wor-ried that girls exposed to street influences might marry wastrels, or find themselves unwed and pregnant, or even become prostitutes. The latter concern haunted the minds of many in an era in which women's legitimate vocational opportunities were often restricted. One settlement worker lamented how normal the presence of vice seemed to the numerous children who were regularly exposed to such activities in crowded tenement buildings. Girls observed that while they themselves lacked food and clothing, the prostitute lived in "ease [and] comfort . . . [in] wonderfully furnished apartments." Thus the prostitute's persona all too often possessed an aura of "luxury, and . . . of that which seems . . . beautiful."[6]

More generally, child welfare activists asserted that without the parental supervision that middle-class parents were routinely able to provide, the slum child channeled a natural desire for social contact into an involvement in a peer-dominated street culture, before his or her character was sufficiently developed to discern right from wrong. When this was reinforced by the despair arising from the squalor of slum life, the child all too often failed to internalize a sense of lawfulness and middle-class virtues such as thrift, sobriety, cleanliness, and perseverance, which were considered prerequisites both to personal advancement in life and the future stability of society as a whole. One New Yorker who worked with children at the University Settlement challenged his fellow citizens to take action, reminding them that kids "are the citizens of a few years hence, [and] they will constitute a large part of the moral sense of the community." Another settlement worker declared that "the future of . . . civilization" depended on the positive development of the child's "moral nature."[7]

Reformers viewed adolescence (especially early adolescence) as a crucial period in child development, believing that young people during this stage become more and more emotionally independent from their families and increasingly dependent on their peers instead. Activists wondered anxiously whether adolescents would think through to their "own ideas of duty and morality," or instead simply "drift through life without purpose or standard"; whether they would develop "habits of personal cleanliness, both in body and in mind," or instead just go along with "the dictates of . . . [their] senses"; whether they would broaden their horizons, becoming more capable of finding meaningful livelihoods and other avenues of individual fulfillment; and whether they would become citizens concerned with the polity beyond their family or ethnic doorstep. Given an unstructured environment and unsavory friends, a youngster could develop destructive tendencies. As frightening social problems such as crime, alcoholism, family desertion, and prostitution reached alarming proportions in slum districts, reformers developed the juvenile street cleaning leagues, numerous other youth clubs, and related activities that they believed would help families to more effectively socialize their children.[8]

Viewing these programs as means for advancing child development, reformers believed that the programs afforded children access to broader horizons, and greater opportunities for the development of their individual capacities than would typically have been available in the home setting or the streets. The reformers sought to co-opt the children's yearnings for peer camaraderie and recreation, channeling these desires into positive activities and providing structured settings in which they could have fun while gaining peer approval and the approval of adult supervisors for acting responsibly.[9]

The juvenile street cleaning leagues were also part of a broad effort to educate city residents, both young and old, in the "gospel of civic cleanliness"—inculcating, for example, the need for clean streets and the negative effects incurred when people littered or spread soot and trash throughout their neighborhoods by overfilling ash and garbage barrels (or by failing to place covers over these barrels). It was not unusual to spot people tossing heaps of trash out of tenement apartment windows directly onto sidewalks and streets. This was more likely to take place when apartments were overcrowded and contained little storage space; when the woman in charge of household protocol was harried from overwork; or when she was of rural origin and unaware of urban ways, particularly with regard to the disposal of the many new consumer items introduced into her life by residence in the American city. The sporadic failure of DSC workers to collect refuse on the appointed days aggravated the problem.[10]

The era's holistic conception of health and well-being—including the notion that unsanitary conditions erode not only physical health but also personal aspirations, morality, and civic spirit—was a foundation stone of efforts to raise sanitary consciousness. Joseph E. Kean, an official of the Central Mercantile Association, a business group involved in a drive to stimulate citizen cooperation with the DSC in 1914, asserted that the ability of the city to maintain clean streets "directly affects the health of its people and the physical and moral condition of the City at large."[11] Hoping to educate the mostly middle-class readers of the periodical *Woman's Forum,* the Reverend Caroline Bartlett Crane, a nationally renowned sanitary reformer, likewise lamented that "dirt and disorder" in Progressive Era cities was eroding the sense of "civic responsibility" needed to maintain "civilized" conditions. Far too many Americans lacked a "loving regard for order and cleanliness and honor." While praising the City Beautiful movement's drive to erect inspiring civic sculpture, she warned that civic art without civic cleanliness was "as diamond rings on dirty hands." Dirty streets were "a menace to public health and a destroyer of civic beauty," and were a sign that we "have not yet mastered the fine art of living decently together." Readers were urged to think not only of the cleanliness and order of their own personal dwellings but also to become civic activists, to "feel their share of responsibility for the cleanliness of their city." Only then could cities attain a decent degree of "municipal housekeeping . . . [and the level of] civic cleanliness . . . [that is] the foundation of civic art and of civic pride and civic self-respect."[12]

Many Progressive Era reformers emphasized that cleanly habits engendered self-respect, and that this then generalized into greater respect for one's household and the civic environment. Ellen Scrimgeour, the president of the Brooklyn branch of the Women's Health Protective Association, a group active in sanitary reform, believed that a neat, properly filled ash barrel is "a sign of righteousness. The ash barrel reflects the mind of its owner." People who placed overfilled barrels out for collection were inconsiderate of the fact that the barrels spilled ash particles all over the sidewalk, spreading dirt and disorder onto the streets with each incoming wind and "demoralizing" the populace. Reflecting the influence of Social Gospel beliefs, Scrimgeour added that "when Christianity takes upon itself the burden of making cities, then will the Kingdom of Heaven begin upon the earth. When we are all righteous, even the women, in so simple a thing as the ash barrel, when we are all ready, then will it come."[13]

Scrimgeour and many other activists believed that the unstable moral environment associated with filthy civic conditions made a child's choice of life-style—which determined health and well-being as much as did actual germ infestation—a more perilous undertaking. As we have seen, an increasing awareness of the difficult environment faced by the poor helped sensitize progressives to the notion that society could finance services or enforce regulations that would make a certain level of middle-class comfort available to the poor. An improved environment might then permit tenement residents that modicum of hope and confidence that would, in turn, increase the likelihood that they would adopt the values considered prerequisite to self-improvement and social order. Even many traditionalists who retained the habit of blaming poor people for their conditions and failings could nevertheless think of children within an Enlightenment-inspired framework, in which each child's character is a blank slate (tabula rasa) at birth, possessing the potential for good if provided decent care. The perceived innocence of children, and the related perception that they were more pliable than adults (who were already set in their ways), helped win middle-class support for many social reform measures that could directly or indirectly affect the young—including, for example, child labor legislation; the founding of juvenile court systems; foster care; vocational training; playgrounds and other alternatives to street play (including juvenile street cleaning leagues); in-school health screenings and instruction in disease prevention; measures to ensure a tuberculosis-free milk supply; more rigorous tenement housing standards; and minimum wage legislation.[14]

Given the importance of children in the reformers' worldview, it is not surprising that they placed crucial responsibilities on childhood education. Accordingly, Scrimgeour looked to the juvenile street cleaning leagues to stimulate youthful interest in the ensemble of values and behaviors embodied in the phrase "cleanliness and decency." But the street cleaning leagues were merely one of many programs that progressives hoped would provide alternatives to the street gang, raise self-esteem, and foster a sense of cooperation and civic ethics. Progressive Era settlement workers, church and civic group activists, and school administrators established children's clubs—often with an element of self-governance—that catered to a variety of interests, from health education to literary pursuits to cooking classes, that commonly emphasized some elements of civic education.

Likewise, progressive educators initiated civics courses and sought to use school and playground facilities for after-school and summer recreational-educational activities. Reformers hoped that as children at risk engaged in youth club and related activities, they would see aspects of American life that they would begin to value, and that these activities would increase their aptitude for personal success and help immunize them against political apathy or the obverse specter of radical politics. The end product of this vision would be an assimilated adult contributor to society, rather than another tragic byproduct of overwhelming conditions who would worsen that complex of individual and environmental pathology known as the slum. And, in the process, reformers hoped that adults in what was a highly flawed urban environment would themselves learn from the cooperation and civic-mindedness modeled by the children participating in the various clubs and related activities.[15]

Because of the moral, medical, and civic importance attached to cleanliness, activists used various means to promote greater awareness of sanitation issues among all age groups. City officials and members of civic groups such as the WML spoke at teacher and parent meetings, student assemblies, and various church, youth, and civic organizations. At least some instruction in personal or civic sanitation issues was a feature in numerous types of children's clubs. Schools held essay and poster contests to stimulate awareness of DSC work and the importance of civic cleanliness, and multilanguage circulars were distributed in immigrant districts explaining street cleaning ordinances and their significance, and asking for the residents' cooperation. The WML sponsored the distribution of civics books in the public schools that dealt with practical issues such as street cleaning. Through these activities, reformers acted in the spirit of advice given by Commissioner Woodbury of the DSC in 1902, when he told WML members that "the city cannot be legislated into goodness, but the [Woman's Municipal] League can help educate it into cleanliness."[16]

Commissioner Waring had originally founded the juvenile street cleaning leagues in 1895. His imagination was sparked by conversations with Mrs. William Schieffelin, who would be an activist in the WML, and with James B. Reynolds, who at that time headed the University Settlement. Reynolds told Waring about a youth club recently established at the settlement that inspected neighborhood streets and conveyed criticisms or suggestions to DSC officials. Settlement houses and other private philanthropic organizations subsidized the juvenile leagues that subsequently formed under Waring's auspices. Among the early sponsors were the University Settlement, the College Settlement, the Educational Alliance, and branches of the Children's Aid Society. Mainly geared toward poorer, crowded districts, forty-four juvenile street cleaning league clubs counted approximately a thousand children as members by the end of Waring's term in late

1897. By that time, Waring had gained the cooperation of public school officials in efforts to introduce the leagues as an extracurricular school activity. This goal was cut short after the establishment of only two school clubs, however, after the Strong administration was succeeded by the Tammany-dominated mayoralty of Robert Van Wyck.[17]

Because of Waring's success in cleaning the streets and the national renown gained in doing so, Van Wyck initially appointed James McCartney as DSC commissioner, who tried to maintain Waring's policies whenever politically feasible. DSC officials interested in the leagues, such as Reuben S. Simons—who had gone blind while in the department's service—continued to work with the children. But after McCartney died, in February 1900, Van Wyck appointed a more antediluvian style of Tammany administrator, Percival E. Nagle. A real estate developer and contractor with investments in poolrooms and gambling houses in the city and in the "Little Monte Carlo" district just over the Westchester County line, Percy Nagle was not very interested in the juvenile leagues. Ironically, without administrative support and guidance, some clubs regressed to a state of antagonistic intergroup rivalry that resembled the street gang behavior that advocates had sought to shield the children from in the first place. The leagues subsequently disbanded in August 1900.[18] Nevertheless, the publicity engendered during Waring's term had spurred the creation of numerous civic-minded children's clubs throughout the nation that became involved in street cleaning or other types of municipal work.[19]

In New York, after Nagle sloughed off the leagues, the WML took up where the DSC left off. Beginning in 1902, it established the first of its own juvenile street cleaning clubs, similar in nature to the prior groups.[20] Meanwhile, Reuben Simons, still employed by the DSC, gave lectures to school assemblies and civic organizations on the need for cooperation with the department. Although the WML street cleaning clubs were few in number, their existence helped create a climate in which the DSC commissioner, Macdonough Craven, in 1907 authorized Simons to expand his talks to additional areas of the city and help private organizations form new juvenile street cleaning clubs. The University Settlement initiated a club for girls, while the WML sponsored two additional clubs, officially designating its groups the "Waring Juvenile Citizens' League." Prefiguring future developments, one of these clubs was formed at a public school (P.S. 165), to be supervised by its principal.[21]

In 1908, the DSC commissioner, Foster Crowell, approved the formation of juvenile leagues that would again be directly under the department's auspices. This time, DSC leagues were to be operated more often in connection with the public schools. There were nine clubs by the end of 1908. In 1909, under William "Big Bill" Edwards, then the DSC commissioner, twelve more clubs were formed, and league formation began to gain greater momentum. By 1915, there were four hundred branches with over twenty-five thousand members. (A club was sometimes referred to as a branch, a league, or a post.)[22]

Branches were formed in response to student and teacher interest after officials from civic groups or the DSC spoke at student assemblies, or after children learned about street cleaning issues in civics classes. Usually an interested teacher would supervise club meetings as an after-school activity. Individuals from groups such as the WML also served as supervisors at several schools. The WML meanwhile retained at least three of its own previously established "Waring posts" outside of the aegis of the public schools, though the schools provided meeting rooms and a membership base for several new WML-supervised juvenile league posts after 1910. The WML encouraged the children in these posts to participate in the additional recreational opportunities that the WML afforded its posts' members.[23]

Another focus for youth involvement was established in the schools in 1916, when the Merchants' Association began sponsoring an "Anti-Litter League." This organization recruited over a thousand high school students to become "block captains"; each was assigned a block in which they would engage in the same sort of activities as did the older members of the juvenile leagues. Since the quality of participation in youth activities often depended on the personality of an adult leader, the DSC welcomed the involvement of organizations such as the WML and the Merchants' Association.[24]

There were some differences in procedure between the juvenile street cleaning leagues of the 1890s and those of the 1910s, as there were between DSC clubs and those primarily associated with private sponsors. Nevertheless, there were many elements common to all of these groups. A composite picture of a typical club would include members who were nine to fifteen years of age. Both boys and girls were eligible for membership but clubs were segregated by gender. This reflected the belief of most educational theorists that the developmental and social needs of boys and girls differed significantly. (Moreover, one child welfare advocate observed that "constant intimacy between maturing boys and girls fosters an undesirable precocity and introduces unnecessarily perplexing problems.")[25]

Juvenile league members typically would pick up litter in the area of their schools and deposit it in the black-and-red city refuse cans ("red robin cans") placed in the vicinity through the cooperation of the DSC. Depending on the level of enthusiasm of a particular branch, the children might also clear crosswalks near their schools on snowy mornings or hand out bilingual circulars in their neighborhood requesting behaviors that would enhance civic cleanliness. The most motivated club members would approach strangers that they observed littering, asking that they place the object in a red robin can instead. Some would inform the litterer of the relevant city ordinance or explain why they felt it was important to have a litter-free city. The older youths would visit neighborhood residences and businesses, to instruct tenants and building janitors on issues such as refuse separation, ash barrel etiquette, and the danger and illegality of blocking fire escapes with large household objects. On occasion, the more exuberant league members acted in a manner akin to the medieval charivari, invoking community sanction on the city's streets by loudly ridiculing DSC employees who consistently neglected their duties.

All league members showing a good-faith effort were awarded a badge, with an inscription on it: "WE ARE FOR CLEAN STREETS." This helped attract club members; a youngster in the juvenile league could wear a badge and feel like a figure of authority, rather than experiencing the usual feeling of being subject *to* authority. The number of children per street cleaning club varied. Though usually in the twenty- to fifty-member range, branches could have as many as 150 to 200 children. The branches held parliamentary-style meetings every week or two. In the meetings, members would present oral or written reports on the unkempt or dangerous conditions spotted in their neighborhood since the previous meeting (citing, for example, filthy vacant lots and streets, missing street signs, dead animals in roadways, broken curbs, and what we would today call potholes). And members related their discussions with litterers or others about civic sanitation. The number of litterers and other ordinance violators who had been approached were tabulated at the meetings. In 1911, for example, members of three WML posts with a total of approximately 150 members recorded 6,000 incidents for the year. Members sometimes also debated public issues at their meetings, especially when relevant to civic sanitation.

The adult branch supervisor would report missing street signs and other such conditions, after confirming them, to the appropriate city department. When league members reported chronic DSC employee negligence at meetings, the club supervisor would then attempt either to speak with the employee or, if impractical, to report the problem to a DSC official. In addition, if there was no redress regarding such items as overfilled cans and blocked fire escapes after league members had spoken with the transgressor, the club supervisor would report the offending landlord, janitor, or tenant to the appropriate city department.[26]

An egregious example of the types of conditions that were reported to city authorities was that of a restaurant in which the cellar floor had been torn up. Sewer water flowed out of broken pipes protruding from beneath the surface onto the cellar floor, upon which stood the restaurant's vegetables ready for preparation. After prompting the amelioration of these conditions, league members maintained a watchful eye to preclude a return to the status quo ante.[27]

Answering criticism that the juvenile street cleaning leagues encouraged children to be pompous and to "spy upon" others, David Willard spoke for the Waring administration in asserting that the emphasis was rather on teaching "clean habits" to league members, and on "stirring up in them a spirit of civic pride" and a sense of "the child's individual responsibility to his own city and his own best self." Insofar as the rest of the community was concerned, the primary aim was to spread the consciousness of a league member by "the example which he sets to others."[28]

After the pattern set by Nazi and Communist youth who ferreted out what they considered to be the subversions of their elders, it may be difficult for present-day readers to stomach the reporting aspect of the juvenile leagues. There was indeed potential for the abuse of league practices, but a sense of perspective mitigates any facile correlation of the impulses of the American progressives with those of later totalitarians. Pre–World War I America had a far different cultural climate than postwar Germany or Russia. Especially before the destabilizing effects of the war and the subsequent Red Scare, progressives generally cherished, to a far greater degree than future supporters of totalitarian regimes would, the personal liberty aspects of the American tradition. Most progressives were wary of any overarching power, including that of the government. To foster prosocial conduct, their major emphasis was on the encouragement of voluntary internal restraints, on creating a normative sense, as exemplified by Waring's desire to teach the populace through the example set by the children.[29]

To stimulate esprit de corps at branch meetings, league members sang patriotic songs or popular songs with lyrics about civic sanitation substituted for the usual words. Although the popular melodies were mostly ones unrecognizable to the average person today, one club sang the following lyrics to the tune of "Yankee Doodle":

> We will keep our city clean
>   We'll not be unruly,
> What we say we really mean—
>   Yes, we do, most truly.
> We'll not throw upon the street
>   Anything, no, never;
> That's the way to keep it neat
>   Always and forever.
>
> We'll not trespass in our play,
>   Break the trees or hedges,
> Pluck the flowers that bloom so gay—
>   We will keep our pledges.
> If we do, then all will know
>   We are grateful really—
> To our city much we owe
>   We must love it dearly.

We'll not spit upon the street,
    In cars nor public places;
This is far from being neat,
    Leaves unwholesome traces.
And disease is spread about
    By such selfish doing;
We will try to put to rout
    Smoking, spitting, chewing.[30]

At each meeting, the children also recited the juvenile street cleaning leagues' "Civic Pledge," composed during the Waring administration: "We, who are soon to be citizens of New York, the largest city on the American continent, desire to have her possess a name which is above reproach. We, therefore, agree to keep from littering her streets and, as far as possible, to prevent others from doing the same, in order that our city may be as clean as she is great and as pure as she is free."[31]

Members of WML posts had access to club rooms stocked with games and magazines. The WML boys met weekly in gymnasium facilities, where they took basketball and gymnastics lessons or played refereed basketball contests. Dancing and first aid classes also were popular. One boy related that "the dancing class is great sport. We have the two-step and barn dance down fine and are working hard on the waltz." Some months after the introduction of a WML post for girls in 1910, one boy, in commenting on his fondness for the dance class, remarked proudly that he and the other boys were acquiring some manners, as signified by their learning to walk a dance partner to her chair rather than leaving her standing in the middle of the room.[32]

The private sponsors of the juvenile street cleaning leagues of the 1890s often provided recreational opportunities similar to those of the WML posts that were established a few years later. And it is probable that at least some of the clubs affiliated with public schools during the latter part of the Progressive Era had access to gymnasiums and other recreational facilities provided through the public school system's Evening Recreation Centers.[33] Child welfare advocates often encouraged the inclusion of physical recreation as an auxiliary activity for various types of youth clubs. They believed that supervised athletics afforded opportunities for physical development and lessons in fair play, cooperation, and self-control. And they considered athletics and other recreational activities to be a lure with which to attract children to the more serious purposes of the groups. "It is not difficult," remarked a WML official, "to influence . . . boys and girls by appealing to their natural tastes." Some child welfare activists also theorized that kids would more quickly learn moral lessons through physical activities because of the emotional wallop generated by the mixture of physicality with emotionally instilled lessons. These lessons would thereby be impressed upon the child's whole body (psyche included). Thus, the fear of garnering team members' censure would greatly reinforce lessons in cooperation, and the physical-affective impressions so imprinted would, in turn, facilitate the brain's adoption of corresponding, yet more abstract, notions of right and wrong.[34]

To honor league members, once or twice each year sponsors convened special meetings of the children from several clubs, or schools would hold special assemblies attended by all of their students. Parents were invited to these events, and a visiting dignitary such as Waring, Reuben Simons, or a WML official would give a speech on the children's work, urging the audience to emulate the league members' civic consciousness. The children would read essays they had written on related topics, and medals or certificates were awarded to those who had shown particular resolve in their work.[35]

To further maintain the children's interest and promote awareness of DSC operations, there were occasional field trips, even including boat excursions to view the department's fill operations at Rikers Island. And the DSC periodically treated all of the juvenile league members to a grand picnic held in their honor. There, the kids would march with banners flying, and then play baseball and other games. The children also cherished participating in the annual DSC employee parade down Fifth Avenue. In part, Waring had instituted the DSC parade, like the juvenile leagues, to promote citizen interest in the department's work. As in the case of the juvenile leagues, the parade idea was dropped after Waring's term but was reinstituted in 1909 (only a few months after the DSC juvenile leagues had been reestablished). The revival of these two activities was a sign of a general intensification of the progressive zeitgeist during that part of the era.[36]

In sponsoring the juvenile street cleaning leagues, Waring hoped at the very least that this would cut down on the number of kids who tossed litter onto the streets and sidewalks of New York. But he was also mindful that these kids could be publicity agents for the cause of civic sanitation, especially among older family members "who do not understand our language, and who still feel the influence of the country where they grew up." Waring hoped that league children would speak with relatives and peers concerning, for example, the virtues of a litter-free environment, the importance of separating household wastes, and the laws pertaining to these issues.[37]

During his term in office, Waring asserted that the children's example was generating a "contagious cleanliness" within their communities and spreading a sense of personal responsibility for civic sanitation. When added to the fact that his DSC was improving street cleaning and trash collection services, tenement district residents now experienced a higher level of civic sanitation that contrasted favorably with the demoralizing street conditions of the past. Waring believed that these improvements, and an awareness among tenement residents that they or their children had helped create such conditions, reinforced not only a greater appreciation of personal and civic cleanliness but also greater levels of self-respect and self-esteem. This connoted a rise not simply in levels of physical comfort but in levels of hope and vigor as well, which in turn helped residents garner greater personal power in the struggle for a sufficient livelihood. Charity case workers made this connection as they visited tenement apartments that they claimed were cleaner, cheerier, and more orderly. They praised Waring's more effective street cleaning policies and the work of the juvenile leagues for contributing to these improvements, while school teachers related that children involved in juvenile league activities appeared more eager in their lessons.[38]

The Educational Alliance maintained that its hygiene classes for immigrant mothers produced similar results. These classes reportedly engendered in their matriculants "an appreciation of cleanliness and pleasant surroundings, [which] stimulates the desire to make their own abodes more attractive, and when the spirit of something better once possesses those who are huddled together in unhealthy quarters, the problem of crowded tenements will find easier solution."[39]

Such remarks typified the progressives' perception that cleanliness, health, and morality were interrelated concerns, a viewpoint embodied in the stated goal of one New York citizens' lobby group to "keep the streets of this city in a condition consistent with decency." Reformers believed that the civic pride resulting from clean streets and homes would inspire citizens to work for the improvement not only of their own individual lives but also for the improvement of the city at large.[40]

In particular, DSC officials and sanitary reformers hoped that by educating New Yorkers about the negative effects of dirty streets and the value of clean streets, the juvenile leagues would help build a critical mass of public opinion supportive of DSC efforts to improve services. The city administration faced the dilemma that without heightened levels of citizen cooperation, the streets would remain in such poor shape that taxpayers, discouraged about DSC services, would be reluctant to support the use of more city funds to upgrade the department. A correspondent for the *Times* declared that if citizens would show "moral support for the [DSC] servants of our greater home" by refraining from littering, the resulting clean streets would spark an awakening of civic pride and higher expectations, which in turn would make New Yorkers more inclined to support the DSC or proposed improvements in mass transit or other urban reform measures. But until that day, people would hesitate to spend their money on civic ventures. After all, the writer declared, taxpayers do not like to throw money into pigsties, since "pigsties are not paying investments except to dealers in pigs."[41]

Supervisors of children's clubs that were interested in civic education and related topics sometimes recruited members by inviting existing youth street gangs to participate. This was usually practical only with gangs that were not "tough," that is, those that had not suffered the dehumanizing experience of habitual engagement in seriously antisocial activities. In one example of gang co-optation, a matron in charge of one of the public toilet facilities in a city park complained to WML members "that her life was made unbearable by a gang of rowdy girls" from the neighborhood. Women of the WML's Waring Juvenile Citizens' League Committee then visited the girls. Their ensuing discussion resulted in the formation of a new juvenile league post. According to WML committee chairwoman Marion Peters, this opportunity had "transmuted the gang spirit into a spirit of civic co-operation. The matron is no longer disturbed by these girls."[42]

A University Settlement worker discussed another instance, in which, through outreach efforts, a gang of boys formed a club that regularly played basketball at the settlement house. During one of the club meetings, two of the boys began to fight. The rest of the group would have accepted such an event on the street as just another byproduct of the Darwinian street culture to which they were accustomed. But in the settlement club an adult supervisor broke up the fight. Club members then pleaded with the supervisor to "make them friends. . . . [It] is not right for the club," and they themselves harangued the brawlers, telling the two boys that they were "disgracing this club." Their remonstrances did in fact help foster a reconciliation. To the settlement worker, the incident illustrated the theory that if children are provided positive group experiences in which they feel appreciated and opportunities to shine within positive social channels, then they will feel proud of the group, and loyal to it and to the greater community that provides such worthy resources.[43]

With safe and secure play experiences, education in civic matters, and an awakening of hope for a brighter future, reformers believed that children would be more likely to adopt an active, proprietary interest in civic affairs. The child's inclination to cooperate and consider others' views in civic matters would be strengthened all the more when school civics classes or after-school recreational programs fostered participation in practical public-oriented projects—through means such as the juvenile street cleaning leagues and student government. Advocates envisioned a city in which tens of thousands of children would grow up to help generate an orderly but just society, one in which citizens would consider the well-being of the whole rather than caring only for narrow interests when choosing candidates or policies.[44]

Julia Richman was a prominent figure in educating New York's children about considerate civic habits. As a school principal and then an assistant superintendent within the city's public school system, she helped institute educational practices that were more sensitive to the needs of Lower East Side immigrant students. She established one of the first juvenile street cleaning league branches (at the Educational Alliance) during the 1890s. And as part of the general movement within progressive education to bring greater relevance to the study of civics, she coauthored a book, entitled *Good Citizenship* (1908), to instruct students in the practical functions of municipal government and the ways in which children could help their city. She informed her young readers that without citizen cooperation, it is "impossible to keep the city streets clean," as it would likewise be impossible to keep an apartment clean if family members constantly discarded trash onto the floor after it was swept.[45]

Like most progressives, she did not hesitate to speak out when she perceived a slackening of personal virtue. Indeed, if the behavior in question could adversely affect the well-being of the broader society, the progressives said so, loudly, seeking to evoke a sense of personal responsibility or guilt in ways that would sound harsh to many in the present day. Richman thus informed her readers that people who tossed garbage from apartment windows lacked pride in the city's appearance, possessing an uncaring and lazy attitude that was "a sign of bad breeding . . . [and a] disgrace to themselves and to their neighborhood."[46]

Character was a key concept in the progressive mindset, which regarded the development of a child's personal character and his civic consciousness to be inextricably intertwined matters. Waring had praised the juvenile street cleaning leagues' propensity to "react on . . . [the children's] characters; the citizen in embryo is obviously developing," and he appreciated a colleague's witty characterization of the leagues as "Citizen Factories." Waring hoped that the leagues were making "citizens who will be interested in the city and who will do what they can to improve its ways as well as its highways."[47]

Similarly, while the chairman of the Educational Alliance's Committee on Education expressed gratitude that the settlement's juvenile street cleaning league club helped keep neighborhood streets more tidy, he believed that "the main object . . . [of the club is] rather the influence which reacts upon the character of the members, preparing them for active interest in civic duty." Another Educational Alliance spokesperson emphasized the connection between personal and civic virtue, asserting that the settlement's "religious, moral, and mental training shall go hand in hand. . . . The duties of citizenship will be treated as religious obligations . . . inculcating a high sense of moral duty." And Henry M. Leipziger, chairman of the Educational Alliance's Committee on Moral Culture (which supervised the settlement's juvenile street cleaning league club), noted that "when we say that the Alliance Americanizes those who come within its influence, we mean that it makes them better citizens in the broadest sense of the term, and that can only be accomplished by the building of character."[48]

Indicating the commonly perceived nexus of cleanliness and virtue, another Educational Alliance leader noted the settlement's intertwined goals of teaching "a love for personal cleanliness and moral rectitude" through its after-school classes and clubs. Alliance officials did not doubt that they should encourage habits conducive to personal and civic cleanliness. "To inculcate proper appreciation of purity of mind and purity of body," the organization's president, Isidor Straus, claimed, "reaches the fundamental basis on which the uplifting of mankind rests."[49]

The principles underlying the work of the juvenile leagues and related groups were exemplified in the community "cleanup" campaigns common to the era. Like the juvenile leagues, cleanup drives exemplified the progressives' desire to promote community awareness of issues that required a cooperative citizenry. The drives were one among many other campaigns that aimed to educate the populace and foster civic involvement concerning a variety of public issues during the era, from childhood disease prevention to automotive safety.

The cleanup drives grew in popularity during the latter part of the era. Business and civic groups typically organized publicity campaigns that aimed to spur citizens to use a special one-week period to clean out their yards, clear their cellars and attics of accumulated rubbish, and beautify the city's appearance—for example, by planting flower boxes in their apartment windows. City street cleaning departments concurrently made special efforts to collect the additional rubbish and clean the streets with exceptional care.[50] Adult cleanup drive organizers spoke to school assemblies to enlist students to inform their parents about the campaigns and hand out educational leaflets to neighborhood residents. Juvenile street cleaning league youths and members of related clubs served as the core battalions in these efforts throughout the nation.[51]

Sometimes cleanup drives would include attempts to ascertain whether householders were complying with a municipality's sanitation laws. In 1915, for example, the Hartford, Connecticut, chamber of commerce sponsored a campaign in which 257 Boy Scouts, with a polite yet "business-like" approach, distributed health and fire department literature and inspected the yards of 10,085 dwellings. Householders had plenty of lead time in which they were informed of the campaign. Once under way, those who had not cooperated were reported for possible nuisance citations. A journalist stated that the campaign had a big "moral effect on the householders." The writer related that when the scouts arrived in the poorer sections, "strenuous cleaning commenced at once." Homeowners and landlords there vigorously implored the boys not to report them, claiming that they had just been preparing to clean their yards. The Boy Scout office received calls from every section of town, from people fed up with the filthy yards of neighboring properties, who asked that the scouts inspect those addresses.[52]

Sanitary reformers thought that the majority of citizens wanted to cooperate with cleanup drives and related efforts, and that the civic cleanliness ideal had an inherent appeal among people of all classes. They believed that an approach that focused mostly on education (but was backed up by enforcement) strengthened people's regard for this ideal, as did the very feelings of hope and civic pride engendered by the more cleanly appearance of those neighborhoods involved in the cleanup drives.[53]

Some reformers criticized the cleanup campaigns, asserting that people should abide by sanitary norms year round and that one-week spectacles evoked spasms of public interest that made citizens feel good without truly resolving ongoing civic sanitation problems. Cleanup advocates replied that the campaigns helped foster positive attitudes and behavior patterns that would become habitual. The historian and civic activist Mary Beard praised juvenile leagues and cleanup drives for bringing parents "the message of prevention and the feeling of public interest which [the children] have acquired at school or at their little meetings." The aggregate result was a greater likelihood of an "every-day-in-the-year campaign for the elimination of disease-breeding germ and dust provokers."[54]

Beard singled out for praise the important role that women's civic groups played in supporting cleanup campaigns, juvenile leagues, and other civic sanitation efforts. These efforts serve as an interesting lens for viewing the Progressive Era "maternalist" vision of reform. Historians in the past generation have used this term to describe late nineteenth- and early twentieth-century social reform efforts that were grounded in a common belief that women possessed particularly strong nurturing qualities and heartfelt concern for their fellow human beings—characteristics that traditionally undergirded their role as homemakers but that could rightly metamorphize into a robust concern for the public sphere that so deeply affects the well-being of many people.[55]

In this vein, Beard believed that women found the civic sanitation ideal particularly appealing because their historical function involved guarding the cleanliness and health of the household, a function that she believed was strengthened by instinctual urges. She hoped that civic sanitation advocates would prompt numerous women to associate private cleanliness with the need for improved public cleanliness, by reminding housewives that the dust and dirt of the street tended to seep, slowly but surely, into their own houses.[56]

The progressives' search for the root causes and ramifications of public problems helped many women and men alike to recognize the interconnectedness of issues. Motivated in part by a sense of compassion for the needy that was enhanced by their experience as nurturers, many Progressive Era women came to recognize what trailblazing female social reformers had said for years: that, contrary to hierarchical assumptions, the public sphere should be of great concern to women (rather than just to men), and that even middle- and upper-class women in fine homes could not escape their ties to the problems affecting the city as a whole by walling themselves off into a traditionally insular domestic role. Instead, the requirements of home life in the city demanded public involvement and a sense of responsibility for "municipal housekeeping."

Julia D. Perry of the Women's Health Protective Association of Brooklyn, for example, viewed women as guardians of the household who "by nature and education" were concerned with preserving the order thereof. As good housekeepers, they sought to eliminate waste, dust, and vermin from their homes, and by logical extension, "as the city is but the aggregation of homes, and its conduct materially affects the individual home, thoughtful philanthropic women have felt the necessity of entering into municipal life and using their common sense and persuasive powers to influence legislators and officials to abate dangerous nuisances and pass and enforce sanitary ordinances."[57]

A WML leader, in exhorting women to join in her organization's reform efforts, likewise spoke of the connectedness of different social spheres:

> The day is past when a woman's life is bounded by the four walls of her home; there lies undoubtedly the principal sphere of her daily activities, but to make these activities sane and intelligent, she must connect them, as her life is inevitably connected by circumstances, with the welfare of the city of which she is, whether she will or not, a part. That the city shall be clean and healthy, that the tenements shall be as well administered as the law provides, that the police shall be vigilant and faithful, on these things her own personal comfort and safety and her family's, to a large extent depend. One woman alone is powerless to effect much, but thousands of women banded together with this object in view will supply a disinterested public opinion seeking nothing but the public good, before which officials and departments must in time bow, and on the individual woman herself the effect of associating her life with the activities of the city makes her a better citizen, a more intelligent human being, and therefore a completer wife, mother, and home-maker.[58]

In extending the functions of the guardian of the home, female reformers asserted that women were specially qualified to educate the public in civic matters because of their traditional role in the socialization of children. "It is peculiarly appropriate," noted one WML member, "that women should be doing this work, for after all it is to the mothers that we turn for the teaching of our children." In accepting the challenge of educating the public about civic sanitation issues, Ellen Scrimgeour stressed that women must "stand straight and square for righteousness" in both their private and their public lives, because they "stand before the public as teachers."[59]

The idea of expanding the educative role of women from the private home and schoolhouses to the more public sphere was considered particularly appropriate when this involved issues affecting children and the family. And given the environmental-causation ethos shared by numerous sanitary/social reformers, many issues indeed were believed to affect children and the family.

In working with the juvenile street cleaning leagues, WML members asserted that they were instilling the civic counterpart to the "sense of fairness and duty, . . . [of] ideals and ethics" that women had from time immemorial tried to instill in their own children. The WML's monthly *Bulletin* proudly celebrated its organization's efforts to "educate our boys along practical lines of good government." In resurrecting Waring's vision of the juvenile street cleaning leagues as an important vehicle for securing a broader public consciousness, the women believed that their activities would "go down in the annals of civic accomplishment."[60]

In effect, the idea of being a nurturer within the broad civic home allowed numerous Progressive Era women, who usually thought of themselves as traditionalists, to feel that it was legitimate to become social reform activists (and allowed many to feel free to work for woman suffrage as well).

Activism in the cause of sanitary/social reform also seemed legitimate to many women because it resonated with their self-concept as admirers and nurturers of beauty. The mass appeal of the City Beautiful movement during the Progressive Era exemplified the belief that the aesthetic sense was an important element in sustaining health, order, and personal and civic improvement.

Influenced by the legacy of the pioneering nineteenth-century landscape architect Frederick Law Olmsted, City Beautiful proponents believed that the polluted air, noise, congestion, and fast pace of urban life jangled human nerves and weakened the body's ability to cope with physical and mental disease. They proposed building parks, wide boulevards, and civic monuments to strengthen the health, morals, and civic spirit of urban residents who might otherwise fall prey to the temptations of the street or the saloon. Theorists believed that ample city greenery would provide psychological relief from the crowded urban environment. And, influenced by theories of miasmatic disease, they believed that the greenery would help cleanse city air polluted by congested conditions. Though housing was typically not directly addressed in City Beautiful campaigns, many proponents also supported housing reform proposals that would mandate adequate ventilation and plumbing, believing that this would help people maintain an industrious disposition and good health. While some City Beautiful advocates hoped that civic sculpture and monumental government structures would simply awe immigrants into a rigid respect for civic norms—much as some people of the era hoped that flag-waving appeals would instill an unquestioning sense of patriotism—most progressives were attracted to a type of civic model, derived from the study of Periclean Athens, in which civic sculpture and the like would inspire both a sense of respect for society's norms and a yearning to participate assertively and thoughtfully as citizens in community life.[61]

Consistent with the common perception that beauty was an important civic good, officials of the New York City Board of Education asserted that through cooperation with programs such as the juvenile street cleaning leagues, "the maintenance of order and beauty in the surroundings of school children . . . [is] contributing toward the development of character." Likewise, WML periodicals reminded members that green plants in the environment were an important ingredient in "health and uplift." Establishing middle-class comforts and pleasures such as these in the surroundings of the poor would help create "an atmosphere . . . that will revive both body and spirit in these sordid districts." One WML article emphasized that "beauty is almost as essential to well-being, usefulness and happiness as any of the more commanding and more insisted upon civic virtues—good sanitation, honest [housing code] inspection and the like."[62]

In this view, people would be more likely to gain a proprietary feeling for their personal and civic environment if it was one in which individuals could find beauty and comfort, an environment of which they could be proud. WML members hoped to "arouse civic pride and stimulate interest in a City Beautiful, because we believe that our city and country under-rate the value of beauty in the environment. We believe that aesthetics make for orderliness and a higher standard of living, while ugliness and sordidness make for vulgarity and shiftlessness."[63]

Women seeking more beautiful and healthful urban surroundings through sanitary reform measures were at times ridiculed, both by people that the women had criticized for creating filthy conditions and by those who saw their work as unladylike. Ellen Scrimgeour lamented that Women's Health Protective Association members were "subjected to ridicule" when they tried to persuade streetcar conductors to enforce the regulation against spitting on the floors of the cars. Many people in fact resented crusades such as those against spitting that challenged the prerogatives of unfettered individualism and brought to public attention subjects that were not considered appropriate for "ears polite."[64]

In 1897, Mary E. Trautmann, president of the Manhattan branch of the Ladies Health Protective Association, recalled pioneering sanitary reform projects that the association had initiated, including the drive in 1884 to force the removal of a manure pile, thirty feet high by two hundred feet long, that was stored, for sale as fertilizer, in an open lot close to her house (very near the location of today's United Nations headquarters). Trautmann spoke of the hostility that her group incurred: "Even the women looked upon our efforts with distrust and thought we were entirely outside of woman's sphere in our undertakings. In some respects, they were right, for the work was very disagreeable and far from aesthetic. We were housekeepers, and knew the health of our families as well as the public health could only be maintained by having pure food, pure water and pure air." This insight gave her and her colleagues "the courage to go on," to organize themselves and take a leading role in what one member described as a "conflict with the powers of avarice and selfishness entrenched behind bulwarks of filth."[65]

Scrimgeour spoke in a similarly idealistic manner of the hopes that she and many other women held for the promotion of both sanitary reform and child development through the work of the juvenile street cleaning leagues. She was proud that her own civic group's sponsorship of the leagues had stimulated young people's interest in "cleanliness and decency." She believed that through such work children would attain "a cleanliness that springs from within, whose fruit will be civic honor and integrity, and when these prevail we will have clean streets, pure water, righteous laws honestly executed, and cities which will vie with any . . . [for] our admiration. To hasten this millennial day, women can become 'terrible as an army with banners' and teach, by precept and example, that political strength is the culmination of individual service from each and all."[66]

In pushing into cultural and political frontiers, at times by advocating government intervention to improve social conditions, women's civic groups were an important element in Progressive Era politics. Combined with the growing belief in environmental causation, activist women's concern for civic cleanliness and their inextricably connected desire to nurture health and attain order and beauty—in households and in society at large—were potent factors strengthening the innovative search for root causes and solutions that marked Progressive Era social reform.[67]

The ideal of service touted by Scrimgeour and other activists generally entailed a sense of mutual obligations. A New York settlement worker, Charles S. Bernheimer, for example, maintained that, through participation in largely self-governing youth clubs, a child can more effectively develop his powers of self-expression and self-assertion, while also learning that he must to some extent curb these powers if he is to reap the rewards of a viable group. The child learns the lesson that there are entities beyond his familial world that have "aims worth striving for," and the paradoxical lesson that while he enjoys his freedom, if it remains unrestrained it will destroy that larger group from which he derives so many benefits. In short, he learns of the inherent tension between liberty and order, and the need to augment self-expression with cooperation and "self-restraint." One WML official accordingly praised the juvenile street cleaning leagues' role in socializing adolescents, characterizing the local post as "a brave little David to war on the oldest Goliath, a boy's enmity toward authority."[68]

To encourage a sense of mutual obligation among the young that would, in time, translate into good citizenship, the civic activist William H. Allen urged adults to provide "boys and girls . . . tasks that compel them to feel for civic ideals." He related civic-oriented children's clubs and the work of student governments within schools to the experiential learning approach that John Dewey, Jane Addams, and others were advocating during the Progressive Era. Allen presented the hypothetical case of student government members who grappled with the problem of thievery within their school. Students would be forced to come to grips with a real-life question that faces the broader polity. And the tangible issue of crime would help the students learn the more abstract lesson that a widespread diffusion of solid moral traits is a necessity if problems such as thievery are to be controlled in a democracy. Students would come to understand that the average citizen needs to help "carry the load" if society and government are to function effectively. Allen also subscribed to the Progressive Era international peace movement's tenet that efforts to enhance the well-being of the nation's poor and disadvantaged could provide alternative, non-jingoistic channels for patriotic expression, commenting that children's involvement in civic work and student government constituted a "training for peace . . . [which] is infinitely more important than training for war."[69]

In civics classes, settlement house lectures, and other educational venues, progressives stressed the mutual, reciprocal nature of rights and duties in a democracy. Writing on the topic of citizenship, a contributor to one of the University Settlement's periodicals emphasized that "citizenship implies two obligations—one on the part of the government, the other on the part of the citizen." In this vein, the New York City public school system's model syllabus for civics courses (1914) encouraged teachers to promote a sense of "civic virtue." Ideally, the pupil would "have the desire to be an honest, industrious and useful member of the community, because he has been taught to feel that his happiness and the welfare of the community depend on his efforts to live right." The syllabus reminded teachers that "while a pupil should be taught that a citizen's rights are the most important things he can possess, . . . he should be . . . persistently reminded that every right has a corresponding duty."[70]

Teachers were to illuminate this concept in the earliest grades by pointing to examples of reciprocality within the home: "the love of parents [is] shown in care, protection and support of children. . . . Reciprocal duties of children [are] to love their parents . . . and be truthful to them; to show gratitude by helping the parents, . . . and by obeying the rules of the family." As the student advanced further in school, students were encouraged to participate in practical civics activities, including school government, cleanup drives, and juvenile street cleaning leagues, which demonstrated first-hand to students "that mutual assistance and cooperative service are the fundamental principles of all healthy self-government." The syllabus looked to programs such as the juvenile street cleaning leagues, which had "offset much of the destruction of the street gangs," to help teach that community enterprises and self-government in general could succeed only if young people adopted virtuous behaviors. Students, in turn, would come to understand "that without law, liberty is impossible; and . . . that it is the duty of each citizen . . . to aid in the enforcement of the law."[71]

In *Good Citizenship*, Julia Richman also emphasized the reciprocal nature of rights and duties. She informed her young readers that "little citizens . . . are members of society just as they are members of their family and of their school. As such, each one has certain rights and also certain duties. The city protects the rights, and in return it exacts the duties. This is fair, is it not? . . . People are not likely to forget their rights. When they also remember their duties, they become an honor to themselves and a credit to their city and country." Richman added that immigrant children should be anxious to learn the duties "of good citizenship," and she singled out abstention from littering as a prime example. She asserted that many foreign-born New Yorkers were eager to learn these duties, which was why immigrant children "often make the best kind of American citizens."[72]

WML women likewise emphasized reciprocality in the free workshops that they held at settlement houses and churches for immigrant mothers and girls. They informed their listeners of "what help they have a right to expect from the city government, and what help the city government has a right to expect from them; in other words, to give them information in regard to health ordinances, tenement housing laws and labor regulations for their protection, and to make them realize what women can do to promote the cleanliness, healthfulness, and orderliness of the city."[73]

WML members emphasized reciprocality in their conception of their own duties as well. The organization's president in 1915, Alice Bartlett Stimson, reminded her middle- and upper-class membership that "no one is exempt from the obligations of community life while living under its protection, and accepting its opportunities."[74]

In like manner, the reform-minded DSC commissioner John T. Fetherston commented on the reciprocal nature of his department's relationship to city residents in the DSC annual report of 1914: "The Department of Street Cleaning has a contract with the people of the city to perform certain work . . . ; the people of the city are parties to this contract, and it is their duty to carry out their . . . obligations." And a nationally prominent sanitary engineer (and occasional adviser to the DSC), George A. Soper, asserted that in a democracy, responsibility is placed upon both the beneficiaries and the providers of municipal services. While the DSC should elicit citizen cooperation, he insisted that it cannot expect people to curb slovenly habits unless the department in turn strove to "keep good faith with the public" by conscientiously performing its work.[75]

In 1897, Ellen Scrimgeour described a recent encounter that illustrated her belief that children are receptive to the idea that an individual's rights should be tempered by respect for the rights of others within the community. She had just recently inspired a cleanup drive in her neighborhood, during which participants had cleaned and fenced off a nearby vacant lot that had become an informal trash repository. Soon thereafter, she spotted a boy trying to cut "that sacred fence with a knife." She asked him, "Is this fence yours?" He replied by asking whether the fence was hers. She then answered that "it is mine and yours also." Scrimgeour reflected that this "seemed to appeal to the boy, for he shut up his knife and went away."[76]

An adolescent boy discussed the nexus of civic responsibility and mutual obligations in a report on the work of his juvenile street cleaning league post, in 1914. He admitted that like "most of our boys," he had originally joined the league "on account of the gymnasium," where he could have fun and build up his body. Although other boys at league meetings regularly discussed the group's goals and philosophy, he did not initially understand "the meaning of the club." At each meeting, however, he "got a little better meaning of what the club stood for. . . . What interested me was the fact that I had a share in governing the city; that as a citizen I had a right to dictate that my streets should be clean, that my [apartment] house should be in good condition, and that my whole city should be healthy, clean and convenient to live in. But I found that I also had a responsibility of keeping these things in order. In this I found I could help by keeping my own house clean and in order."[77]

Implicitly recognizing the link between civic benefits and personal responsibility, and between self-expression and self-restraint, the lad went on to relate that while he previously had never thought twice when he walked past unsatisfactory civic conditions, his eyes now truly began to see the dirty streets and overflowing refuse cans. His walks to and from school were now more interesting, as he would contemplate how to overcome these conditions. His appreciation of the constructive part he could play in his city helped him feel empowered. He proudly stated that most of the boys in his post, as in his own case, sooner or later do gain a broader consciousness, and that the boys "are making some very good citizens, which we are all trying to be."[78]

While the progressives encouraged (and at times coerced) people to act responsibly in their personal and civic lives, their emphasis on reciprocality reinforced the belief that society should provide the type of support, through governmental means if necessary, that would make it credible to prescribe individual responsibility in the first place. A nationally known writer on urban issues, Delos Wilcox, for example, believed that the "health and morals" of children were generally well cared for "where the physical surroundings make health and morality possible," but that blighted urban conditions "tended to destroy the homes of the poor altogether, by crowding, unsanitary conditions, or immoral surroundings." Consequently, society must intervene, not only by training children in "citizenship and civic cooperation" but also by providing inexpensive transit, water, and lighting services, and improved housing in tenement areas. (In this vein, in addition to its work to improve civic sanitation and provide child recreation opportunities, the WML lobbied for affordable mass transit and effective factory safety codes.) Wilcox chastised the "laggard taxpayers" who resisted this approach because of its expense, insisting that "the realization of freedom through democracy depends upon costly effort." He warned that the failure to undertake such effort would condemn the populace of the cities to "degenerate physically, mentally and socially."[79]

In many children's programs, an emphasis on both the "rights and duties of citizens" encouraged the young to realize that the flip side of adherence to personal and civic responsibilities included the right to assert one's own opinions and concerns. While exhorting members of juvenile street cleaning leagues to refrain from littering, for example, their supervisors also taught that the good citizen presses, in an orderly way, for the government to provide effective street cleaning and other functions that citizens deem appropriate for a just society. The law-abiding emphasis featured in the previously mentioned board of education civics syllabus was balanced by an emphasis on rights, and on the importance of political involvement and citizen input. The syllabus encouraged teachers to urge students, in their future role as adult citizens, "to vote, . . . to be well informed on city, state and national affairs; . . . to inquire into public activities of the neighborhood; to join such political, religious and social societies as in [the individual's] opinion contribute most to the welfare of the community and the country."[80]

Likewise, the University Settlement Directress of Girls' Work, Blanche L. Kelley, maintained that the settlement's youth clubs encouraged the child "to the expression of her own individuality," and as a girl's involvement in the clubs deepened, her participation in the management of club activities fostered "self-reliance, and . . . self-control." Opportunities for self-expression afforded by the drama club, trips to the museum, and civic involvement provided a young girl "much of which, in her narrower tenement house existence, she might never become aware." Another staff member paid tribute to the girls, who were "eager for life," and remarked that it was the settlement workers' responsibility "to help them discover their own interests and carry them out." The historian Peter C. Baldwin has emphasized that reformers at times felt it advisable to modify aspects of child recreation programs, as they negotiated with the expressed wishes of the children.[81]

The children's club movement fostered a wide range of youthful self-expression, from the serious to the more lighthearted. One group of Lower East Side settlement club adolescents helped lead the successful struggle to block the city's plans to locate an elevated ("el") train down Delancey Street. And a branch of juvenile street cleaning league boys learned behaviors that would allow them to function more successfully in the wider world, by mastering suggestions on "gentlemanly manners" that were printed on cards that the WML distributed to them. (The supervisor of one post reported that the boys were "really trying" now to tip their hats to their elders, that they had made it an act of pride to behave in ways outlined on what they called the "how to become a sport" card.)[82]

Citizen assertion was considered an important element in building the political momentum that was needed to improve street cleaning and other municipal services. Reformers throughout the era attempted to build an advisory relationship between citizen groups and the DSC. By the latter part of the era, this type of relationship became the norm even within Tammany-led administrations, signifying the machine's increased recognition that effective departmental operations were a necessity if complex services were to be provided continually to city residents. Reformers also hoped to elicit input regarding DSC services from people who did not belong to activist civic groups. With greater citizen involvement, well-meaning administrators believed they would be able to present evidence of a high level of demand for services, which would provide the political cover that they needed to help obtain adequate funding or even undertake bolder initiatives in their work. Commissioner Fetherston told New Yorkers that "we want to get you interested in clean streets; we want to have your co-operation in making New York the cleanest city in the world. It can be done, if you want it; it *will* be done, if you make enough noise about it." A WML member echoed these sentiments in declaring that if every woman in the city publicly insisted on clean streets in her neighborhood, then street cleaning problems would virtually disappear.[83]

In sponsoring the juvenile street cleaning leagues and related activities that might enhance children's sense of personal and social responsibility, the progressives hoped to foster a normative orientation, an inner moral compass based on self-restraint rather than on the fear of external punishment. Social theorists recalled the premodern world in which a more close-knit community purportedly was keenly aware of the conduct of people within its orbit and expressed a pervasive moral censure when individuals transgressed community norms. Given the pressures to conform that were attendant to this way of life and to the authoritarian forms of family life, religion, and government that predominated as well, it was easier to inculcate traditional behavior patterns and to prescribe which path a person was to take in his or her life. People knew what they were supposed to do. In contrast, the modern city's relative anonymity and its multitude of choices necessitated more of an internal exercise of free will by the individual. Urban dwellers were said to possess a show-me attitude, in which they must be convinced of the consequences of a behavior before deciding to adopt or reject it. Although the more imperious Progressive Era reformers tended to make ex cathedra pronouncements of rules that the poor should follow, many activists recognized the need for explanation, even if given in rather simplified form. Such activists hoped that children's experience with the juvenile leagues would increase the likelihood that they would *freely choose* habits of social cooperation and later choose to become active citizens as adults.[84]

We can recognize these types of goals in the work of Sophie Loebinger, a middle-class housewife in what was then a largely Italian and Jewish neighborhood, in the area between Seventh Avenue and St. Nicholas Park in Harlem. On her own she organized an informal coed "Junior Park Protective League" in 1913, which provided activities akin to those of the juvenile street cleaning leagues as well as warm personal guidance for the troubled and sometimes criminally inclined children living in nearby tenement housing.

Prior to her league work, Loebinger had observed that many of the neighborhood kids possessed a disquieting lack of normative guideposts, and a skepticism toward adults who claimed self-evident authority when demanding that children obey directions about personal conduct. Sadly, Loebinger later recalled that the children "took no pride in their environment; they had not even crude ideas of the aesthetics. It was clear . . . that they were victims of the circumstances which sometimes surround youth in a great city." Bored after school, without "any really active interest to keep them good," the kids would destroy the trees and flowers in St. Nicholas Park, finding it a "sweet and thrilling dissipation" to get away with ruining what they considered to be mere "fancy fixings." And Loebinger cited, as a particularly egregious sign of the children's vacuousness, the fact that some had tortured dogs and cats, "scarcely [realizing] that they were giving pain to sentient, living things."[85]

According to Loebinger, many of the kids' parents were unable to restrain them, in part, because the parents were too busy or exhausted to show a great amount of interest in their children as individuals. In these "underdeveloped" households, overburdened parents would return home wearied from long hours at work, and all too frequently family life would be cut short all the more when a father would linger after work in a neighborhood saloon.

Moreover, parents often sought to forbid behaviors in their children simply by issuing "ukase [edict] after ukase without offering an explanation or giving any reason whatsoever except 'must' and 'mustn't'"—which Loebinger declared an inadequate approach in "the land of liberty." In contrast to the customary mindset in areas of Europe in which their parents had grown to maturity, children in America were not so highly conditioned to obey external social authority. Here, instead, they were "under the influence of a sense of . . . freedom so intense that it intoxicated, unrestrained by the strict police supervision to which they have been accustomed, [and] taught, possibly, by the very newspapers they read and by the talk they hear to feel a certain definite contempt for the police." While in the children's ancestral lands "their home cities . . . had been absolutely strict," here "the authorities being absolutely lax, they naturally decided that the land of liberty was also the land of license, and behaved themselves accordingly."[86]

Loebinger patiently guided the children, perhaps following the child welfare writer William B. Forbush's advice to boys' club supervisors "to moralize these boys by the power of friendship." She understood the need to offer explanations of normative behavior—that the children should be kindly and nonchalantly "instructed . . . in the fact that right is far more pleasurable and profitable than wrong"—while at the same time providing the children opportunities to channel their energies into positive activities in which they could gain recognition, a sense of usefulness, and opportunities to socialize with their peers. In the league work, she found that kindness and "a little ethical teaching" went a long way. According to Loebinger, the children, with what was at times a "pitiful" eagerness, grasped at the opportunities that her club provided to feel a valued part of something with a higher purpose than they had found in their previously self-centered way of life. Dozens of eager children now picked litter off of nearby streets and cultivated bushes in the neighborhood park rather than tearing them out by the roots as had been their previous sport.[87]

Progressive educational reformers' attempts to reduce the amount of rote learning in New York classrooms exemplified their belief that children would want to develop their intellectual and creative potential if provided stimulating educational experiences. Rote learning and rigid classroom discipline had been the favored pedagogical approach of the often ill-educated teachers appointed before the progressives' late nineteenth- and early twentieth-century drives to professionalize the New York public school system. While not denying the wisdom of retaining some memorization work (and a significant degree of discipline in the classroom), reformers emphasized the need to replace much of the rote work with activities that would reinforce the child's powers of observation, reasoning, and analysis.[88]

Understanding this context can help us better comprehend the motives of sponsors of the juvenile street cleaning leagues and related programs, who hoped to build a critical mass of thoughtful citizens who would feel responsible to grapple with civic sanitation issues. David Willard, for example, spoke of the efforts of juvenile league members under Waring's auspices to disseminate to their parents and friends a "knowledge of the [DSC] ordinances *and the reasons for them*" (my emphasis). Later in the era a Merchants' Association spokesman praised "the work of [young Anti-Litter League] block captains in educating those on their blocks as to the [civic sanitation] laws and the reasons for them."[89] And at a conference on street cleaning in 1914, Donald B. Armstrong, an executive of the New York Association for Improving the Condition of the Poor, noted that effective city services depended on the existence of a healthy democracy and the high level of citizen awareness that that entailed. In contrast to the practices of an absolute monarchy, he observed that a democracy delegates power, "the enforcement of which is made effective through cooperation and understanding between the governing and the governed. Essential to this form of government is public instruction and public intelligence. No multiplication of laws in the Street Cleaning Code will give a clean city if the citizen is not told how and why to maintain civic cleanliness and is not taught the value of cleanliness."[90]

In their educational approach, juvenile street cleaning league sponsors relied to an extent on the glamorous allure of marching in parades and wearing shiny badges, but the sponsors also possessed a democratic faith that rational explanation and a receptivity to what they presumed to be universal ideals would appeal to people across class and ethnic bounds. This faith in reason and in the ideal of citizen responsibility for community improvement was borne out in the unsophisticated yet touching letters that juvenile league members wrote to Commissioner Waring. Young Yetta Tobolsky, for example, wrote of "seeing a girl throwing an apple skin on the sidewalk. I said, 'Please don't throw anything in the street because we want to have our city clean.' And she said, 'Thanks for telling me; if I had thought, I wouldn't have thrown it down.'"[91]

Another league member, Rachel Shapiro, spoke to a girl who had thrown a piece of paper onto the street: "I told her that she must not throw any papers in the street because it made the streets dirty, and she said 'Thank you for telling me' and she said she would carry it home and . . . she would tell all her friends that they must not throw anything in the street."[92]

One child, though hardly a spelling expert, instructed a man in the proper way to dispose of an old mattress that he was illegally dumping on the street. She related that the man then "picked it up and thanked me for the inflammation I gave him." In another missive, David Hamff, a juvenile league member who sold newspapers after school near the Brooklyn Bridge, wrote that "I tell all the other newsboys about our club, and show them my badge, and we all try now to keep the street clean by the Bridge."[93]

In asserting that improved DSC services would reinforce a sense of civic responsibility among juvenile league members (and among other New Yorkers), Progressive Era reformers recognized that the physical/social environment and individual responsibility are not mutually exclusive factors, and that these factors, together, are keys in attaining a good society. Reformers thus embraced what the social scientist Philip Brickman and his colleagues have recently termed a "compensatory" approach to social problems. The compensatory model assumes that people in need are not responsible for the origin of their problems, but that they are responsible for applying solutions to those problems to the fullest extent possible.[94] In this view, those with ample resources in society should provide a helping hand to deprived individuals, but it is also incumbent upon the needy to strive to overcome adversity and diligently use the help that is offered. The deprived person thus earns the respect of others by shouldering what most see as her rightful duties. Likewise, the deprived individual can more readily maintain self-respect, because she and the broader society do not ascribe the origin of her problems to a paucity of moral traits and because the emphasis on self-responsibility enhances feelings of competency.

A deficit of moral traits is more strongly emphasized in what Brickman refers to as the "moral model." In this traditional, more conservative approach, individuals' maladaptive behaviors and attitudes are considered to be primarily responsible for both the origins of and solutions to their main problems. The best way to help people is to remind them of their responsibility to change their behaviors and attitudes. While agreeing that individual responsibility is an important factor, the social reform progressives' environmental-causation outlook prompted them to dispute a rigid moral model viewpoint in their struggle for public opinion, and in struggles within their own minds.[95]

Brickman also contrasts the compensatory approach with what has come to be known as the "social control" approach to social problems. People adhering to this model tend to maintain that deprived individuals have dysfunctional or morally objectionable value systems that underlie their own (and thus many of the broader society's) problems. Not surprisingly, people possessing a social control perspective tend to value "a strong degree of submission [by the needy] to agents of social control"; that is, they emphasize the need to "enlighten" individuals "as to the true nature of their problem." (Hence Brickman uses the term "enlightenment model" interchangeably with "social control model.") Because deprived people at times resist proposed solutions, helpers become preoccupied with the need to socialize the individual into accepting the prevailing view of proper behavior, through the use of carrots and sticks. Because this approach carries an implication of guilt and posits solutions over which the needy have little influence, it tends to foster a negative self-image in the deprived individual.[96]

Within the past two decades, important trends in historical scholarship have emphasized the agency of the needy and other out-groups in history, and have sought to comprehend the complexity of reformers' views and the context in which they operated.[97] Nevertheless, many historians in the past forty years have conceptualized Progressive Era reformers as acting in ways consonant with the social control model. These historians have tended to castigate the era's reformers for assuming that the needy should follow the behavioral prescriptions of middle- and upper-class progressives, and they have maintained that while the progressives ostensibly blamed the environment for the origins of social problems, their tone at the very least betrayed the strong burden of guilt that they, in reality, still fastened onto individuals in need.[98]

Alternatively, in Brickman's compensatory model, a certain authority is ascribed to persons in need, concomitant to the active role that these individuals take in remedying their conditions. This perspective is more in line with this study's view that the progressives emphasized non-rote education in promoting normative behaviors. Juvenile street cleaning league activists, for example, hoped that league children would of their own free will use their newly acquired knowledge of civic affairs to think through to a philosophy prescribing greater personal and civic responsibility. The progressives had an idealistic faith that the children would, in their philosophical deliberations, recognize that high levels of personal and civic sanitation would garner long-term benefits for themselves, their families, and the broader society.

Seeking to actualize their budding civic philosophy, juvenile league members at times created tension within their neighborhoods, arising from a conflict in values, particularly when they chided other New Yorkers about their civic sanitation habits. These conflicts arose along a traditional fault line within American political culture that dates back to the nation's founding, a fault line that the philosopher-journalist Herbert Croly spoke of during the Progressive Era when he famously advocated the use of Hamiltonian means to serve Jeffersonian ends. Croly believed that a Jeffersonian esteem for the common man could more effectively be actualized in an urban-industrial society if the nation would be less Jeffersonian in its hesitancy to use government to help develop the potential of individuals and the economy.[99]

Rather than using the very early republic as a framework, it is perhaps more useful to our study to conceptualize this key political-cultural division in relation to the mid-nineteenth-century inheritors of the Hamiltonian-Jeffersonian fault line—that is, the Whigs and the Jacksonian Democrats. In asserting their differences, the Whigs and Jacksonians responded to a more wide-ranging set of issues than those that had challenged their forebears during the days of Hamilton and Jefferson, including issues of urban development and massive immigration that are more like those of the Progressive Era.

The mid-nineteenth-century Whigs were challenged by the growth of a heterogeneous urban society. While many were elitist like their Hamiltonian-Federalist forerunners, the Whigs, at least theoretically, were more optimistic about the potential of the common man. And while they were condescending in some ways, they did embrace a measure of community-oriented concern for the less fortunate, which was buttressed by the traditional noblesse oblige concept that those with education, wealth, or inherited status have a special responsibility to help ensure the long-term well-being of society. In their outlook, voluntary agencies (or, when necessary, the government) should intervene to promote individual and broad social improvement. Thus, many Whigs advocated municipal sanitary reforms and state and federal measures to foster regional economic development, humane care for the mentally ill, penal reform, and sometimes even a modicum of legal protection for Indians and African Americans.[100]

They were also the strongest advocates in creating public school systems that were meant to instruct the young in the literacy and computational skills needed in the new commercial and industrial society; teach the middle-class virtues of punctuality, perseverance, and thrift, which were also considered prerequisites to success in the urbanizing world; and disseminate the civic virtues that were considered necessary to maintain a healthy democracy. Favoring centralized school systems that would be committed to the economic, social, and moral improvement of the child, Whigs maintained that the complex nature of the emerging society required an educational system that would take on functions that had previously been within the province of the family.[101]

Jacksonians, on the other hand, generally emphasized their non-elite origins (although many Jacksonian leaders, in reality, were quite wealthy) and favored neighborhood control of schools. They often resented paying taxes for government-sponsored programs of mass improvement, which many believed would not benefit the common man but would instead be used in potentially meddlesome ways (or used to line the pockets of insiders). In short, the Jacksonians preferred smaller government and wanted to leave personal improvement to the individual, his family, or his church.[102]

In the Gilded Age following the Civil War and Reconstruction, the Republican Party inheritors of the Whig community-oriented tradition were often overruled within party circles, which were increasingly dominated by corporate interests. The ensuing Progressive Era movements to improve education, workplace safety, child welfare, and civic sanitation, and to address many other social problems, can be seen, in part, as a renaissance of community-oriented enthusiasm within urban middle- and upper-class circles. And, as already noted, the Progressive Era cross-fertilization of ideas, between middle- and upper-class reformers on the one hand and representatives of working-class interests on the other, helped modify the beliefs of many adherents of the Jacksonian political tradition (and the beliefs of many within the moralistic Whig reform tradition). Jacksonian-rooted activists concerned about urban social problems became increasingly reconciled to the use of government intervention to assist the common man, a figure who was very important within the Jacksonian sense of self-identity.[103]

In the process, the American reform tradition gained a predominantly urban working-class, multicultural constituency by the 1920s, as the progressive tradition evolved into what would become the core of the New Deal Democratic coalition.[104] The story of reformers' attempts, through the juvenile street cleaning leagues, to spread an ethic of responsibility for civic cleanliness (while simultaneously pushing for improved DSC services) can be seen, in part, as a case study of efforts by middle- and upper-class progressives to sell the notion that the Jacksonian reverence for freedom, equality, and individual fulfillment would best be served in an urban, industrial society by a shift toward a more community-oriented approach to complex social problems.

To the progressives, the work of the juvenile leagues embodied what "Big Bill" Edwards once called "street cleaning morals." On one level, Edwards was simply referring to litter and other problems directly related to civic sanitation. But more figuratively his phrase signified the promotion of guidelines for living together peaceably in an urban environment, the spread of a code of conduct that was considered necessary for attaining a decent quality of life for all. Essentially, the prospect that numerous people would gain an enhanced awareness of the effect of their civic sanitation-related behaviors on others held forth the promise that people would become more considerate generally of their fellow New Yorkers.[105]

Like other reformers, the street cleaning activist and WML official Ida Cohen believed that all too many New Yorkers lacked the heightened civic consciousness embodied by the phrase "street cleaning morals." Cohen, who wrote a book used in New York schools to educate students about civic sanitation issues, approvingly quoted a New Yorker who declared, in community-oriented terms, "The average citizen is prone to do the easiest thing always, and it is the easiest thing to throw the useless newspaper, the banana skin, the candy box or the advertising dodger [handbill] in the gutter. . . . [The city should] compel such untidy people to take thought for others and remove the reproach that the second city in the world is . . . [the] dirtiest." Although community-oriented tendencies and Jacksonian individualistic tendencies coexisted to some degree within the psyches of most Americans during the Progressive Era, the persistent conflict between those who considered themselves stewards of the city's cleanliness and those "prone to do the easiest thing" was undergirded by the tension between these two poles of the American temperament.[106]

Like the largely Whig-sponsored reform movements of the decades preceding the American Civil War, middle- and upper-class adherents of the late nineteenth- and early twentieth-century progressive movement were influenced, in part, by a paternalistic noblesse oblige tradition of community responsibility for the down-trodden—a type of paternalism that the social commentator John B. Judis believes is sorely missed in today's polity—and a popular religious belief in the possibility of individual uplift. This religious sensibility was augmented during the Progressive Era by Social Gospel adherents, who maintained that improved social conditions would help people to achieve a more godly existence (which in turn would help them gain entrance into heaven) and that people should, above all, seek to actualize the ideal of human brotherhood among their fellow corporeal human beings on earth. Though religious in nature, Social Gospel beliefs were influenced by a more secular strain of thought as well, inherited from the eighteenth-century Enlightenment tradition, which had fostered the environmental view of poverty and degradation, a view that strongly influenced those progressives who looked to social science to legitimate their reform impulses.[107]

Even though many progressives (particularly the younger ones) took pains to insist on the social science basis of their beliefs, their goals and their emotional enthusiasm were actually often rooted in an idealistic yearning for righteousness and uplift. It is true that some progressives cared more for money-saving efficiency than they did for people's problems. The city planner Robert Moses, who worked in New York during the Progressive Era as a young assistant to Mayor John Purroy

Mitchel, later derisively characterized Mitchel's reform administration as "an honest outfit committed to saving rubber bands." But most progressives were neither cold-hearted nor naïve enough to believe that social science could in itself map out the best decisions on all public issues. Rather, they were aware that values and ethics were as important as empirical study in considering those issues.[108]

The reformers' spiritual and ethical concerns produced fervent hopes that can be seen in their commentaries on the juvenile street cleaning leagues and related programs. In discussing the civic sanitation work of organizations such as the juvenile leagues, a writer for the reform-oriented periodical *American City* expressed his wish that the nation's children would "become truly educated in civics . . . before they enter upon their personal activities and have learned to center all of their thoughts around these activities. It gives them the broader view of life and points out . . . that the ideal life is the life that is good for all the people of the community. A generation universally educated along these lines would bring the practical millennium."[109]

Likewise, in advocating government action for social problems, R. Fulton Cutting, a Citizens' Union leader and philanthropist, in 1901 praised the example that Waring had set in his street cleaning work: "There is a swelling tide of human brotherhood that seeks to express itself through democratic institutions, and the religion of the Twentieth Century is destined to employ Government as one of its principal instrumentalities for the solution of social issues."[110]

This impassioned concern for community well-being was reflected in a memorial piece written three years earlier in Waring's honor, in which a child recreation advocate, William Potts, pointed to the colonel's work for the city as a harbinger of a new sense of individualism: "Today the individual realizes more or less dimly that though he is first of all an individual, and his individuality must be cherished as the chief hope of the world, that individuality can only be developed and perfected by . . . communion with his fellow men. . . . Is it not clear that he is at length emerging into a broader light which shines upon him as a member of an ever-advancing body, the complete health of which depends upon the fullest development of all its members, himself among the rest?"[111]

The growth in popularity of such community-oriented ideals during the Progressive Era stemmed in part from the fact that many within the Jacksonian tradition were reevaluating their commitment to the small-government ideal. The rise within Tammany Hall itself of a powerful social reform wing attested to this trend during the latter part of the era, when Democrats with urban immigrant constituencies began advocating systematic government programs and regulatory measures to address social problems.[112]

Nevertheless, Tammany Hall was still more in tune than were most middle- and upper-class progressives with the Jacksonian facet of the American temperament. One settlement worker ruefully observed that police usually turned the other way when they spotted children lighting bonfires on the streets, a practice that seriously damaged roadways, created fire hazards, and added quantities of ash to the streets' accumulation of litter. The writer hypothesized that the policemen implicitly asked themselves, "Are not the boys future voters, and why should Tammany molest them?" Although taking office a few years after the demise of the Progressive Era, Mayor James J. Walker, who was affiliated with Tammany Hall, signified the continuing strength of the Jacksonian ethos in a speech to the Cleaner Brooklyn Committee of that borough's chamber of commerce. Walker ostensibly praised children's voluntary attempts to clean vacant lots and awaken interest in a clean city. Nonetheless, insisting that "developing pride in the home city will do much more than would making such actions a crime," he disavowed those New Yorkers who favored the actual enforcement of litter laws.[113]

Not surprisingly, Tammany-appointed magistrates (judges) usually would acquit defendants brought to court simply for violating DSC ordinances. In 1919, for example, Magistrate O'Neill of Brooklyn upbraided a policeman who had issued a summons to a woman for throwing litter from her automobile window. O'Neill complained that "this is a shame to bring this woman all the way from the Bronx on this trivial matter." Earlier in the era, a WML member wondered how serious Magistrate "Battery Dan" Finn could be about sanitary code cases when he himself habitually spat on the floor during court proceedings.[114]

In the 1890s, Waring's attempts to elicit juvenile street cleaning league support for antilitter efforts had garnered derisive comments from Tammany officials. The house organ *Tammany Times* mocked the "tender heart . . . [whose] latest economic plan is that . . . school children should give fruit skins to horses instead of throwing them on the sidewalk. Hereafter, if your animal doesn't need that kind of diet, you must muzzle it." Tammany was still uncomfortable with the increasing pressure to change the role of government in order to take on regulatory and related functions that might intrude upon individual prerogatives. In contrast to the traditional Tammany conception of government as a vehicle for a highly personalized distribution of public resources, the progressives counterposed the idea of government as a vehicle for the regulation of group differences and the systematic adjustment of social problems. In this new pattern, some people would receive benefits, but others might be inconvenienced by government action.[115]

A letter to the editor published in the *New York Sun* indicated resentment of these paradigmatic changes within political culture, in criticizing Colonel Waring's requirement that a special card be placed on a building's front door when a resident wanted the DSC to collect paper and other nonorganic refuse (rubbish). Under this regulation, rubbish had to be kept indoors until collection time, or placed under the stoop, in order to keep it out of sight and protect it from being scattered by the wind and rain, and the matter had to be placed in a box or a barrel, or tied into a secure bundle, to further ensure that the contents would not spill onto the streets. The correspondent sought to use individual liberty as a trump card, proclaiming that the new rules came "from the despot who cleans our streets." The letter writer demanded "to know where our despot gets authority to make . . . this absurd rule as to bundles?"[116]

The writer also mockingly portrayed Waring as effeminate, rhetorically asking the colonel if he wanted the rubbish bundles to be "tied with a bow-knot, and must it be a single or a double bow?" This type of mockery paralleled that used by the *Tammany Times* when it derided the masculinity of "Miss . . . Sissy Waring" and others trumpeting concern for civic sanitation and for reform in general, who thought themselves "better and purer" than the average person. The attempt to feminize Waring signified the traditional Jacksonian inclination to reinforce a sense of equality and dignity among white males by stigmatizing others as occupying the sorts of social strata that allowed, and indeed invited, ridicule.[117]

The Jacksonian attitude toward civic sanitation points to a dichotomy within American culture, between a community orientation and a Jacksonian-individualistic drive for equal status and personal expression that is at times heedless of the needs of the community. In this vein, a mid-twentieth-century essay by the American studies scholar John A. Kouwenhoven used the example of contemporary attitudes toward littering as a means to help readers understand the persistence within America of certain concepts of freedom and equality (and the tensions arising from these concepts). Pointing to the omnipresent "beer can by the highway," Kouwenhoven asserts that people who see this detritus as merely signifying "contempt for the rights of others" fail to take into account the broader meaning that such litter holds for the American character. In the societies of most of our forebears—and particularly in the European societies from which we have inherited so many cultural traits—hierarchical status and station of birth mattered a good deal more than in America's more open social milieu. Kouwenhoven maintains that American society's traditional ideal of social equality and our incessant search for individual social mobility are factors that transmute into questions implicit in the minds of many litterers. In effect, before tossing their beer or soda can they ask, "Whose highway is it anyway?" In a sense, the litterer insists "that he is what Pearl Bailey elegantly calls 'the character that owns the joint.'" The spirit of American individualism, with its "open-ended conception of abundance . . . [and of] man's potentialities" created here what Ralph Waldo Emerson referred to as "a sloven plenty . . . an unbuttoned comfort, not clean, not thoughtful, far from polished," an atmosphere in which even a lower-income individual can feel entitled to the sense that he or she is "the character that owns the joint."[118]

Progressive reformers such as Ida Cohen resented what they perceived as a lack of responsibility in people that Kouwenhoven would later portray as self-styled owners of the joint. Cohen hoped that the juvenile street cleaning leagues would raise the level of awareness in slum neighborhoods where all too often "parents are foreigners . . . whose ideas of a free city is to do what one pleases on the streets, throwing refuse out of the windows, and using back yards for dirt heaps." Believing that community interests overrode the freedom of individuals to toss garbage, Julia Richman declared that those who threw garbage from kitchen windows "have no right to do it."[119]

In some ways, juvenile street cleaning league members and their supervisors sought to bridge the fault line between the Jacksonian and the more community-oriented aspects of American consciousness. Supervisors were aware of the inherent conflict in values during encounters in which league members asked strangers to adhere to stricter civic sanitation habits. Recognizing that most people were quite sensitive when others, in effect, questioned whether their morals measured up to proper standards, supervisors cautioned the kids to be tactful and polite when advocating street cleaning morals. Waring informed his young charges that many people simply did not realize that littering was wrong. He asked the children to "speak to people pleasantly when you see them throwing things into the street. Don't scold, and people will remember." Julia Richman advised prospective juvenile league members that if they learned of tenants who would "dare to go so far in wrongdoing as to throw garbage . . . [from their windows] into the street," they should "speak to them about it in a pleasant way; explain that it is against the law, and . . . tell them what your club is aiming to do, and perhaps you may awaken in them a spark of civic pride. Who knows?"[120]

Juvenile league supervisors reported that the children in their clubs were, in fact, usually polite in encounters with city residents. During the first year of their work with the leagues, a WML official stated that there had been no reports of "impertinent or offensive conduct" by the children; "they go about their work in a business-like manly way that commands the respect of all." In discussing how to respond when a litterer snubbed one of their requests, a juvenile league member during the 1890s, Harry Bernstein, told his companions that "youse boys . . . can just pick it up yourself and put it in your pocket if there isn't a barrel." (Dignity was an important consideration in this as in all other things for young Mr. Bernstein, as evidenced by the handkerchief he wore over the sharp point of his standing collar, to preserve it in immaculate condition.)[121]

While most New Yorkers did not argue with juvenile league members' entreaties, conflict was not unknown, particularly in the early years before some supervisors realized the need to teach a proper regard for tact. In 1896, for example, young Isidor Finkel pressed the bartender at a saloon owned by Charles "Silver Dollar" Smith, a notoriously rough-hewn and sometimes violent Tammany district leader, to remove a messy barrel of ashes that had been wrongfully placed on the sidewalk after regular DSC pickup hours. Finkel later related that the bartender "asked me what business it was of mine, and I told him that I was a volunteer aid to the Street Cleaning Department and showed him my certificate. He didn't do anything, so I reported him and told the newspapers." Waring publicly praised Finkel, but the newspapers viewed the lad's efforts as rather brazen and impolitic.[122]

In another incident, after observing William Sanger, age seventeen, throw a load of old tin cans in the gutter, Joseph Liebergall, who was thirteen, displayed his badge and informed Sanger that he was under arrest. Sanger then vigorously kicked the boy. For this he was arrested (by a real policeman) and brought to court, whereupon Liebergall withdrew the complaint. The magistrate then discharged Sanger with a reprimand. The *Times* anticipated the thoughts of concerned juvenile league supervisors in commenting that these types of incidents threatened to turn the leagues more into a source of amusement than respect for many New Yorkers.[123]

A more typical pattern can be found in a letter that Sam Berkowitz, a young member of a Lower East Side branch, wrote to Waring: "Our housekeeper [building superintendent] did not keep the yard clean, and I said to him, 'Why don't you keep the yard clean'? And he said, 'That is not your business,' and I said, 'It is my business, because I belong to the Street Cleaning Department.' So now he sweeps the yard clean everyday."[124]

Reformers hypothesized that while the offender in an encounter such as this might be angry and defensive, he or she would also be caught in the moral dilemma of at least partially realizing, often after the heat of the incident, that the youth was right. Usually, the offender would become more self-conscious when on the verge of littering in the future, and would consequently be less likely to engage in such behavior.[125]

Aware of a need for sensitivity when asking others to change their behaviors, a WML official observed that juvenile league girls generally were better at speaking to building superintendents than were the boys—"but we are gradually persuading the latter that if they are really working in the city's interest they can accomplish more by being friends with people than enemies." Relatedly, because girls were generally considered to be less aggressive than boys, people usually felt a bit more threatened when approached by the latter. And boys were usually less adept at the heart-to-heart sharing of concerns that evoked positive responses in people. Likewise, a WML official noted that girls were "more closely in touch with the home and . . . [a girl's] influence in reaching the interest of her parents concerning civic responsibility" was accordingly more effective.[126]

Hoping to stimulate a sense of responsibility for civic sanitation among the immigrant poor, James H. Hamilton, head worker of the University Settlement, related in a letter in 1907 to a colleague that the "very weightive" problem of tenants' tossing garbage out of their windows could be reduced if "many of our offending

[Lower East Side] neighbors are thoroughly spanked. . . . A season of wholesale arrests would be most salutary." Such a policy would frighten many area residents and "the rest [would be] awakened to the enormity of their offense."[127]

While reformers' attempts to promote tougher enforcement of sanitation laws did yield a modicum of success (especially during the terms of reform mayors), activists believed that greater public awareness about civic sanitation issues was the more essential goal. If this objective could be attained, the ensuing normative pressure on the police and judiciary would result in more consistent enforcement and, more important, there would be much less need for such enforcement.[128] Ida Cohen observed that "there are many city laws . . . which make it a crime to do certain things. But, why should we be obliged to arrest people in order to keep our city clean? Why should we not take a pride in our city?"[129]

In short, if Americans thought of themselves, in the words of John Kouwenhoven, as "the character[s] that own the joint," then progressives concerned about the urban environment replied, in effect, that citizens ought to learn (and internalize) the duties that accompany ownership. Otherwise, the piece of pie that each person exercising his own sense of individuality wanted ultimately would be ruined, along with the rest of the pie. In this community-oriented view, the egalitarian thrust for social mobility was a more positive element in American life when it was channeled into civic-minded directions rather than into an unabashed scramble for "sloven plenty." In the reform solution, education in civic rights and responsibilities, along with the provision of social services and regulatory measures to help spark hope in the poor, would make the enforcement of litter laws a far less urgent matter. Nevertheless, enforcement of these and other laws restricting certain types of individual behavior would always be a necessary deterrent.[130]

While James Hamilton prescribed rather harsh enforcement measures in his letter, he emphasized education in it as well, praising the recent formation of a girls' juvenile street cleaning post at the settlement, which was "seeking to educate . . . as many children as possible in the matter." Considered as a whole, Hamilton's letter reflected the ambivalent feelings many progressives held concerning the coercive use of government power. While the progressives are known for hastening greater acceptance of government intervention, such acceptance nevertheless involved a large mental leap for people with roots in the nineteenth century. There existed a Jacksonian component even within the mindset of progeny of the community-oriented mid-nineteenth-century reform tradition. Progressive Era activists thus approached social problems with the view that government should use its powers when needed, even at the federal level, but that people should take care of their problems themselves as much as reasonably possible, which should reduce the need for government intervention.[131] In part because of this rationale, social reformers hoped to reinforce self-reliant features and internal restraints among the poor. Although numerous Americans, particularly within the lower-middle class, were content to mainly slap coercive measures onto the populace when there was a social problem, many reform leaders wanted the government to "spank" the people as little as necessary.[132]

This observation does not negate the fact that a considerable amount of anxiety underlay many progressives' desire to promote a broader civic consciousness and middle-class values within immigrant communities. Witnessing immense waves of immigration and the despairing squalor attendant to life in tenement neighborhoods, much of the American middle class feared that these conditions would breed disorder. Although reformers typically believed that the majority of immigrants actually possessed a strong work ethic and wanted to help maintain a stable social order, many reformers also believed that numerous immigrants had not yet generated the internal restraints and consciousness necessary to maintain individual and civic well-being in a free society. The director of the Educational Alliance, David Blaustein, a generally sensitive observer of Lower East Side life, wrote that for some immigrants from more oppressive societies, "tyranny has taught them to regard all public institutions as instruments of oppression." They had come to America to be "free" and enjoy "equal rights" (as well as economic opportunity), but had been conditioned "under a paternal form of government, [in which] they are never called upon to exercise their duties as citizens." Like Sophie Loebinger, some commentators worried that immigrants would take their newfound liberty as license to answer to no one, rather than understanding the responsibilities inherent in a democratic system and in the web of mutual obligations binding society and the free individual. Many reformers also worried that the discouraging prospect of low wages, economic insecurity, and slum life depressed the energy and hope needed to remain internally disciplined and civic-minded.[133]

Activists were frank in stating that reforms were needed if society hoped to curb crime, reduce the attraction of the youth gang among children, avert violent labor and political strife, and check outbreaks of communicable disease. Following the nineteenth-century English statesman and historian Thomas Macaulay's injunction to reform in order to preserve, progressives asserted that if a free society wished to preserve itself, it must co-opt the forces of potential disorder by instituting reform measures. While citizens' fears of disorder have often been used to fuel or justify repressive and reactionary measures, the progressives used such fears as a framework to better inform the public (and themselves) about the need for a stronger educational system and new social programs, helping in this way to gain a mass middle-class base of support for the pioneering use of government resources in addressing social problems. Progressive Era reformers believed that the three-pronged "Americanization" recipe of education, external aid, and enforcement of the law—with major emphasis on the first two elements—would reinforce immigrants' aspirations, social mobility, and loyalty to the polity, thus allowing the continued coexistence of order and freedom. And the reformers correctly surmised that the presence within immigrant communities of numerous successful, hard-working compatriots would powerfully model middle-class values as well.[134]

Whether by appealing to compassionate feelings or to an enlightened sense of self-preservation, activists convinced numerous citizens during the Progressive Era that the political and economic system was capable of creating healthier environments through social reform, which they believed would, in turn, enable almost all individuals to respect values such as cleanliness, industry, sobriety, and thrift, which marked the self-improvement approach to living. In this view, through the juvenile street cleaning leagues and other non-rote educational endeavors, children would be more likely to develop their reasoning skills and the corollary desire to grapple through to a more highly developed sense of personal and civic ethics. The progressives, with their combination of religious fervor and secular rectitude, believed that a generation of ethically sensitive children would, as future citizens, honestly engage themselves in the challenge of building a better society. Although progressives at times voiced harsh judgments of the poor, most of them maintained a faith in democracy's potential, if society and politics were guided by an assertive, yet orderly, citizenry. Reformers did not seek to create sheep-like automatons that would simply accept social conditions as laid down from on high. They hoped to cultivate a frame of mind within children that would allow kids to choose, more intelligently and for themselves, concepts of the good—which reformers believed would resemble, in its basics, the ideals that they themselves espoused.[135]

Nevertheless, while it is reasonable for a polity to attempt to uphold certain standards in order to maintain a viable society (for example, standards of civic sanitation), some progressives were in fact intolerant of a healthy diversity. This intolerance exacerbated the conflict between immigrant parent and child, as both the reformers and the broader culture induced the young to assimilate more quickly and thoroughly the dominant modes of behavior. An emphasis on conformity could be seen in the workplace and in social situations, when young people hungry to gain status in a largely prejudiced society felt compelled to veil ethnic characteristics that would have otherwise stood out sharply.[136]

Probably in part because of ethnic prejudice, WML attempts to establish a collaborative relationship with impoverished immigrant women in slum neighborhoods met with mixed results. Mrs. Henry M. Hall lamented that her WML branch found it difficult to gain the cooperation of immigrant women in her neighborhood on the Lower East Side, where the "streets teem with millions of foreigners totally ignorant of the first principles of civic cleanliness." The WML had tried to form groups "among the more intelligent of the Italian and Jewish women who could further our work, but the women approached were too busy or too indifferent to possess any interest in city cleaning." She and her colleagues were merely able to obtain an agreement among neighborhood grocers' wives to place outdoor vegetable stands high enough to prevent dogs from urinating on the contents.[137]

Julia D. Perry of the Women's Health Protective Association certainly must not have seemed warm and reassuring to the poor. Consider her reaction to the previously mentioned letter writer who had criticized Waring in the pages of the *Sun.* Perry declared that the writer's attitude was one of "license," a condition that promotes lawlessness and which, based on her reading of history, could be expected to lead to political counterreaction and tyranny. She concluded that "those who think must govern those who toil," and that immigrants should, relatedly, be educated in the "simple rules of hygiene and cleanliness." To inspire activism among the women of her organization, she then quoted Plato's injunction to "every virtuous citizen to rescue the state from the usurpation of vice and ignorance."[138]

It is true that many immigrant women were too busy for WML activities, being so overworked that they had little time to spend on even some of the basic household sanitation chores that they would have liked to accomplish. The immigrants' response to WML overtures was probably further muted when they observed the condescending tone of individuals such as Mrs. Hall. There was, indeed, potential for abuse in prescribing tenets of behavior for what Delos Wilcox termed "the training of future citizens and . . . the fusing of conflicting race habits and race interests into a common Americanism." Many reformers should be given credit for attempting to overcome historically engrained ethnocentrism, but an offensive message all too often came across to immigrants that their own culture was considered inferior.[139]

At times activists' attempts to curb what they believed to be antisocial behavior in the immigrant community did conflict with the values held by individuals within these communities. Sometimes this values-conflict arose when reformers spoke about the long-term good while many struggling immigrants were focusing, rather, on their more immediate needs. All complex democratic societies face tough choices between conflicting public goods, choices that are more difficult when there are significant cultural and financial gaps between social groups. As we have seen, public policy regarding the enforcement of sanitation and pushcart ordinances at times engendered such conflict.[140]

Many proud tenement dwellers, moreover, resented the notion that they were the objects of anything smacking of charity. No matter how sensitive the external helper, this perception prompted feelings of dependence and loss of control over one's life, feelings that eroded the immigrant's self-image; this reinforced a determination to avoid using external sources of aid if at all possible.[141]

A general distrust of external institutions also reinforced a wariness concerning agents or agencies of reform, a distrust inherited from long residence in some of the more authoritarian and hierarchical lands of Europe. The power that American charity workers and reformers at times held over immigrants naturally brought to the forefront of many immigrants' minds reminders of the asymmetrical power relations with authorities that they had hoped to leave behind in Europe. (Here, in part, is a basic seedbed of support for the Jacksonian view of the good society.) One can imagine, for example, the fear and resentment felt by immigrants during the aforementioned cleanup campaign in Hartford in which Boy Scouts called in the authorities to issue summonses if they were not satisfied with the neatness of residents' yards. Resentment toward reformers was reinforced as well by a layer of envy and ill-feeling that people with lower social status often feel, though perhaps in a vague and unstructured way, toward those occupying higher social strata, feelings that Tammany appealed to in its often successful quest to win the ethnic vote.[142]

The gap between impoverished immigrants and social reformers belonging to groups such as the WML constituted a Catch-22 situation. The needy did not typically feel that reformers were directly tied in with their lives in a way that would build trust; this, in turn, reinforced a resistance among the poor to programs that would have increased a tie-in, programs that often could have both benefited the poor and served as broadening experiences for the reformers.

When we consider prejudiced remarks such as those of Mrs. Hall and Julia Perry, it is instructive to bear in mind that these women were rooted in an Anglo-American culture that had traditionally blamed individuals for their failures and accepted ethnic stereotypes as a given. Ethnic prejudice was a common feature in a period in which most people were not even aware that negative stereotyping of other cultures was unfair and harmful. Certainly most people had not developed the greater level of respect for other cultures that the more advanced strains of progressivism were promoting. Instead, they were typically influenced by rumors and stories that they had heard since childhood about the squalor of the slums, stories that featured sensational examples of individual depravity, brutishness, and neglect. This type of information reinforced the tendency to judge harshly. When we consider that many social reformers operated without the experience of ongoing relations with individuals who lived in the slums—individuals who they could comprehend as human beings rather than as abstract objects of disdain or pity—it is actually impressive that so many middle- and upper-class people sincerely struggled to understand the poor from an environmental perspective, fighting and overcoming at least the harshest aspects of their prejudices.

This was possible because many engaged in an inner war within their own minds, a war that paralleled the lively dialogue in which they participated within public discourse. The environmental-causation ethos, with its recognition of the

potential for reason and good within members of all ethnic groups, and its related recognition of the need for government instrumentalism, vied with a more
traditional conservative ethos that primarily blamed individuals for their lack
of success. An inner war often erupted because the progressive stance—which
faulted the external conditions that inhibited human flowering while still focusing
on those behaviors over which individuals did have power—involved a complex
mental reckoning. It did not allow adherents the psychological benefit of being
able to easily and assuredly categorize those in need. By contrast, moral model
proponents who advocated small-government/laissez-faire solutions could blame
the individual without ambivalence, and devotees of far left philosophies could
simply blame structural faults and go no farther.

Commissioner Macdonough Craven of the DSC was among those within the
civic sanitation bureaucracy who put stock in the notion of individual blame. In
1907, in replying to the pleas of settlement workers (before the fateful strike of
that year) to more faithfully clean the streets of the Lower East Side, he declared
that "the disease breeding filth which you speak of is thrown in the streets by
the people themselves, and they alone are to blame in regard to this matter." He
implored the settlement workers to press the people in their neighborhoods to
behave better.[143]

Again, we see reformers caught in the middle, facing the objections of conservatives while trying at the same time to empathize with the demoralization and
heartbreak felt by the poor as they faced difficult circumstances. At the same time
that settlement workers, women's civic club members, and other activists tried
to reconcile these cross-pressures within their own conscience-driven psyches,
they pleaded with other middle- and upper-class New Yorkers for political support, asking them to understand self-defeating behaviors among the poor from
an environmental-causation perspective, rather than writing off large segments
of the population as irresponsible knaves or fools.[144]

These activists hoped to attract support for programs that would bring out the
best in people who lived under very difficult circumstances, programs that would
strengthen the self-reliant values that they believed were key in rising out of the
slums. While self-reliance could help limit the need for government programs,
the progressives considered the supportive services and regulatory measures that
were deemed necessary to be elements of a reciprocal social bargain between the
haves and the have nots that made it fair to expect self-reliant behaviors. And
reformers trusted that individual self-fulfillment would be enhanced rather than
suppressed in this process of buttressing self-reliance.[145]

Thoughtful progressives realized that their work would be much more effective
if they could gain the cooperation of individuals within immigrant communities. They believed that it was possible to do so, in part, because they assumed
that significant common ground existed. In this view, while unhealthy environ-

ments twisted all too many people onto the wrong path, a basic universal set of values, along with some education, allowed sensible individuals of all cultures to recognize the ill effects of inebriation, bad work habits, and unhygienic practices upon family life (and to recognize that a landlord's neglect of tenement facilities could take its toll as well).

In a speech at the University Settlement in 1902, Jane Addams, the nation's foremost exponent of settlement work and social reform, addressed the challenge of working effectively with people from diverse backgrounds, people who were not always inclined toward friendship with outsiders. She emphasized first that she believed strongly in the toleration of cultural differences. But she then observed that there was plenty of common ground upon which to build a better society, one which would help nurture and sustain more fulfilled and ethically aware individuals. The "cultivated man," she declared, forgets "differences of dress, of language, of manner and other superficial distinctions because he is able to perceive and grasp the underlying elements of identity and comradeship." The much discussed "'Social Gulf' [is actually] an affair of the imagination, and curiously enough appears deepest to those of the shallowest imagination." The study of history and literature could help settlement workers and other reformers understand the potential for common ground, which in turn would allow them to tackle their challenging work with greater spirit and "moral energy."[146]

Addams and other advanced social reform progressives felt a duty to try to dampen the prejudices that older-stock Americans harbored toward immigrant groups. To do so, it was important to stress commonalities, in order to lower the natives' anxiety levels. Only then could settlement workers and their allies hope to gain a respectful hearing for more sophisticated messages about the need to accept cultural differences.

While less well known for community outreach than settlement workers, members of more staid civic groups such as the WML frequently reached out with a fair level of toleration, openness, and understanding to connect with tenement dwellers. Thus, in addition to their work in lobbying for social reform legislation and in pressing the DSC and other municipal departments to provide effective services, the WML worked in more personalized ways to enhance directly the well-being and comfort of tenement residents. And these efforts often helped modify attitudes on both sides of what turned out to be a traversable culture gap.

In 1914, for example, a group of girls from a juvenile street cleaning league on the Lower East Side suggested to their WML supervisors that cooperation between the WML and neighborhood residents could be enhanced by appealing to the latter in their native tongue. Securing WML approval, the girls, who were already accustomed to handing out multilingual DSC and health department leaflets, then distributed invitations to a proposed meeting of Italian mothers from the area. The WML paid an Italian speaker to address the one hundred mothers (and one father) who attended the gathering. Ida Cohen reported that the audience "seemed greatly interested. . . . Appeals were made to them to learn their duty to the city of their adoption." After the address, juvenile league girls served coffee and cake and "all joined in singing popular Italian songs." Both the juvenile league girls and the mothers "begged for a repetition of the meeting."[147]

The WML then organized a series of lectures in Italian, with titles such as "The Danger from Unsanitary Surroundings," "Child Punishment," "Manners," and "Prevention from Infection." WML members also organized drama clubs and classes in subjects such as first aid, cooking, and dressmaking (the last being particularly popular); subsidized the sale of saplings and flower plantings for tenement window boxes, offering prizes to those who helped beautify their blocks; donated water fountains for public use in tenement neighborhoods (and purchased great amounts of ice to chill the water during the summers); operated a summer recreation (swimming) pier; and held neighborhood dances.[148]

In discussing the effects of their outreach efforts, a WML member commented that "the [immigrant] women were eager to learn the ways of this strange new country and very responsive to our teaching. We know of no greater service to the city than by advice and direction to help these immigrant women to become useful citizens." The trust forged by such efforts helped neighborhood immigrant women feel more inclined to use the resources of settlement houses, consult with teachers about their children's school work, and cooperate with health department efforts to isolate people with cases of communicable disease.[149]

In another type of outreach effort, WML members spoke with neighborhood storekeepers, DSC personnel, and policemen, urging them to do their part to fulfill civic sanitation ordinances, and dialoguing to promote a mutual understanding of the difficulties experienced by all of the parties involved. In what became an ongoing liaison in at least one district, WML women recurrently accompanied policemen on neighborhood foot patrols, encouraging the officers to remind violators of the laws concerning overfilled ash cans, litter, blocked fire escapes, and the like, and to issue summonses if the violations were not addressed after a reasonable time.

The policemen were usually sympathetic to the women's concerns once a sense of rapport and understanding was established. This frequently prompted police officers not simply to remind residents of the laws but to explain their importance as well. The dynamic WML leader of this outreach effort, Louise Morgenstern, commented, "The street work has brought us into contact with many classes of people and studying the violations from their point of view as distinct from that of the law has been most interesting and has helped us to handle some of the problems." She observed that as a result of the drive, "at least in certain localities there is a vast improvement."[150]

Despite the differences at times dividing immigrants and reformers, Morgenstern's work and the WML's outreach efforts with Italian mothers highlight the fact that many reformers were sensitive enough to realize the need for negotiation and dialogue with individuals within the neighborhoods. And although immigrants generally were selective about which elements of American culture they chose to assimilate, there was significant congruence between their values and those of middle- and upper-class reformers. In discussing the supervised after-school playground activities organized by the city's public schools during the 1890s, one school official wrote of overhearing the "great relief" expressed by working-class parents that such a program was available. "Many an anxious mother . . . [can now] know her children are off the streets, out of the danger of carts and cars, and away from its evil influences."[151]

There were other issues of mutual interest as well, although details about particular public policy choices could be hotly contested. Most reformers and immigrants worried about the effects of unsanitary slum conditions, and there was a common longing for quality education. There was mutual apprehension concerning the effects of near-open prostitution and drunkenness on family life (although many disagreed about whether to target saloons to ameliorate the latter problem). And most immigrants did not have to be pushed to adopt a self-improvement ethic, which so many had sought to actualize by coming to America in the first place.[152]

Most immigrant parents, in fact, hoped to see their children "Americanized." Basically, they wanted their young to have the greater opportunity for individual fulfillment that existed in America. At times, conflict arose between parents and children when the former felt their ways being discarded or when the new ways seemed to imply a disdain for the old, but most looked upon their children's adoption of an American identity as a source of at least bittersweet pride. The children themselves typically felt proud to say the words "our forefathers" in referring to the nation's founders and the ideals that they represented. In point of fact, if more immigrants had wanted to, they could have formed communities such as those of the Amish or Hutterites, maintaining a separate identity from the cultural mainstream, and indeed some of New York's ultraorthodox Jewish immigrants did choose this option.[153]

Historians during the past generation have corrected some of the exaggerated estimations of the cultural gap that existed between Progressive Era immigrant parents and their children, and have reminded us that the immigrants' prior culture significantly affected the larger American culture over the course of time. Still, ethnic ways significantly diminished among the younger generation, partly due to social pressures to conform to middle-class American culture and also because many young people freely chose to internalize the standards of the new culture. The pull of American popular culture particularly reinforced the cultural rift between immigrant parent and child. Numerous children of eastern and southern European parents, like their native Anglo-Saxon counterparts, adopted elements of popular culture that reformers actually considered as unsavory as did the youths' parents. The pull of American culture and pressures to conform were common within all social strata and were more potent factors in exacerbating the cultural rift between immigrant parent and child than were the reformers' efforts to Americanize immigrant offspring per se. In carrying out these efforts, Progressive Era social reformers worked within the currents of powerful social trends, which they helped to humanize more than they made worse.[154]

Most immigrants and progressives would have agreed with the sentiments expressed in 1904 by James H. Hamilton, when he answered critics' charges that the University Settlement was an intruder on the Lower East Side and that such organizations fostered unhealthy dependencies among the immigrant poor. It seemed that the critics believed that indigenous self-help was the only valid approach and that even the wisest external guidance was suspect. Hamilton replied that a successful settlement house must truly connect with the spirit and desires of neighborhood folks; otherwise it would never attract enough participants to continue to exist. He added that, above all, the settlement aimed to promote self-help. He hoped, for example, to encourage the development of indigenous leaders on the Lower East Side who would conduct the University Settlement's activities and assert the needs of the community in civic affairs. Hamilton declared that resentment of outside help is "narrow, provincial and bigoted. A community of [foreign birth] should welcome . . . Americanizing agencies." He offered the analogy of a nation putting a tariff on art works, to highlight how mistaken a community would be if it refused to allow the influence of healthy elements because those elements were of outside origin. And he observed that "a receptivity to the best that other neighborhoods or people in other conditions have to offer is a desirable quality in any community. Neighborhood growth in culture consists largely in adapting to local needs what comes in or is brought in from the outside."[155]

Certainly, policies aimed at individual and social improvement could conflict with the Jacksonian part of the American temperament, which was a potent factor within immigrant communities. Judith Walzer Leavitt's work on late nineteenth-century Milwaukee keenly illustrates how this conflict could flare up when public health reform policies were applied in a heavy-handed manner.[156]

Drawing on a different type of cultural evidence, John Kouwenhoven relatedly warns against a tendency on the part of some community-oriented individuals to fixate on a sense of security and order, seeking a buttoned-up certitude, as if people can thoroughly take care of and fix up into a neat package all potential contingencies of life and all potential foul-ups in society or in the economy. Although he certainly does not condone littering or similar behaviors, Kouwenhoven fears that if society too rigorously follows the buttoned-up path, it could take on aspects of a soulless machine. By radically eschewing elements of what

I have termed the Jacksonian ethos, we would sacrifice a degree of freedom and individuality, and greater opportunities for wealth and individual fulfillment. Kouwenhoven's concerns may seem somewhat superfluous in the present day, in which social well-being is threatened much more by an often unreasoning Jacksonian resurgence and related government cutbacks. He does imply, however, that if we wish to gain adequate support for (and successfully implement) policies that address problems of litter, waste, and other social questions as well, we must attempt to creatively address the egalitarian urge for self-fulfillment, freedom, and mobility.[157]

CONCLUSION

In part, Progressive social reformers worried about clean streets, refuse collection, and refuse disposal because of a set of attitudes that they shared regarding sanitation, health, and social and moral order, attitudes that undergirded a broad range of urban social reform concerns. George E. Waring Jr. and his Progressive Era disciples believed that filth in public places bred not only disease but also hopelessness, fear, crime, and other indicators of disorder. They associated cleanliness with wholesomeness and with the health and well-being of individuals and the community as a whole. Accordingly, the moral condition of individuals and the stability of society at large depended on the existence of adequate public sanitation.

The legacy of the miasma theory and the traditional concept of the body as a porous system strongly affected by the physical, social, and even psychological environment made sanitation issues seem all the more crucial during the Progressive Era. An individual's level of well-being, comfort, and health reflected both the quality of his or her environment and what we would today term his or her "lifestyle." This holistic outlook, which implicitly recognized a link between impoverished living standards and disease, was an important component of the progressives' semi-utopian vision of the good society, a vision of widespread improvement in individual and community health, well-being, and morality.

In seeking to correct unsanitary conditions and other deficiencies in the social and physical environment, the progressives sought to hinder disease-breeding microbes and foster conditions in which people could more easily maintain healthy and orderly lives. Many reformers concerned about public health did not conceptualize medical problems primarily as issues needing the attention of scientific researchers devoted to finding relevant therapies. This expansive approach resonates with the views of the late Rene Dubos and other modern-day advocates of "social medicine." Dubos emphasized that health issues are inseparably intertwined with social issues; medical problems tend to arise "whenever the conditions of healthy life are wanting." Civilization can most effectively gain control over disease and premature death "by reforming itself . . . [through] organized effort . . . for the creation of a healthier, happier world." Persons interested in this approach to health (and to social justice) would find the study of Progressive Era sanitary and social reform to be a rewarding endeavor.[1]

To a significant extent, progressives succeeded in attracting middle-class support for the notion that individual and social improvement depended upon an active approach toward urban environmental conditions. Reflecting their deep concern for the development of individual character, the progressives asked, in effect: "What do folks need in their environment to maintain a keen sense of morality?" And the progressives would have easily alternated the words "health and well-being" with "morality" when asking that question. Cleanliness (as an emblem of well-being and moral order) and dirt (as a presumed breeder of disease, immorality, and disorder) were important symbols in promoting a greater awareness that the urban environment can powerfully affect health and human character. This outlook, in turn, reinforced acceptance of the concomitant need to foster environmental conditions that brought physical and moral improvement.

Sanitary reform was thus expansive in scope. A broad approach to individual and community needs, it allowed many people more readily to conceptualize the factors necessary to maintain healthy, moral lives. This type of approach reinforced the perception that sanitary and other social needs were related elements along a continuum. The meaning attached to cleanliness and dirt helped many people to realize that a variety of social problems affect public health and well-being. Progressive Era sanitary reform, then, is a fruitful avenue for examining the emergence of the concept that poverty and related conditions reflect, to a significant extent, broader underlying problems in the social and physical environment. In effect, Progressive Era sanitary reform can be equated with social reform.[2]

In this vein, clean streets were considered an integral part of an ensemble of interrelated human needs within the city. While reformers believed that the fulfillment of these needs often depended upon the cooperation of tenement district residents, many understood that if these residents were to have the wherewithal to participate as responsible moral agents in community life, then they should be provided with the prerequisites of a healthy and moral lifestyle. Thus government was obliged to hold up its end of what was, in effect, the Progressive Era social contract. It was necessary, for example, to upgrade street sanitation, housing conditions, and workplace safety, in order to complement the efforts of individuals in poorer districts who were striving to improve their own personal prospects and conduct their lives in ways that were not injurious to the community as a whole.

In this context, juvenile street cleaning leagues provided much needed after-school recreational opportunities, an environmental amenity considered crucial for the prevention of juvenile delinquency. My own contemporaries are usually amazed when I note that reformers paired their concern for clean streets with a movement to provide wholesome childhood recreation. But in the progressives' expansive, values-oriented notion of sanitation and public health, the reform of street sanitation did not simply oblige the city to find more efficient ways to push a broom across a slab of paving. Because cleanliness symbolized individual and community well-being, morality, and the potential for individual and community improvement, it is not surprising that it became a springboard for efforts to address the problems that children coming of age faced in an urban industrial society.

Controversies involving public sanitation often reflected the strains affecting urban society as a result of rapid growth. And the meaning ascribed to public sanitation helped make it a lightning rod for fundamental public debates over the most suitable ways to raise living standards and reform society. Consequently, sanitary reformers often faced considerable opposition from those who sought more individualistic-oriented solutions to social problems. Public sanitation issues, then, can serve as a lens through which scholars can examine the dichotomy between a more community-oriented (social reform progressive) approach and a more individualistic (quasi-Jacksonian) approach within late nineteenth- and early twentieth-century political culture—which, in turn, can help us better understand a conflict within the American temperament that remains pertinent in the present day.

This dichotomy was significant within political culture, in part, because it denoted differences of opinion concerning the development of individual character and morality. Progressives insisted on the importance of a moral component in social policy, believing that this was a necessary concomitant to successful long-term reform. They agreed with conservatives that the attitudes and behaviors of the needy were key factors in determining whether individuals would be able to attain prosperity, health, and well-being. Nevertheless, unlike conservatives, who often simply demanded behavioral change in the poor, many progressives recognized a reciprocal obligation to help upgrade the urban environment and living standards of city residents. With adequate external resources, individuals could more readily change their attitudes and behaviors.

In blending moralism with an awareness of the external needs of the poor, this synthesis proved politically attractive to many middle-class citizens. Recognizing that a moralistic quality suffused the outlook of the leaders of social reform movements, the middle class more readily accepted the proposition that government social programs or regulations were sometimes necessary. Indeed, in advocating measures to promote health and welfare (especially among children) while at the same time retaining expectations of individual moral responsibility, the progressives attracted a strong middle-class base of support for innovative voluntary and government-sponsored social programs and policies. And although recent historical works have rightly emphasized that working-class and immigrant groups significantly influenced the trajectory of Progressive Era reform, the era's reformers, nevertheless, were mainly of middle-class origins. Clearly, historians concerned about social justice issues in the present day can find the study of Progressive Era middle-class reform a fruitful avenue for exploration.[3]

The historian Leo Ribuffo, relatedly, has urged scholars to more closely examine the Progressive Era, implying that it would be constructive to creatively use its legacy to inform the politics and policies of present-day liberalism. He suggests that the types of attitudes held by Progressive Era activists are about the farthest that most middle-class Americans since that period have been willing to venture in the direction of social reform (with the New Deal seen as an emergency sort of exception). The historians Otis L. Graham Jr. and Elizabeth Koed have encouraged scholars to examine and reflect upon what Progressive Era reformers found, through their own experience in working with struggling immigrants, to be a "minimalist core . . . of skills, behaviors, and values" that should be encouraged in order to maintain a functioning society. To help make this sort of information useful in the present day, historians can try to discern those behaviors and values that were imparted in a noncoercive manner, and those that were generally agreed upon as normative by both the native middle class and struggling immigrants. A tentative list includes literacy skills, a work ethic and punctuality, hygienic practices, democratic political participation, and the rule of law. At the same time, it would be useful to examine those goals and methods that went beyond the bounds of consensus and were considered repugnant by people on the receiving end of the reformers' efforts.[4]

While Graham and Koed mainly refer to the assimilation of Progressive Era immigrants, in a broader sense the study of that period's assimilation efforts can help inform our attempts in the present day to grapple with the plight of any individuals or groups who are at risk of becoming enmeshed in the web of negative environmental factors that foster poverty and related social problems. In this regard, it is instructive to read portions of the last book written by Eleanor Roosevelt, *Tomorrow Is Now.* Although she rose to the height of her influence during the New Deal presidency of her husband Franklin, she (like Franklin) was originally a Progressive Era reformer, and she was able to powerfully influence many Americans to think more progressively, up to the time of her death in 1962. Writing in the early 1960s, she reflected on her struggles against the Jim Crow restrictions that still affected African Americans, and her concern about the poverty that plagued the African American community. In addressing these issues, she urged blacks, as individuals, to assume personal responsibility: "Too often, it is true, Negroes from underprivileged areas move into apartments or neighborhoods and, because they have been taught no better, clutter the hallways with filth and arouse reasonable resentment and alarm in the white tenants, who naturally do not want to see their way of life deteriorate. The function of democratic living is not to lower standards but to raise those that have been too low."[5]

Roosevelt's concern for behavioral change among the poor would have been recognizable to her Progressive Era contemporaries, as would the near-totemic view of sanitation as a sign of decent living conditions. Just as recognizable was her main thrust in that part of her book, which was to advocate equality for African Americans and espouse social policies that would help impoverished blacks move into the middle class. Realistically, the political support of the white middle class was necessary to achieve these ends, and Roosevelt, like many other figures from the Progressive Era, was able to express her ideals in a manner that was saleable to many within the middle class. In her book she related some of the hurdles that she had encountered in advocating programs to provide adequate housing for urban blacks to a skeptical white middle class: "People said, 'It is ridiculous to give a bathroom to these people. They don't know how to use it.' . . . Our answer was to put a director in charge who helped people to learn about their new surroundings and to adapt to them." Her realistic appraisal of the necessity of middle-class political acceptance prompted her, as well, to urge "that men like Martin Luther King might well perform a great service to the cause of equality for which they fight so gallantly, if they were to help some of the underprivileged Negroes to prepare themselves to fit in to better surroundings."[6]

Thus Eleanor Roosevelt, like Progressive Era activists generally, appealed to a desire for both order and social justice. Like her colleagues of the Progressive Era, she believed that a free society can attain these potentially contradictory ends only if the populace involves itself in the civic process. This, in turn, necessitates the development of that aspect of character that traditional reformers labeled "civic virtue": "In a democracy, it is your business. Democracy requires both discipline and hard work. It is not easy for individuals to govern themselves."[7]

Eleanor Roosevelt's continuing relevance across the decades of the twentieth century highlights the possibility that elements of the Progressive Era social reform ethos might help today's moderates and liberals (whom I will term today's "progressives") frame social justice issues in ways that could prove attractive to moderate conservatives—many of whom might welcome an alternative to right-wing ideologues who portray themselves as the only true conservatives—and increase the likelihood of building successful reform coalitions. A revival of concern among today's progressives for moral issues and for "the stability of the social order" (as the late Daniel Patrick Moynihan recommended) would make it harder for political opponents to portray today's progressives as people who are outside the fold of moral America. But instead of using moral concepts to seek to impose lifestyle choices when there is no popular consensus concerning such choices, or to use an "us versus them" framework that plays on the public's fears and insecurities, progressives could attempt to build consensus and compromise. They could also attempt to provide educational measures and other resources that can help individuals make wiser moral decisions (for example, with regard to issues such as teen pregnancy).[8]

Progressive activists might also emphasize that they seek many of the same basic goals as conservatives (such as safe neighborhoods and, ideally, stable two-parent families), but that their solutions in some ways differ—in that problems such as crime, drug use, teenage pregnancy, and unstable families cannot adequately be addressed merely by instituting tough sentencing laws, tough welfare laws, or other band-aid measures. By highlighting the connection between complex social problems and phenomena such as family instability, and by emphasizing how social policy measures—from smaller classroom sizes (particularly for younger children), to the broader provision of after-school recreational opportunities and drug rehabilitation services, to higher minimum wage rates and more generous Earned Income Tax Credit benefits—would help address these problems, progressives could assert that the cry for moral order and family values is rather hollow when trumpeted by leaders who would simultaneously cut the taxes that would fund such preventive measures. One could also appeal to the long-term self-interest of today's middle class, by emphasizing that tough law-and-order policies are not as effective against crime as is a toughness that includes the provision of preventive measures, and that we should provide high-quality (and lifelong) educational opportunities and related supports if we want to cultivate a future in which our country is economically competitive.[9]

A reinvigoration of elements of the Progressive Era Social Gospel tradition might challenge many evangelical Christians to think in broader terms about social problems and go beyond the belief that individual charitable acts can adequately address poverty and related social problems. Similarly, by legitimating the notion that there are structural and environmental bases of maladaptive behaviors, the Social Gospel tradition might encourage many evangelicals to go beyond a singular emphasis on individual morality in identifying the genesis of crime, poverty, and other symptoms of social dysfunction. The concept of reciprocal obligations, a concept entailing responsibilities not only on the part of society's have-nots who seek help but also on the part of those who possess the means to provide help, might resonate powerfully with many evangelicals. Such an idea could strengthen support for programs and policies that provide the social and physical conditions that foster opportunity and hope among the poor. And by emphasizing their desire for a stable social order and for communities in which children can grow up safely, progressives might help reassure evangelicals that a societal superego would not vanish if progressive candidates were to gain political power.

More fundamentally, there is a good chance that many of today's citizens, whether evangelicals or not, would relate positively to the moral message, which is at the heart of all great religions, that we as a people are responsible for aiding the poor and disadvantaged (as long as the progressives who tout this message emphasize that the recipients of aid must also reciprocate). Relatedly, the historian James Morone has pointed out that although Americans in the past have usually attributed social problems to individual moral failings, there has also been a strong progressive strain within American political culture that has garnered significant success through emphasizing the immorality of unjust social and economic conditions that foster poverty.[10]

Elements of the Progressive Era municipal housekeeping tradition (minus the sexist elements) might also help popularize a social justice agenda in the present day. As we have seen, Progressive Era reformers emphasized the positive attributes of cleanliness and the belief that filthy environments undermined individual and social order—with special emphasis often given to those conditions considered threatening to the health and spirit of children and the family. The social commentator Jean Bethke Elshtain has noted Jane Addams's view that the uncleared garbage in her settlement house neighborhood assaulted not simply the physical health of slum dwellers but that such conditions were also "an assault on the human soul, which says that the city cares so little about taking away this garbage because it regards the human beings compressed into [such neighborhoods] as refuse, too."[11] In the municipal housekeeping outlook, which was an expansive framework, filth was a prominent symbol reinforcing the belief that almost any factor that could be considered a threat to children or the family was, perforce, a social problem that needed to be addressed—not only by uplifting individuals but by also ameliorating the relevant environmental conditions. Improved street cleaning and garbage collection services were just two of the many policy prescriptions meant to address the interconnected social and physical ills that could weaken individual morale, family stability, and social order. In pointing out the ramifications of negative physical conditions, Progressive Era reformers helped many people recognize the ways in which more abstract problems threatened child welfare, family stability, and social order—helping many to understand, for example, how low wages negatively affected so many marriages.

A sense of concern about unwholesome or dangerous physical conditions—from crumbling school buildings to inadequate housing to dirty streets—still resonates with many citizens in the present day. And an emphasis on the threat that these conditions pose to child welfare and family stability (and, hence, to social order) might sharpen this resonance and increase the public's sensitivity to broader and more abstract social problems.[12]

If limited when applied to individual behaviors by the guidelines of consensus and compromise, a social policy approach rooted in the Progressive Era emphasis on reciprocal obligations—which was highlighted in recent years when President Clinton spoke about the mutual responsibilities of both the haves and have nots—need not degenerate into a tool for stigmatizing the poor or merely policing their behaviors. In today's society, with persistent crime, poverty, and great numbers of rudderless children, will humane scholars accept responsibility to help set behavioral and attitudinal standards (while at the same time promoting structural improvements)? Those so inclined can examine programs of the Progressive Era such as the juvenile street cleaning leagues, to help illuminate the nuanced viewpoint of the era's reformers toward individual character and the good society, a viewpoint that valued self-expression and social justice while at the same time valuing order, and that recognized the need for powerful government (and the social programs and regulations that only government could provide), while hoping to minimize the need for such by fostering a self-disciplined population.

APPENDIX

Mayors of New York City, 1893–1945

Thomas F. Gilroy	1893–94
William L. Strong	1895–97
Robert A. Van Wyck	1898–1901
Seth Low	1902–3
George B. McClellan Jr.	1904–9
William J. Gaynor	1910–13
Ardolph Loges Kline	1913
John Purroy Mitchel	1914–17
John F. Hylan	1918–25
James J. Walker	1926–32
Joseph V. McKee	1932
John P. O'Brien	1933
Fiorello H. LaGuardia	1934–45

Source: *The Green Book,* official directory of the City of New York, online, http://www.nyc.gov/html/dcas/html/features/greenbook_mayors.shtml (accessed August 24, 2005).

Commissioners of the New York City Department of Street Cleaning, 1893–1918, with Date of Appointment

William S. Andrews	July 21, 1893
George E. Waring	January 15, 1895
James McCartney	January 1, 1898
Percy E. Nagle	February 10, 1900
John McGaw Woodbury	January 1, 1902
Macdonough Craven	October 22, 1906
Walter Bensel	July 8, 1907
Foster Crowell	November 23, 1907
William H. Edwards	January 1, 1909
John T. Fetherston	January 1, 1914
Arnold B. MacStay	January 30, 1918

Source: New York Department of Street Cleaning, *Report for the Year 1918* (n.p., n.d.), 62.

NOTES

Frequently cited newspapers are identified by the following short titles.

Globe and Commercial Advertiser	*Globe*
Jewish Daily Forward	*Forward*
New York American	*American*
New York Call	*Call*
New York Daily News	*Daily News*
New York Daily Tribune	*Tribune*
New York Evening Post	*Evening Post*
New York Evening World	*Evening World*
New York Herald	*Herald*
New York Sun	*Sun*
New York Times	*Times*
New York World	*World*
The Worker	*Worker*

Introduction

1. Richard Harrison Shryock, *The Development of Modern Medicine: An Interpretation of the Social and Scientific Factors Involved* (London, 1947; repr., Madison: University of Wisconsin Press, 1979), 211–47; John Duffy, *The Sanitarians: A History of American Public Health* (Urbana: University of Illinois Press, 1990), 79–192; Suellen Hoy, *Chasing Dirt: The American Pursuit of Cleanliness* (New York: Oxford University Press, 1995), 25–87; Walter I. Trattner, *From Poor Law to Welfare State: A History of Social Welfare in America,* 5th ed. (New York: Free Press, 1994), 141–43. On the nineteenth-century British public health movement, see Anthony S. Wohl, *Endangered Lives: Public Health in Victorian Britain* (London: J. M. Dent, 1983).

2. John C. Burnham, "The Cultural Interpretation of the Progressive Movement," in *Paths into American Culture: Psychology, Medicine, and Morals,* ed. John C. Burnham (Philadelphia: Temple University Press, 1988), 225; Leo P. Ribuffo, "From Carter to Clinton: The Latest Crisis of American Liberalism," *American Studies International* 35 (June 1997): 4–29.

3. Suzanne Lebsock, "Women and American Politics, 1880–1920," in *Women, Politics, and Change,* ed. Louise A. Tilly and Patricia Gurin (New York: Russell Sage Foundation, 1990), 35–62; Robyn Muncy, "Gender and Professionalization in the Origins of the U.S. Welfare State: The Careers of Sophonisba Breckinridge and Edith Abbott, 1890–1935," *Journal of Policy History* 2 (1990): 290–315; Anne Firor Scott, "On Seeing and Not See-

ing: A Case of Historical Invisibility," *Journal of American History* 71 (June 1984): 7–21; Kathryn Kish Sklar, "The Historical Foundations of Women's Power in the Creation of the American Welfare State, 1830–1930," in *Mothers of a New World: Maternalist Politics and the Origins of Welfare States,* ed. Seth Koven and Sonya Michel (New York: Routledge, 1993), 43–93.

Chapter 1: The Garbage Workers' Strike of 1907

1. Richard L. McCormick, "The Discovery That Business Corrupts Politics: A Reappraisal of the Origins of Progressivism," in *The Party Period and Public Policy: American Politics from the Age of Jackson to the Progressive Era,* ed. Richard L. McCormick (New York: Oxford University Press, 1986), 311–56.

2. Richard L. McCormick, *From Realignment to Reform: Political Change in New York State 1893–1910* (Ithaca: Cornell University Press, 1981), 212–13.

3. New York City Board of Aldermen, *Report on the Administration of the Street Cleaning Department of the City of New York* (New York, 1906), 3–7, 20–35, 71, 119–32; *Times,* May 18, 26, 1906, October 24, 1906 (unless noted otherwise, all *Times* citations refer to sec. 1 of the issue); *Evening World,* June 25, 1907; *Herald,* July 1, 1907; Benjamin Miller, *Fat of the Land: Garbage in New York the Last Two Hundred Years* (New York: Four Walls Eight Windows, 2000), 114–20.

4. George B. McClellan Jr. to John McGaw Woodbury, October 13, 1906, McClellan Papers, New-York Historical Society; *World,* October 14, 1906; *Times,* October 23, 24, 1906, March 5, 6, 1907, April 5, 30, 1907. While in office, Waring forged the nation's first reliable urban street cleaning and garbage collection operation. Martin V. Melosi, *Garbage in the Cities: Refuse, Reform, and the Environment, 1880–1980* (College Station: Texas A&M University Press, 1981), 59–78; Richard Skolnik, "George Edwin Waring, Jr.: A Model for Reformers," *New-York Historical Society Quarterly* 52 (October 1968): 354–78; James H. Cassedy, "The Flamboyant Colonel Waring: An Anticontagionist Holds the American Stage in the Age of Pasteur and Koch," in *Sickness and Health in America: Readings in the History of Medicine and Public Health,* ed. Judith Walzer Leavitt and Ronald L. Numbers, 2d rev. ed. (Madison: University of Wisconsin Press, 1985), 451–58; John Duffy, *A History of Public Health in New York City,* vol. 2: *1866–1966* (New York: Russell Sage Foundation, 1974), 125–26.

5. "Streets," *Guild Review* (publication of the University Settlement) 1 (February 1907): 7, in the *Papers of the University Settlement Society of New York City* (Madison: State Historical Society of Wisconsin, 1972), microfilm, reel 3.

6. Woman's Municipal League (hereafter WML), *Bulletin* 5 (April 1907): 3.

7. WML, *Bulletin* 5 (March 1907): 5; (April 1907): 3, 8–9; (May 1907): 5–7 ("incapacity and indifference"); (June 1907): 1–2 ("hoary system").

8. Haven Emerson, "The Report of the [New York Academy of Medicine] Section on Public Health for the Year 1907," in "Annual Reports 1907–1909," ms., Rare Books Room, New York Academy of Medicine, New York; "Resolution Concerning Street Cleaning Adopted by New York Academy of Medicine, May 2, 1907," Minutes of the Section on Public Health and Legal Medicine, Rare Books Room, New York Academy of Medicine, New York; WML, *Bulletin* 5 (April 1907): 6–9; (June 1907): 3; "Clean Streets," *Guild Review* 1

(May 1907): 40, *Papers of the University Settlement Society of New York City,* microfilm, reel 3; *Times,* March 4, 5, 8, 1907, April 5, 30, 1907, May 12, 17, 1907.

9. Macdonough Craven to George B. McClellan Jr., July 8, 1907, McClellan Papers, Municipal Archives, New York; *Tribune,* June 26, 1907; *American,* June 26, 1907; *Times,* June 30, 1907; Mark H. Maier, *City Unions: Managing Discontent in New York City* (New Brunswick, N.J.: Rutgers University Press, 1987), 11–13.

10. *Tribune,* June 26, 1907.

11. Ibid., July 1, 1907; *Sun,* June 26, 1907; *American,* June 26, 1907; *Times,* June 30, 1907; *Evening World,* June 25, 1907.

12. John Duffy, *The Sanitarians: A History of American Public Health* (Urbana: University of Illinois Press, 1990), 145 (Memphis statistic); John Duffy, "Social Impact of Disease in the Late 19th Century," in Leavitt and Numbers, *Sickness and Health,* 414–21; Martin V. Melosi, *The Sanitary City: Urban Infrastructure in America from Colonial Times to the Present* (Baltimore: Johns Hopkins University Press, 2000), 153; Richard Charques, *The Twilight of Imperial Russia* (New York: Oxford University Press, 1958), 32 (Russian statistic). For the endemic-epidemic dichotomy, see Richard Harrison Shryock, *The Development of Modern Medicine: An Interpretation of the Social and Scientific Factors Involved* (London, 1947; repr., Madison: University of Wisconsin Press, 1979), 215–17; Rene Dubos and Jean Dubos, *The White Plague: Tuberculosis, Man, and Society* (Boston: Little, Brown, 1952; repr., New Brunswick, N.J.: Rutgers University Press, 1987), 209–10; Edwin H. Ackerknecht, *A Short History of Medicine,* rev. ed. (Baltimore: Johns Hopkins University Press, 1982), 211.

13. For New Yorkers' concerns about epidemics, see Duffy, *History of Public Health in New York,* 2:143–47, 161–62.

14. George Rosen, *A History of Public Health* (New York: MD Publications, 1958), 288–89; Richard Harrison Shryock, *Medicine and Society in America: 1660–1860* (Ithaca: Cornell University Press, 1960), 62–71; Ackerknecht, *Short History of Medicine,* 159, 175.

15. Jon A. Peterson, "The Impact of Sanitary Reform upon American Urban Planning, 1840–1890," *Journal of Social History* 13 (Fall 1979): 83–103; Stanley K. Schultz, *Constructing Urban Culture: American Cities and City Planning, 1800–1920* (Philadelphia: Temple University Press, 1989), 126–42; Duffy, "Social Impact of Disease," 414–21; Dubos and Dubos, *White Plague,* 218; John M. Eyler, *Victorian Social Medicine: The Ideas and Methods of William Farr* (Baltimore: Johns Hopkins University Press, 1979), 97–122; Gert H. Brieger, "Sanitary Reform in New York City: Stephen Smith and the Passage of the Metropolitan Health Bill," in Leavitt and Numbers, *Sickness and Health,* 399–413; Duffy, *Sanitarians,* 1–192; Nancy Tomes, *The Gospel of Germs: Men, Women, and the Microbe in American Life* (Cambridge, Mass.: Harvard University Press, 1998), 23–47; Ackerknecht, *Short History of Medicine,* 210–17; Shryock, *Development of Modern Medicine,* 211–47; Howard D. Kramer, "The Germ Theory and the Early Public Health Program in the United States," *Bulletin of the History of Medicine* 22 (May–June 1948), 235, 243; Shryock, *Medicine and Society,* 161–62; Rosen, *History of Public Health,* 288–89, 338–39; Gordon Atkins, *Health, Housing, and Poverty in New York City, 1865–1898,* lithoprinted Ph.D. diss. (Ann Arbor, Mich.: Edwards Brothers, 1947), 259; Charles E. Rosenberg and Carroll Smith-Rosenberg, "Pietism and the Origins of the American Public Health Movement: A Note on John H. Griscom and Robert M. Hartley," in Leavitt and Numbers, *Sickness and Health,* 385–98. Manhattan alone contained 60,000 horses, which excreted 2.5 million pounds of manure (and 60,000

gallons of urine) onto the streets daily. Miasma-related anxieties were reinforced by the existence of such great quantities of this matter, and the dust containing this matter, on the city's streets. Moreover, increasing smoke emissions from industry and coal-burning stoves and furnaces heightened concern about airborne contaminants. The germ theory, in combination with the traditional fear of foul air, produced a heightened concern about dust that was exemplified by the term "germ dust." The fearful implications of germ dust during a garbage workers' strike can be easily imagined. Parenthetically, it may be that the replacement of large numbers of horses by automobiles within a few years after the strike sounded the death knell for remnants of the miasma theory. *Tribune,* July 2, 1907; *Times,* August 22, 1907; O. Chisholm, "Street Cleaning Difficulties in New York," *Charities and the Commons* 18 (August 17, 1907), 594; New York Department of Street Cleaning (hereafter, DSC), *Clean Streets through Education and Cooperation: Report of Exhibition and Tests of Street Cleaning Appliances* (New York, 1914), 21; Edwin G. Burrows and Mike Wallace, *Gotham: A History of New York City to 1898* (New York: Oxford University Press, 1999), 1194; David Stradling, *Smokestacks and Progressives: Environmentalists, Engineers, and Air Quality in America, 1881–1951* (Baltimore: Johns Hopkins University Press, 1999), 48–57; Tomes, *Gospel of Germs,* 96–98; Melosi, *Garbage in the Cities,* 142.

16. On these matters and related issues, see Tomes, *Gospel of Germs,* 26–38; Shryock, *Development of Modern Medicine,* 282–83; Ackerknecht, *Short History of Medicine,* 177–83.

17. David Rosner, "Introduction," in *Hives of Sickness: Public Health and Epidemics in New York City,* ed. David Rosner (New Brunswick: Rutgers University Press, 1995), 9, 12; Harold L. Platt, "Invisible Gases: Smoke, Gender, and the Redefinition of Environmental Policy in Chicago, 1900–1920," *Planning Perspectives* 10 (1995): 70, 90–92; Kramer, "Germ Theory," 246, DSC, *Clean Streets through Education,* 20.

18. On these matters and related issues, see Thomas Darlington, "Civics and Sanitation," in *Proceedings of the New York Conference for Good Government and the Eleventh Annual Meeting of the National Municipal League,* ed. Clinton Rogers Woodruff (n.p., 1905), 197–205; P. M. Hall, "The Collection and Disposal of City Waste and the Public Health [with discussion]," *American Journal of Public Health* 3 (April 1913): 314–15; William Paul Gerhard, "A Half-Century of Sanitation," *American Architect and Building News* 63 (March 11, 1899): 75–76; Rosner, "Introduction," 13–14; Naomi Rogers, "A Disease of Cleanliness: Polio in New York City, 1900–1990," in Rosner, *Hives of Sickness,* 117–18; *Times,* August 21, 1908; Tomes, *Gospel of Germs,* 46–57, 67, 127; Barbara Gutmann Rosenkrantz, "The Search for Professional Order in 19th-Century American Medicine," in Leavitt and Numbers, *Sickness and Health,* 228–29; George Rosen, *The Structure of American Medical Practice, 1875–1941,* ed. Charles E. Rosenberg (Philadelphia: University of Pennsylvania Press, 1983), 7–12, 88–91; Duffy, *Sanitarians,* 199; Platt, "Invisible Gases," 71, 81–82, 85; John Shaw Billings, "Public Health and Municipal Government," *Annals of the American Academy of Political and Social Science,* supp. (February 1891): 13. The era's medical profession was moving toward greater occupational specialization based upon the theory of disease specificity and the corresponding view of the body as a collection of discrete parts. An enhanced professional authority resting on this basis reinforced the sway of medical expertise in the field of public health and a corresponding movement of public health leaders away from an emphasis on social reform issues to those issues that were more specifically germane to laboratory-based medical science. The decline of a general reform ethos after World War I and the competition of government agencies

for limited public funds reinforced this trend. George A. Soper, "The Work of Boards of Health," with discussion, in *Proceedings of the National Municipal League,* ed. Clinton Rogers Woodruff (National Municipal League, 1908), 8–21, 378–87; A. W. Hedrich, "Recent Public Health Reports," *National Municipal Review* 6 (May 1917): 379–86; "The Function of the Engineer in Government," *National Municipal Review* 12 (May 1923): 271–72; M. N. Baker, "Garbage and Refuse Disposal a Matter of Cleansing Rather Than Health," *National Municipal Review* 13 (December 1924): 675–78; *Tribune,* October 9, 1906; *Times,* August 25, 1907, sec. 2; James H. Cassedy, *Charles V. Chapin and the Public Health Movement* (Cambridge, Mass.: Harvard University Press, 1962), 98, 216–19; Russell C. Maulitz, "'Physician versus Bacteriologist': The Ideology of Science in Clinical Medicine," in *The Therapeutic Revolution: Essays in the Social History of American Medicine,* ed. Morris J. Vogel (Philadelphia: University of Pennsylvania Press, 1979), 91–107.

19. *Times,* June 27, 28, 1907; *Tribune,* June 27, 1907 (quote).

20. *Tribune,* June 27, 1907; *World,* June 28, 1907 ("ready to spread"); *Evening World,* June 26, 1907 ("heated air").

21. *Evening World,* June 26, 1907; *World,* June 28, 1907; *Globe,* June 28, 1907 (quote); *Sun,* June 28, 1907; *Times,* June 30, 1907.

22. *Evening Post,* June 27, 1907; *Times,* June 28, 30, 1907, July 1, 1907; *Tribune,* June 28, 1907; *Brooklyn Eagle,* June 29, 1907; *Sun,* June 28, 1907; *World,* June 28, 1907 (quote).

23. *American,* June 28, 1907; *Times,* June 29, 1907.

24. *Evening Post,* June 27, 1907 (quote); *Times,* June 29, 1907; *Worker,* July 6, 1907; *Sun,* June 28, 1907; *Evening World,* June 27, 1907.

25. Transcript of meeting, Craven and labor representatives, June 29, 1907, McClellan Papers, Municipal Archives, New York ("Jersey justice"); *American,* June 28, 1907; Board of Aldermen, *Report on the Administration,* 5–7.

26. Chisholm, "Street Cleaning," 590–94; Board of Aldermen, *Report on the Administration,* 5–7, 131; WML, *Bulletin* 5 (June 1907): 2; *Times,* October 24, 1906, July 10, 1907; *Tribune,* July 10, 1907.

27. *Worker,* July 6 (slavery analogy), 20, 1907; *Tribune,* June 30, 1907, July 1, 1907; *Evening Post,* June 27, 1907; *Evening World,* June 27, 1907; *Herald,* December 14, 1906; John McGaw Woodbury to George B. McClellan Jr., January 6, 1905, McClellan Papers, Municipal Archives, New York; June 29, 1907, meeting, McClellan Papers, Municipal Archives, New York; DSC, *Report for the Year 1906* (New York: Martin B. Brown, 1907), 4–5. On related matters, see Robert Dishon, "The New York City Department of Street Cleaning, 1881–1929," manuscript, 1988, New York City Department of Sanitation.

28. DSC, *Report for the Year 1906,* 4–5; *Evening World,* June 25, 1907; *Herald,* June 26, 1907.

29. MacDonough Craven to Central Federated Union, July 1, 1907, McClellan Papers, Municipal Archives, New York; June 29, 1907 meeting, McClellan Papers, Municipal Archives, New York; DSC, *Report for the Year 1906,* 4–5; *Worker,* July 6, 1907; *Sun,* June 30, 1907; *Herald,* June 26, 1907; *Evening Post,* June 27, 1907.

30. Louise Bolard More and Robert Coit Chapin, as noted in David C. Hammack, *Power and Society: Greater New York at the Turn of the Century* (New York: Russell Sage Foundation, 1982), 90, 341; New York State Department of Labor, *Seventh Annual Report, 1907* (New York, 1908), 2:xxv–xxvii; *Times,* June 11, 1897; Melosi, *Garbage in the Cities,* 148–49; Dishon, "New York Department of Street Cleaning," 22.

31. *Times,* June 28, 1907; *American,* June 28, 1907; *Sun,* June 28, 1907.

32. *American,* June 28, 1907 (quote); *Tribune,* June 28, 1907.

33. *Tribune,* June 28, 1907; *Sun,* June 28, 1907; *American,* June 28, 1907; *Evening World,* June 27, 1907.

34. *Tribune,* June 29, 1907 (quotes); *Sun,* June 29, 1907.

35. *Tribune,* June 29, 1907.

36. Ibid.

37. *American,* June 29, 1907.

38. Ibid.; *Tribune,* June 29, 1907; *Sun,* June 28, 1907.

39. Shryock, *Development of Modern Medicine,* 244, 280–93; Thomas McKeown, *The Role of Medicine: Dream, Mirage, or Nemesis?* (Princeton: Princeton University Press, 1979), 78, 89, 117; Shryock, *Medicine and Society,* 161–66; Rosen, *History of Public Health,* 338–39; Schultz, *Constructing Urban Culture,* 135; Barbara Gutmann Rosenkrantz, *Public Health and the State: Changing Views in Massachusetts, 1842–1936* (Cambridge, Mass.: Harvard University Press, 1972), 75–77, 103, 123–27; Paul Starr, *The Social Transformation of American Medicine* (New York: Basic Books, 1982), 136–38; Rosen, *Structure of American Medical Practice,* 44–47.

40. Rosenkrantz, *Public Health and the State,* 75–77, 123; David P. Thelen, *The New Citizenship: Origins of Progressivism in Wisconsin, 1885–1900* (Columbia: University of Missouri Press, 1972), 10, 33, 44–85; Alexander B. Callow Jr., commentary in *The City Boss in America: An Interpretive Reader,* ed. Alexander B. Callow Jr. (New York: Oxford University Press, 1976), 176.

41. McCormick, *From Realignment to Reform,* 31, 106, 219, 254; Augustus Cerillo Jr., "The Reform of Municipal Government in New York City from Seth Low to John Purroy Mitchel," *New-York Historical Society Quarterly* 57 (January 1973): 51–71; Eric F. Goldman, *Rendezvous with Destiny: A History of Modern American Reform,* rev. ed. (New York: Vintage, 1955), 155; John C. Burnham, "The Cultural Interpretation of the Progressive Movement," in *Paths into American Culture: Psychology, Medicine, and Morals,* ed. John C. Burnham (Philadelphia: Temple University Press, 1988), 223–24.

42. *Tribune,* June 29, 1907 ("God help"), July 1, 1907; *American,* June 29, 1907 ("situation in hand"), July 1, 1907; *Globe,* June 28, 1907; *Times,* June 30, 1907, July 1, 2, 1907, August 23, 1907.

43. *Tribune,* June 29 ("beyond description"), 30 ("the smells," "the rain"), 1907; *American,* June 29, 1907 ("ready to carry," "never before knew"), July 1, 1907 ("deadly vapor"); *Times,* June 29, 1907 ("if we don't clear"); *Globe,* June 28, 1907. In addition, the *Times* reported that one woman kept all of the windows of her apartment closed, to protect against "vile odors and germ-breeding accumulations," after her infant daughter came down with diarrhea. She decided to get away from the "terribly hot and close" apartment with her daughter, for a cruise to visit relatives, hoping that the sea breezes would restore the baby's health. Unfortunately, the child died while on board. *Times,* July 3 ("vile odors," "terribly hot"), 1907. The *American* was not technically accurate in implying that this was the first time the city's street cleaning service had been crippled by a strike. Indeed, grievances raised in December 1906 during a brief strike adumbrated the issues of 1907. To resolve that earlier walkout, Craven promised to try to limit the use of overtime work; his infidelity to these promises helped fuel the drivers' anger during the weeks preceding the strike of 1907. Nevertheless, no full-blown strike of several days' duration had taken

place during the generation preceding the strike of 1907. N.Y.S. Department of Labor, *Seventh Annual Report, 1907*, vol. 1, 72–73; June 29, 1907, meeting, McClellan Papers, Municipal Archives, New York; *Herald,* December 12, 13, 14, 1906; *Times,* December 13, 1906; *Tribune,* December 14, 1906; Adolf F. Meisen, "History of Street Cleaning in New York City, 1860–1872" (Master's thesis, Columbia University, 1939), 32–35; David Ziskind, *One Thousand Strikes of Government Employees* (New York: Columbia University Press, 1940), 83; Maier, *City Unions,* 11–13.

44. *Times,* June 30, 1907, July 1, 2, 1907, August 23, 1907; *Tribune,* June 29, 1907, July 1, 1907; *American,* June 29, 1907, July 1, 1907; *Globe,* June 28, 1907.

45. *Evening World,* June 28, 1907; George E. Pozetta, "The Mulberry District of New York City: The Years before World War One," in *Little Italies in North America,* ed. Robert F. Harney and J. Vincent Scarpaci (Toronto: Multicultural History Society of Ontario, 1981), 23–24.

46. Samuel L. Baily, "The Adjustment of Italian Immigrants in Buenos Aires and New York, 1870–1914," *American Historical Review* 88 (April 1983): 284–97; "Study of Italian Families in Gramercy District," ca. 1906, in Charity Organization Society Papers (part of the Community Service Society Papers), box 162, Rare Books and Manuscripts Collection, Butler Library, Columbia University, New York; Hammack, *Power and Society,* 84; Melvyn Dubofsky, *When Workers Organize: New York City in the Progressive Era* (Amherst: University of Massachusetts Press, 1968), 17–19, 82; Robert Foerster, *Italian Emigration of Our Times* (Cambridge, Mass.: Harvard University Press, 1919; repr., New York: Russell and Russell, 1968), 401–4; Pozetta, "Mulberry District," 14–22, 27–28. For alternative viewpoints on the role of Italians in the labor movement in urban America during the Progressive Era, see Rudolph J. Vecoli, "Italian American Workers, 1880–1920: Padrone Slaves or Primitive Rebels?" in *Perspectives in Italian Immigration and Ethnicity,* ed. S. M. Tomasi (New York: Center for Migration Studies, 1977), 25–49; Paul Buhle, "Italian-American Radicals and Labor in Rhode Island, 1905–1930," *Radical History Review* 17 (Spring 1978): 121–51; Donna Gabaccia, "Neither Padrone Slaves nor Primitive Rebels: Sicilians on Two Continents," in *Struggle a Hard Battle: Essays on Working Class Immigrants,* ed. Dirk Hoerder (De Kalb: Northern Illinois University Press, 1986), 95–117.

47. Most of the strikebreakers were recent Italian and Hungarian immigrants who arrived with few ties to the New York community, few skills, and hungry for a job. Several Jewish immigrants also served as strikebreakers. The *Forward,* the pro-labor Yiddish-language newspaper, reported that some "green Jews" (new arrivals) were "fooled into being scabs. . . . Green Jews should be on their guard and not let themselves be convinced by charlatans and swindlers." The existence of huge pools of unskilled immigrant labor constituted a serious obstacle to successful union organization in unskilled industries. *Forward,* June 29, 1907; *Herald,* July 1, 1907; Edwin Fenton, *Immigrants and Unions, a Case Study: Italians and American Labor, 1870–1920* (New York: Arno Press, 1975), 254–58. I am indebted to Morris Moskowitz for translating the *Forward* article.

48. *Tribune,* June 29, 1907, July 1, 1907; *American,* June 29, 1907; *Herald,* July 1, 1907; *Evening World,* June 28 (quote), 29, 1907.

49. *Times,* June 29, 1907 (quote); *Tribune,* June 29, 1907; *American,* June 29, 1907; *Evening World,* June 28, 1907.

50. *Times,* June 30, 1907 (quote); *American,* June 30, 1907.

51. N.Y.S. Department of Labor, *Seventh Annual Report, 1907,* vol. 1, part 3, 139–40; *Evening World,* June 29, 1907; *Times,* June 29, 30, 1907; *Tribune,* June 30, 1907.

52. *Tribune,* June 30, 1907.

53. *Times,* July 3, 1907; Melosi, *Garbage in the Cities,* 109–12; Schultz, *Constructing Urban Culture,* 111–49.

54. Darlington, "Civics and Sanitation," 197–205 (quote, 205). A WML flyer dated March 13, 1913, likewise reminded citizens: "For Health and Decency, Clean Up." Box labeled "Woman's Municipal League of the City of New York, New-York Historical Society, New York City." A breakdown of civic sanitation was considered so disruptive of the social order that the stability of private property seemed threatened, as witnessed in the Streets Conference Committee's entreaty to Mayor McClellan during the strike: "Where the public health is menaced, the use of streets attended with universal discomfort, private property injured to a degree difficult to estimate, and real estate values impaired, the situation is of an emergency character, and we ask you to deal with it accordingly." *Tribune,* July 1, 1907.

55. *American Hebrew,* June 28, 1907.

56. Ruth Schwartz Cowan, *More Work for Mother: The Ironies of Household Technology from the Open Hearth to the Microwave* (New York: Basic Books, 1983), 164–72; Suellen Hoy, *Chasing Dirt: The American Pursuit of Cleanliness* (New York: Oxford University Press, 1995), 116–17; Tomes, *Gospel of Germs,* 188.

57. Darlington, "Civics and Sanitation," 197–205 ("sickness," 197); DSC, *Clean Streets through Education,* 32 ("moral condition"); John Morton Blum, *The Republican Roosevelt,* 2d ed. (Cambridge, Mass.: Harvard University Press, 1977), 26.

58. WML, *Bulletin* 7 (November–December 1909): 5.

59. *American Hebrew,* June 28, 1907 (quote); Melosi, *Garbage in the Cities,* 117–33; George Rosen, *Preventive Medicine in the United States 1900–1975: Trends and Interpretations* (New York: Science History Publications, 1975), 47–48.

60. Anne Firor Scott, "On Seeing and Not Seeing: A Case of Historical Invisibility," *Journal of American History* 71 (June 1984): 15–16; Mark Haller, "Urban Vice and Civic Reform: Chicago in the Early Twentieth Century," in *Cities in American History,* ed. Kenneth T. Jackson and Stanley K. Schultz (New York: Knopf, 1972), 301; Rosen, *Preventive Medicine,* 6–14, 25–26; Robert H. Bremner, *From the Depths: The Discovery of Poverty in the United States* (New York: New York University Press, 1956), 123–38; Roy Lubove, "The Twentieth-Century City: The Progressive as Municipal Reformer," in *Bosses and Reformers: Urban Politics in America, 1880–1920,* ed. Blaine A. Brownell and Warren E. Stickle (Boston: Houghton Mifflin, 1973), 82–96; Rosenberg and Smith-Rosenberg, "Pietism and the Origins," 388; Melosi, *Garbage in the Cities,* 109–10, 117.

61. Suellen M. Hoy, "'Municipal Housekeeping': The Role of Women in Improving Urban Sanitation Practices, 1880–1917," in *Pollution and Reform in American Cities 1870–1930,* ed. Martin V. Melosi (Austin: University of Texas Press, 1980), 173–94; Melosi, *Garbage in the Cities,* 36, 105–33; Scott, "Seeing and Not Seeing," 16.

62. WML, *We Are Municipal Housekeepers* (New York, 1908), booklet, in box labeled "Woman's Municipal League of the City of New York," New-York Historical Society; *Times,* February 16, 1913, sec. 5; Melosi, *Garbage in the Cities,* 105–23.

63. Jane Addams, *Twenty Years at Hull-House* (New York: Macmillan, 1910), 205, 283–89, 312–21; *Tribune,* July 2, 1907; *Globe,* June 29, 1907; Cowan, *More Work,* 164–72. Parenthetically,

a concern with cleanliness and other "Americanizing" values did not necessarily preclude a recognition of the effectiveness of labor union activity in obtaining the necessary financial prerequisites for a clean way of life. Dubofsky, *When Workers Organize*, 17, 26.

64. *American*, July 1, 1907 ("malodorous"); *Tribune*, June 30, 1907 (Lehane quote).

65. *Tribune*, July 1, 1907.

66. Ibid., July 2, 1907 (quotes); Tomes, *Gospel of Germs*, 96–97.

67. *Tribune*, July 2, 1907; *American*, July 1, 1907. Doty was an early supporter of Dr. Charles V. Chapin, who, as superintendent of health in Providence, Rhode Island, sought to influence the public health movement in emphasizing personal contact between individuals rather than environmental cleanliness as the most important element in the spread of disease. Cassedy, *Charles V. Chapin*, 115. In general, expert medical opinion concerning the danger of airborne particulates was divided between those who warned about the threat of direct infection from germ-laden dust and others who were alarmed by the potential for *secondary* infection. This latter group believed that lung and throat tissue was irritated when great quantities of dust were present in the air. The concomitant impairment of the body's natural powers of resistance was said to increase the likelihood of infection from the nondust sources to which people are typically exposed. On the whole, there was a tendency among medical authorities to recognize that direct infection was less prevalent than was believed to be the case during the earlier years of the bacteriological age. W. Gilman Thompson, F. M. Gibson, and Rudolph Hering, summaries of their speeches, as well as ensuing discussion by other physicians and sanitarians, in "Synopsis of the Stated Meeting of the New York Academy of Medicine Held April 4, 1907," Minutes of the Section on Public Health and Legal Medicine, Rare Books Room, New York Academy of Medicine, New York; Public Health Committee of the New York Academy of Medicine, "Pathogenicity of Street Dust," report, Rare Books Room, New York Academy of Medicine, New York, reprinted from *The Medical Record* (December 18, 1915); F. P. Gorham, "The Bacteriology of Street Dust," *American City* 3 (1910): 174–76.

68. *American*, June 30, 1907.

69. *Times*, June 30, 1907, July 1, 1907; *Evening World*, June 29, 1907; *American*, June 30, 1907; *Tribune*, June 30, 1907.

70. *Annual Report of the Board of Health of the Department of Health of the City of New York for the Year Ending December 31, 1907* (New York, 1908), 104–17 (quote, 109); *Times*, June 30, 1907, July 1, 1907; *Tribune*, June 30, 1907, July 1, 1907; *Herald*, July 1, 1907; *Evening World*, June 29, 1907.

71. Herald, July 1, 1907; *Times*, July 1, 2, 1907; *World*, July 1, 1907.

72. J. S. Billings Jr. to Haven Emerson, November 18, 1907, Minutes of the Section on Public Health and Legal Medicine, Rare Books Room, New York Academy of Medicine, New York; "Resolution Concerning Street Cleaning," Minutes of the Section on Public Health and Legal Medicine, New York Academy of Medicine; *Tribune*, July 1, 1907; *Times*, July 1, 1907; Melosi, *Garbage in the Cities*, 122–23.

73. *American*, July 1, 1907; *Tribune*, June 30, 1907 (quote).

74. *Sun*, June 30, 1907 (quote). Among a number of other complaints raised during the meeting, one of the drivers' delegates had objected about the fine of one week's pay for drinking a beer. June 29, 1907, meeting, McClellan Papers, Municipal Archives, New York.

75. *American*, July 1, 1907.

76. The AFL at that time was composed mainly of skilled union affiliates and generally lacked the funds or the necessary interest (in part because of ethnic prejudice) to organize unskilled laborers. Nevertheless, when unskilled workers would organize *themselves* effectively, the AFL would rush to aid these efforts. The AFL would thus be able to add to its organizational strength with the least effort and also prevent the alliance of workers with the rival IWW organization. *Times,* July 1, 2, 1907; Blum, *Republican Roosevelt,* 113; Dubofsky, *When Workers Organize,* 47, 54, 70.

77. This is not so far-fetched. On December 9, 1907, in an unprecedented move, Governor Hughes removed a major elected city official, John F. Ahearn, president of Manhattan Borough, who had been beseiged by allegations of corruption and incompetence. This development was clearly anticipated in July 1907. *Times,* June 30, 1907, July 1, 18, 1907; *Sun,* June 30, 1907; *American,* June 30, 1907, July 1, 1907 ("impeach"); *Tribune,* June 30, 1907, July 1, 1907; Cerillo, "Reform of Municipal Government," 60.

78. *Tribune,* July 2, 1907.

79. *American,* July 2, 1907 (quotes); *Times,* July 2, 1907.

80. *American,* June 30, 1907, July 2, 1907 (quote); *World,* July 5, 1907; *Evening World,* June 26, 1907; *Times,* July 1, 2, 4, 7, August 23, 1907; *Tribune,* June 30, 1907, July 3, 1907. In addition to African American employees, accounts refer to strikers with Italian, Irish, and Jewish family names, and it is probable that employees of other ethnic groups participated as well. Nevertheless, the department did attempt to bring in one hundred fifty African American strikebreakers from Baltimore (who did not arrive before the end of the strike), thus exemplifying the classic American strikebreaking pattern in which management would hire members of more economically disadvantaged ethnic groups. This often succeeded not only in breaking strikes but in undermining the potential for the multiethnic cooperation that was needed to achieve ongoing union solidarity. *Times,* July 3, 1907.

81. *Board of Aldermen Proceedings,* July 1–September 17, 1907 (New York, 1907); *Times,* July 2, 1907 ("unjust fines"). While Sullivan felt that a more politic commissioner would have granted enough strategic concessions to prevent the strike in the first place, labor relations were often troublesome during periods in which the political machine held fuller control of the department. Maier, *City Unions,* 11–13, 23; Wallace S. Sayre and Herbert Kaufman, *Governing New York City: Politics in the Metropolis* (New York: Russell Sage Foundation, 1960), 299–300, 442–43. On related issues, see Dishon, "New York Department of Street Cleaning."

82. *Times,* May 20, 1905, July 2, 10, 1907; *Tribune,* July 2, 1907; Dubofsky, *When Workers Organize,* 21; Arthur Mann, introduction to *Plunkitt of Tammany Hall* by William L. Riordon (New York: Dutton, 1963 [repr. of earlier ed., New York: McClure, Phillips, 1905]), xvi, xix; Robert K. Merton, "The Latent Functions of the Machine," in *Urban Bosses, Machines, and Progressive Reformers,* ed. Bruce M. Stave (Lexington, Mass.: D. C. Heath, 1972), 27–37; Oscar Handlin, "Why the Immigrant Supported the Machine," in Callow, *City Boss,* 98–102; Alfred Connable and Edward Silberfarb, *Tigers of Tammany: Nine Men Who Ran New York* (New York: Holt, Rinehart and Winston, 1967), 240–46.

83. *American,* July 2, 1907; *Evening World,* July 1, 1907; *Times,* July 2, 3, 1907; *Tribune,* July 2, 1907; N.Y.S. Department of Labor, *Seventh Annual Report, 1907,* vol. 1, 139–40.

84. *American,* July 2, 1907.

85. Ibid.

86. Resignations file, McClellan Papers, Municipal Archives, New York; *Tribune,* July 9, 1907 (quote).

87. Walter Bensel to George B. McClellan Jr., July 16, 1907, McClellan Papers, Municipal Archives, New York; *Times,* July 10, 1907, October 7, 1907, November 5, 1907. In April 1907, just prior to the New York Academy of Medicine's decision to cooperate with the Streets Conference Committee, the academy's Section on Public Health held a special meeting with the general membership of the academy to inform members about and "protest against the intolerable conditions of the streets of the city." Later in the year, Dr. Haven Emerson, secretary of the Section on Public Health, commented that "the dissatisfaction which our meeting expressed . . . played a useful part in the subsequent action of the Mayor in enlisting the very considerable assistance the city has received at the hands of Dr. Walter Bensel [during the last half of the year]." Emerson, "The Report."

88. *Board of Aldermen Proceedings,* October 1–December 31, 1907 (New York, 1908); *Times,* July 10, 11, 1907, August 7, 16, 1907, October 18, 1907, November 5, 1907, September 17, 1959; *Worker,* July 20, 1907; Maier, *City Unions,* 11–13, 23–24; Sayre and Kaufman, *Governing New York,* 299–300, 442–43; Dubofsky, *When Workers Organize,* 117; Ziskind, *One Thousand Strikes,* 83–86; Richard Fenton, *Outline History of the Department of Sanitation* (New York: Department of Sanitation, 1954).

89. *Worker,* July 6, 20, 1907; *Times,* July 3, 1907; *Tribune,* July 1, 1907; Dubofsky, *When Workers Organize,* 149–50.

90. Dubofsky, *When Workers Organize,* 116–25, 147–51.

91. George B. McClellan Jr. to Joseph M. Price, July 9, 1907, McClellan Papers, New-York Historical Society; WML, *Bulletin* 5 (July–August 1907): 1.

92. WML, *Bulletin* 7 (November–December 1909): 6; Dubofsky, *When Workers Organize,* 23–55, 86–120, 148; Hoy, "'Municipal Housekeeping,'" 187–91. The department's increased recognition of civic group input reflected broad Progressive Era trends in which even city administrations beholden to political machines gradually accepted not only the advice of civic groups but also the principle that it was necessary to have enough expert administrative control to prevent corruption from affecting government operations as blatantly and egregiously as it had in the past. Otis A. Pease, "Urban Reformers in the Progressive Era: A Reassessment," *Pacific Northwest Quarterly* 62 (April 1971): 49–58; J. Joseph Huthmacher, "Charles Evans Hughes and Charles Francis Murphy: The Metamorphosis of Progressivism," *New York History* 46 (January 1965): 25–40; Connable and Silberfarb, *Tigers,* 231–68; Cerillo, "Reform of Municipal Government," 68–71.

93. "Citizens are indignant—wonder why no effort at amicable settlement is made by the Commissioner" (*Evening World,* June 27, 1907; this newspaper also termed the DSC's work rules "intolerable"); "These uniformed men are much in need of enlightenment. It should not come in too harsh a form. But they are in need of being told that they are public servants" (*Times,* July 2, 1907); "Employees have made up their minds to force by intimidation and coercion a change in rules . . . under which they took their jobs" (*Sun,* June 29, 1907); "Commissioner Craven [has] made the most deplorable failure of his official career in trying to cope with the situation" (*American,* June 29, 1907). This newspaper also sympathized with drivers who were often fined for no reason other than a "grudge" (*American,* July 1, 1907); "The garbage 'strikers' . . . are . . . invading the rights of every citizen of New York and impugning the fundamental principles of popular sovereignty"

(*Tribune,* June 30, 1907); "New York has four million residents . . . [who] lay yesterday disgusted and nauseated, but helpless, at the mercy of the handful of disgruntled men who used to drive her swill carts" (*Herald,* July 1, 1907); [If workingmen would not rebel in the face of such conditions] "there would be little hope for the future. . . . [Men] would be only fit for the life of serfs" (*Worker,* July 6, 1907). The press reflected the public's uncertainty about where to place the blame for the strike. With the health and welfare of their children at stake, there was, for example, significant support for the strikebreakers in some working-class districts that were normally pro-labor. While the press tended to portray the employees as lazy and incompetent beneficiaries of political patronage, they commonly lay the ultimate responsibility for the strike upon the shoulders of the DSC administration. *Times,* July 1, 2, 1907; *Evening World,* June 27, 1907; *Globe,* June 29, 1907; *Tribune,* July 1, 2, 1907; *American,* July 1, 1907.

94. Dubofsky, *When Workers Organize,* 118–20.

95. It was to the detriment of the street cleaners that they failed to sustain long-term organized union activities between the two strikes. Tangible demands, rather than the desire for union recognition, motivated the drivers in 1907. Until unskilled workers were able to coalesce behind less violent, long-term, dues-paying attempts at unionization, they were unlikely to attain success beyond temporary gains. If long-term efforts to organize had been linked with sustained support by the CFU (with its array of more powerful *skilled* unions), the garbage workers' bargaining power would have been more formidable in 1911. With the inherent weakness of bargaining power in a crowded unskilled labor market, however, such an organizational feat would have been quite difficult to sustain. Fenton, *Immigrants and Unions,* 188–99, 217, 248–58, 559–76; Dubofsky, *When Workers Organize,* 17–19, 77–82, 115–55.

96. McCormick, "Business Corrupts Politics," 316, 329–32, 342–51. See related quote from the Progressive Era author William Mayo Venable, as noted in Melosi, *Garbage in the Cities,* 105. It is to the credit of the progressives in general that their response to the era's social ills encompassed broader goals than simply the cleansing of corruption. While they of course built on some reform precedents, the progressives, in their greater willingness to use government to address the urban conditions that fostered poverty and disease, diverged from their mugwump predecessors' belief that the rule of honest elites presiding over a spare array of government responsibilities would constitute an adequate response to the problems of industrial society.

97. Dubofsky, *When Workers Organize,* 151.

Chapter 2: George E. Waring Jr. and the Civic Promise

1. Alfred Connable and Edward Silberfarb, *Tigers of Tammany: Nine Men Who Ran New York* (New York: Holt, Rinehart, and Winston, 1967), 209–10; Oscar Handlin, "Why the Immigrant Supported the Machine," in *The City Boss in America: An Interpretive Reader,* ed. Alexander B. Callow Jr. (New York: Oxford University Press, 1976), 101; William L. Riordon, *Plunkitt of Tammany Hall* (New York: McClure, Phillips, 1905; repr., New York: Bedford–St. Martin's, 1994), 49–51.

2. Robert K. Merton, "The Latent Functions of the Machine," Monte A. Calvert, "The Manifest Functions of the Machine," and Joel A. Tarr, "The Urban Politician as Entrepreneur," in *Urban Bosses, Machines, and Progressive Reformers,* ed. Bruce M. Stave (Lexington,

Mass.: Heath, 1972), 27–37, 45–55, 62–72, respectively; Handlin, "Immigrant Supported the Machine," and Daniel P. Moynihan, "When the Irish Ran New York," in Callow, *City Boss*, 98–102, 118–23, respectively; Connable and Silberfarb, *Tigers*, 240–46; Steven P. Erie, *Rainbow's End: Irish-Americans and the Dilemmas of Urban Machine Politics, 1840–1985* (Berkeley: University of California Press, 1988), 58–59, 69.

3. Connable and Silberfarb, *Tigers*, 211–14.

4. *Times*, September 4, 1892, August 8, 1893, November 3, 1893, January 4, 1895 (quotes); Gerald W. McFarland, *Mugwumps, Morals, and Politics, 1884–1920* (Amherst: The University of Massachusetts Press, 1975), 90–97.

5. *New York Times*, November 28, 1897, October 30, 1898; John Duffy, *A History of Public Health in New York City*, vol. 1: *1625–1866* (New York: Russell Sage Foundation, 1968), 176–94, 356–75; John Duffy, *A History of Public Health in New York City*, vol. 2: *1866–1966* (New York: Russell Sage Foundation, 1974), 6–76, 108–28; Adolf F. Meisen, "History of Street Cleaning in New York City, 1860–1872" (Master's thesis, Columbia University, 1939), 2–44; Gordon Atkins, *Health, Housing, and Poverty in New York City, 1865–1898*, lithoprinted Ph.D. diss. (Ann Arbor, Mich.: Edwards Brothers, 1947), 46–52, 189–207, 259–79; Steven Hunt Corey, "King Garbage: A History of Solid Waste Management in New York City, 1881–1970" (Ph.D. diss., New York University, 1994), 10–36; Steven H. Corey, "Garbage in the Sea," *Seaport* 25 (Winter–Spring 1991): 18–23; Robert Dishon, "The New York City Department of Street Cleaning, 1881–1929," manuscript, 1988, New York City Department of Sanitation, 1–16; Gert H. Brieger, "Sanitary Reform in New York City: Stephen Smith and the Passage of the Metropolitan Health Bill," in *Sickness and Health in America: Readings in the History of Medicine and Public Health,* ed. Judith Walzer Leavitt and Ronald L. Numbers, 2d rev. ed. (Madison: University of Wisconsin Press, 1985), 399–413. In addition to Steven Hunt Corey's excellent dissertation and other works cited here and elsewhere in my book, see his forthcoming book *King Garbage: An Environmental History of New York City.*

6. On Waring's background and career prior to 1895, see Martin Melosi, *Garbage in the Cities: Refuse, Reform, and the Environment, 1880–1980* (College Station: Texas A&M University Press, 1981), 53–58; Martin Melosi, *The Sanitary City: Urban Infrastructure in America from Colonial Times to the Present* (Baltimore: Johns Hopkins University Press, 2000), 155–60; Joel A. Tarr, "The Separate vs. Combined Sewer Problem: A Case Study in Urban Technology Design Choice," *Journal of Urban History* 5 (May 1979): 308–39; Benjamin Miller, *Fat of the Land: Garbage in New York the Last Two Hundred Years* (New York: Four Walls Eight Windows, 2000), 62, 81–84; Jon A. Peterson, "George Edwin Waring, Jr.," in *Pioneers of American Landscape Design,* ed. Charles A. Birnbaum and Robin Karson (New York: McGraw-Hill, 2000), 424–27.

7. Stanley K. Schultz, *Constructing Urban Culture: American Cities and City Planning, 1800–1920* (Philadelphia: Temple University Press, 1989), 153–217 (quote, 153). On these matters and related issues, see Melosi, *Garbage in the Cities,* 132–33; Joel A. Tarr, *The Search for the Ultimate Sink: Urban Pollution in Historical Perspective* (Akron: University of Akron Press, 1996), 78, 96.

8. "Street-Cleaning," *Outlook* 66 (October 20, 1900): 426–27; George E. Waring Jr., *Street-Cleaning and the Disposal of a City's Wastes: Methods and Results and the Effect upon Public Health, Public Morals, and Municipal Prosperity* (New York: Doubleday and McClure, 1898), 11–16; *Times,* October 11, 1896 (supp.).

9. Riordon, *Plunkitt,* 51 (Plunkitt quote); Waring, *Street-Cleaning and Disposal,* 10 ("my man"); Miller, *Fat of the Land,* 69.

10. George E. Waring, Jr., "Government by Party," *North American Review* 163 (November 1896): 587–94; *Times,* October 15, 1903; Dorothy Ross, "The Liberal Tradition Revisited and the Republican Tradition Addressed," in *New Directions in American Intellectual History,* ed. John Higham and Paul K. Conkin (Baltimore: Johns Hopkins University Press, 1979), 116–31; McFarland, *Mugwumps,* 35–37; David C. Hammack, *Power and Society: Greater New York at the Turn of the Century* (New York: Russell Sage Foundation, 1982), 11–12; Alexander B. Callow Jr., "Commentary One," in Callow, *City Boss,* 5; Arthur Mann, "British Social Thought and American Reformers of the Progressive Era," *Mississippi Valley Historical Review* 42 (March 1956): 672–92.

11. Irwin Unger and Debi Unger, *The Vulnerable Years: The United States, 1896–1917* (Hinsdale, Ill.: Dryden Press, 1977), 115–22 (quote, 115). On these matters and related issues, see Frederic C. Howe, *The City: The Hope of Democracy* (New York: Scribner's, 1905), 11, 120, 225, 413; Waring, "Government by Party," 587–94; Otis A. Pease, "Urban Reformers in the Progressive Era: A Reassessment," *Pacific Northwest Quarterly* 62 (April 1971): 49–58; Augustus Cerillo Jr., "The Reform of Municipal Government in New York City from Seth Low to John Purroy Mitchel," *New-York Historical Society Quarterly* 57 (January 1973): 51–71; Callow, "Commentary One" and "Commentary Five," in Callow, *City Boss,* 10, 176–77; McFarland, *Mugwumps,* 103–6; Anne Firor Scott, "On Seeing and Not Seeing: A Case of Historical Invisibility," *Journal of American History* 71 (June 1984): 7–21; Robert H. Bremner, *From the Depths: The Discovery of Poverty in the United States* (New York: New York University Press, 1956), 123–38; Roy Lubove, "The Twentieth-Century City: The Progressive as Municipal Reformer," in *Bosses and Reformers: Urban Politics in America, 1880–1920,* ed. Blaine A. Brownell and Warren E. Stickle (Boston: Houghton Mifflin, 1973), 82–96; Paul Boyer, *Urban Masses and Moral Order in America, 1820–1920* (Cambridge, Mass.: Harvard University Press, 1978), 157–59.

12. George E. Waring Jr., *The Sanitary Condition of City and Country Dwelling Houses,* which includes the text of his 1876 paper (New York: Van Nostrand, 1877), 48–62 (quotes, 54, 57); William Paul Gerhard, "A Half-Century of Sanitation," *American Architect and Building News* 63 (March 11, 1899): 75–76; Martin V. Melosi, "Pragmatic Environmentalist: Sanitary Engineer George E. Waring, Jr.," *Essays in Public Works History* 4 (April 1977): 9–12; James H. Cassedy, "The Flamboyant Colonel Waring: An Anticontagionist Holds the American Stage in the Age of Pasteur and Koch," in Leavitt and Numbers, *Sickness and Health,* 451–58; George Rosen, *A History of Public Health* (New York: MD Publications, 1958), 288–89; Paul Starr, *The Social Transformation of American Medicine* (New York: Basic Books, 1982), 38–55, 135–38; Clay McShane, *Down the Asphalt Path: The Automobile and the American City* (New York: Columbia University Press, 1994), 24–25. Waring did stay informed about the newer findings on bacteriology. As a result, he toned down his focus on sewer gas in the later part of the nineteenth century, while still emphasizing filth as a breeding ground for infectious microorganisms. George Edwin Waring Jr., "Sewage Disposal at Isolated Houses," *American Architect and Building News* 35 (March 12, 1892): 166–69; Jon A. Peterson, "New Perspectives on George E. Waring, Jr.: Gilded Age Sanitarian," paper presented to the American City and Regional Planning History Conference, St. Louis, Missouri, November 8, 2003; Jon A. Peterson, "Waring, George Edwin, Jr.," in *Pioneers of American Landscape Design 2: An Annotated Bibliography,* ed. Charles A.

Birnbaum and Julie K. Fix (Washington: U.S. Department of the Interior, National Park Service, Cultural Resources, Heritage Preservation Services, Historic Landscape Initiative, 1995), 155–64.

13. Waring, *Sanitary Conditions*, 51–52.

14. Gerhard, "A Half-Century," 75–76 ("civilization and sanitation"); J. C. Pumpelly, *Clean Streets*, Reform Club Municipal Program Leaflet no. 2 (New York, 1894), Columbia University Library, 1 ("condition of the streets"); Waring, *Street-Cleaning and Disposal,* 9 ("squalid and hopeless"); *Times,* November 21, 1898 ("filth and squalor"), November 23, 1898 ("health and cleanly living").

15. Edward T. Hartman, "The Social Significance of Clean Streets," *American City* 3 (1910): 173; *Times,* February 12, 1898; David Stradling, *Smokestacks and Progressives: Environmentalists, Engineers, and Air Quality in America, 1881–1951* (Baltimore: Johns Hopkins University Press, 1999), 48; Melosi, *Garbage in the Cities,* 60–78, 109–12; Schultz, *Constructing Urban Culture,* 111–49; John Duffy, *The Sanitarians: A History of American Public Health* (Urbana: University of Illinois Press, 1990), 96–99, 128.

16. Waring, *Street-Cleaning and Disposal,* 190.

17. Ibid., 186–88; Hartman, "Social Significance of Clean Streets," 173; Gerhard, "A Half-Century," 75–76; *Times,* August 1, 1895, October 11, 1896.

18. Waring did not need to point out to his readers that the streets would be fouled by horse manure mixed in with the slush. Waring, *Street-Cleaning and Disposal,* 91–109; *Times,* February 26, 1895 (quote), November 3, 1895, October 11, 1896 (supp.); Atkins, *Health, Housing, and Poverty,* 269.

19. *Times,* February 21, 28, 1895, March 1, 7, 8, 1895.

20. *Evening Telegram,* May 18, 1895, October 23, 1897; *Times,* May 19, 28, 1895, June 27, 1895, July 3, 24, 1895, August 1, 1895, January 16, 1896, February 14, 1896.

21. Waring, *Street-Cleaning and Disposal,* 189–91; *World,* October 14, 1897; *Times,* July 1, 1895, October 24, 1895, June 11, 1897, October 21, 1897.

22. Louis H. Rullmann to William Strong, August 14, 1895 (includes September 19, 1984, Rullmann letter to board of health), Strong Papers, Municipal Archives, New York (quotes); Richard Skolnik, "George Edwin Waring, Jr.: A Model for Reformers," *New-York Historical Society Quarterly* 52 (October 1968): 369–70.

23. Transcript of Hearing no. 2, Mayor's Office, February 15, 1895, 24–27, 31–32, Strong Papers; Corey, "King Garbage," 89–93.

24. Hearing no. 2, 24–27, 31–32.

25. On these matters and related issues, see Frederick L. Stearns, "The Work of the Department of Street Cleaning," with discussion following, in Municipal Engineers of the City of New York, *Proceedings* (1913): 196–220; Charles W. Stantiford, *Report on the Disposal of City Wastes* (New York: New York City Department of Docks and Ferries, 1913); George E. Waring Jr., "Review of the General Work of the Department of Street Cleaning of New York," *Municipal Affairs* 2, supp. (June 1898): 79–160; Waring, *Street-Cleaning and Disposal,* 37–90; *Times,* February 2, 1895, January 10, 1896, October 11, 1896 (supp.); Corey, "King Garbage," 68–71, 100–105; Corey, "Garbage in the Sea," 18–23; Steven H. Corey, "The Politics and Practice of Waste Disposal in New York City," *Public History,* Newsletter of New York University's Program in Public History 5 (1988–89): 8–10; Miller, *Fat of the Land,* 89, 129–34; Melosi, *Garbage in the Cities,* 69–73, 103; Dishon, "New York Department of Street Cleaning," 20–48; Richard Fenton, "Current Trends in Municipal Solid

Waste Disposal in New York City," *Resource Recovery and Conservation* 1 (1975): 167–76; Daniel J. Zarin, "Searching for Pennies in Piles of Trash: Municipal Refuse Utilization in the United States, 1870–1930," *Environmental Review* 11 (Fall 1987): 207–22; Daniel C. Walsh, "Solid Wastes in New York City: A History," *Waste Age* (April 1989): 114–24; Daniel C. Walsh, "Will We See a Repeat of 1918?" *Waste Age* (December 1989): 27–32.

26. During the Progressive Era, the health department itself helped reduce mortality rates from two great killer diseases, tuberculosis and diphtheria. Some of the more effective strategies included educating the public in behaviors that would retard the dissemination of tuberculosis; wide-scale bacteriological diagnostic examinations, to attain more precise identification of cases (of both diseases), which in turn allowed for more effective quarantine procedures; and the utilization of the new diphtheria antitoxin on a massive scale, as a preventative and curative agent (one of the few curative measures in the medical profession's armamentarium at that time). One should bear in mind, though, that the general trend of decreased incidence of morbidity and mortality during the era should to a significant extent be attributed to a rise in average levels of nutrition and other basic living standards, which fortified people's resistance to disease. *Times,* September 16, 1897; Duffy, *History of Public Health in New York City,* 2:97–109; Nancy Tomes, *The Gospel of Germs: Men, Women, and the Microbe in American Life* (Cambridge, Mass.: Harvard University Press, 1998), 115; Thomas McKeown, *The Role of Medicine: Dream, Mirage, or Nemesis?* (Princeton: Princeton University Press, 1979), 78, 89, 117.

27. *Times,* March 7, 1897 (quote); George E. Waring Jr. to John S. Henry, March 18, 1895, Strong Papers; Melosi, "Pragmatic Environmentalist," 6–12.

28. Waring, *Street-Cleaning and Disposal,* 186–88; *Times,* August 1, 1895.

29. *World,* October 14, 1897; *Times,* April 4, 1895 (quote), August 24, 1895, June 23, 1897; Dishon, "New York Department of Street Cleaning," 17. In an era in which widespread discrimination seriously inhibited African American economic advancement, breaking the color barrier in an organization that employed as many people as the DSC was no small matter. In the late nineteenth and early twentieth centuries, white immigrant and native white groups, both in the north and the south, often successfully pressured employers to adopt discriminatory practices against African Americans, which even forced African Americans out of many skilled positions that they had customarily held. Jacqueline Jones, *A Social History of the Laboring Classes: From Colonial Times to the Present* (Malden, Mass.: Blackwell, 1999), 133–36, 164. The *Times* (April 4, 1895), in tune with the prejudices of the age, was quick to reassure its readers that the DSC's newly hired African American foreman, who was in charge of forty men of multiple ethnic origins, was "swarthy rather than black. His features are regular and pleasing. He uses excellent English."

30. *Times,* February 10, 20, 28, 1895, February 14, 1896 (quote), October 11, 1896; Waring, *Street-Cleaning and Disposal,* 15, 26–27; John R. Commons, *Labor and Administration* (New York: Macmillan, 1913; repr., New York: Augustus M. Kelley, 1964), 108–19; Mann, "British Social Thought," 682–83; Melosi, *Garbage in the Cities,* 92–93; Eric F. Goldman, *Rendezvous with Destiny: A History of Modern American Reform,* rev. ed. (New York: Vintage, 1955), 152; Melosi, "Pragmatic Environmentalist," 8–9; John C. Burnham, "The Cultural Interpretation of the Progressive Movement," in *Paths into American Culture: Psychology, Medicine, and Morals,* ed. John C. Burnham (Philadelphia: Temple University Press, 1988), 215; G. Edward White, "The Social Values of the Progressives: Some New Perspectives," *South Atlantic Quarterly* 70 (Winter 1971): 72–73.

31. *Times,* March 8, 1895, May 19, 1895, December 10, 1895, October 7, 1896, November 23, 1898.

32. George E. Waring Jr., "The Labor Question in the Department of Street Cleaning of New York," *Municipal Affairs* 2, supp. (June 1898): 515–24; Waring, *Street-Cleaning and Disposal,* 24–36; *Times,* January 8, 30, 1896, October 11 (supp.), 1896, October 31, 1898.

33. *Times,* October 7, 1896 (quote), June 11, 1897.

34. Waring, *Street-Cleaning and Disposal,* 190 ("made up of well-trained and disciplined men"); "Street-Cleaning"; *Times,* October 7 ("highest possible reward"), 11 (supp.), 1896.

35. *Times,* October 11 (supp.), 1896, February 20, 1898.

36. Commons, *Labor and Administration,* 108–19; David Ziskind, *One Thousand Strikes of Government Employees* (New York: Columbia University Press, 1940), 83–86; Mark H. Maier, *City Unions: Managing Discontent in New York City* (New Brunswick, N.J.: Rutgers University Press, 1987), 11–13, 23–24; Wallace S. Sayre and Herbert Kaufman, *Governing New York City: Politics in the Metropolis* (New York: Russell Sage Foundation, 1960), 299–300, 442–43; Dishon, "New York Department of Street Cleaning," 22, 33, 40–41.

37. Department of Street Cleaning (hereafter, DSC), *First Parade of the Department of Street Cleaning, May 26, 1896* (New York, 1896); "Street-Cleaning"; *Times,* May 20, 27 (quote), 1896.

38. DSC, *First Parade; Herald,* May 27, 1896 (all quotes except "Rah! Rah!"); *Times,* February 14, 1896, May 27, 1896 ("Rah! Rah!"); Skolnik, "George Edwin Waring, Jr.," 362–63.

39. *Nation* 61 (August 29, 1895): 1574–75; *Tribune,* October 21, 1897 ("finest pair"); *Times,* October 1, 1896, October 21, 1897; *World,* October 14, 1897 ("To Hell"); Atkins, *Health, Housing, and Poverty,* 277.

40. *Evening Telegram,* October 23, 1897; *World,* October 15, 1897; *Times,* October 31, 1897, January 1, 1910; *Our City: The Story of a Progressive People* (New York: Regular Democratic Organization of Greater New York, 1909), 86–91; Skolnik, "George Edwin Waring, Jr.," 376; Pease, "Urban Reformers," 56–57; J. Joseph Huthmacher, "Charles Evans Hughes and Charles Francis Murphy: The Metamorphosis of Progressivism," *New York History* 46 (January 1965): 25–40; Connable and Silberfarb, *Tigers,* 231–68; Cerillo, "Reform of Municipal Government," 68–71; Atkins, *Health, Housing, and Poverty,* 277–78; Martin Shefter, "Political Incorporation and Containment: Regime Transformation in New York City," in *Power, Culture, and Place: Essays on New York City,* ed. John Hull Mollenkopf (New York: Russell Sage Foundation, 1988), 140–48; Hammack, *Power and Society,* 322–25.

41. Shefter, "Political Incorporation," 140–48; Gary Gerstle, "The Protean Character of American Liberalism," *American Historical Review* 99 (October 1994): 1043–48; Pease, "Urban Reformers," 49–58; Huthmacher, "Charles Evans Hughes," 35–37; John J. Broesamle, *Reform and Reaction in Twentieth-Century American Politics* (New York: Greenwood, 1990), 54; LeRoy Ashby, *William Jennings Bryan: Champion of Democracy* (Boston: Twayne Publishers, 1987), 121–41.

42. Shefter, "Political Incorporation," 147; Pease, "Urban Reformers," 56–57; Connable and Silberfarb, *Tigers,* 231–68; Cerillo, "Reform of Municipal Government," 68–71.

43. *Evening Telegram,* October 23, 1897.

44. Jon C. Teaford, *The Unheralded Triumph: City Government in America, 1870–1900* (Baltimore: Johns Hopkins University Press, 1984), 310; Hammack, *Power and Society,*

143–51; McFarland, *Mugwumps,* 97; Connable and Silberfarb, *Tigers,* 215; Callow, "Commentary Five," in Callow, *City Boss,* 183–84.

45. *Times,* October 28, 29, 30, 1898.

46. "Street-Cleaning," 426–27; "Tammany and the Streets," *Outlook* 66 (October 20, 1900): 427–28; *Times,* July 7, 1896 (quote), November 25, 1898.

47. *Times,* May 28, 1898, October 28, 30, 1898, November 23 (Adler and Roosevelt quotes), 1898; Melosi, *Garbage in the Cities,* 51–52; Melosi, "Pragmatic Environmentalist," 16; Skolnik, "George Edwin Waring, Jr.," 375–77; Edwin G. Burrows and Mike Wallace, *Gotham: A History of New York City to 1898* (New York: Oxford University Press, 1999), 1196.

48. *Times,* November 21, 1898.

49. *Tribune,* October 28, 1897.

50. Callow, "Commentary One" and "Commentary Four," in Callow, *City Boss,* 5, 10, 144.

51. Report of the Ladies Health Protective Association of New York, 1894 to 1896, 26–29, New York Public Library; Tarr, "Urban Politician," 62–72; Moynihan, "When the Irish Ran," 118–23; David P. Thelen, "Social Tensions and the Origins of Progressivism," *Journal of American History* 56 (September 1969): 338–39.

52. "Street-Cleaning," 426–27; *Times,* November 23, 1898; Melosi, "Pragmatic Environmentalist," 3–4; Skolnik, "George Edwin Waring, Jr.," 375–78; Peterson, "Waring." Of course, many elites did not join in the chorus of those demanding environmental amelioration. They should be classified, however, as the conservatives of that era; while sharing many characteristics with progressives, they differed from them in some significant ways. Progressives sympathetic to at least some aspects of social reform are the main focus of our discussion. John Whiteclay Chambers II, *The Tyranny of Change: America in the Progressive Era,1890–1920,* 2d ed. (New York: St. Martin's, 1992), 139, 283.

53. Burnham, "Cultural Interpretation," 227; Tarr, "Urban Politician," 62–72; Teaford, *Unheralded Triumph,* 272; Steven C. Swett, "The Test of a Reformer: Seth Low, New York City Mayor, 1902–1903," *New-York Historical Society Quarterly* 44 (January 1960): 22–40; Jean Bethke Elshtain, *Jane Addams and the Dream of American Democracy: A Life* (New York: Basic Books, 2002), 286–87; Starr, *Social Transformation,* 192; Gerald N. Grob, "Welfare and Poverty in American History," *Reviews in American History* 1 (March 1973): 43–52; Marilyn Thornton Williams, *Washing "The Great Unwashed": Public Baths in Urban America, 1840–1920* (Columbus: Ohio State University Press, 1991), 41–67.

54. Melosi, *Garbage in the Cities,* 74–76, 124–33.

55. Waring, *Street-Cleaning and Disposal,* 177.

56. Ibid., 9; *Times,* July 28, 1895, October 11, 1896 (supp.), November 23, 1898 ("cleanly living"); Boyer, *Urban Masses,* 156–60, 181–87; Mark Haller, "Urban Vice and Civic Reform: Chicago in the Early Twentieth Century," in *Cities in American History,* ed. Kenneth T. Jackson and Stanley K. Schultz (New York: Knopf, 1972), 301; Burnham, "Cultural Interpretation," 218–19; Melosi, *Garbage in the Cities,* 105–33.

57. Waring, *Street-Cleaning and Disposal,* 184.

58. Melosi, "Pragmatic Environmentalist," 14–18; Tarr, *Search for the Ultimate Sink,* 87–96. For alternative views on the relationship of Progressive Era reform movements to the poor, see Boyer, *Urban Masses,* 171–74, 277–83; Samuel P. Hays, "The Changing Political Structure of the City in Industrial America," *Journal of Urban History* 1 (November

1974): 6–38; Samuel P. Hays, "The Politics of Reform in Municipal Government in the Progressive Era," *Pacific Northwest Quarterly* 55 (October 1964): 157–69; Melvin Holli, "Social and Structural Reform," in Callow, *City Boss,* 215–32; Jonas Frykman and Orvar Lofgren, *Culture Builders: A Historical Anthropology of Middle-Class Life* (Liber Forlag, 1979; New Brunswick, N.J.: Rutgers University Press, 1987), 268–72. See Edward T. Morman, "Scientific Medicine Comes to Philadelphia: Public Health Transformed, 1854–1899" (Ph.D. diss., University of Pennsylvania, 1986), vii–4, 32, 243–56, for an alternate viewpoint specifically concerned with the role of public health reform in the late nineteenth-century American city.

59. *Times,* April 6, 7, 1915; "New Hampshire Diarist: To the Head of the Class," *New Republic* 197 (July 27, 1987): 43 (quote).

60. Peter J. Stanlis, ed., *Edmund Burke: Selected Writings and Speeches* (Chicago: Regnery Gateway, 1963), 438–71.

61. *Times,* October 7, 1896; Tarr, *Search for the Ultimate Sink,* 96; LeRoy Ashby, *Saving the Waifs: Reformers and Dependent Children, 1890–1917* (Philadelphia: Temple University Press, 1984), 8–10, 206–10; Broesamle, *Reform and Reaction,* 39–55; Thomas K. McCraw, "The Progressive Legacy," in *The Progressive Era,* ed. Lewis L. Gould (Syracuse: Syracuse University Press, 1974), 199; Richard L. McCormick, "Progressivism: A Contemporary Reassessment," in *The Party Period and Public Policy: American Politics from the Age of Jackson to the Progressive Era,* ed. Richard L. McCormick (New York: Oxford University Press, 1986), 270, 286–88.

62. Broesamle, *Reform and Reaction,* 47–48; McCormick, "Progressivism: A Contemporary Reassessment," 287; McCraw, "Progressive Legacy," 187; Ashby, *William Jennings Bryan,* 143.

63. Tarr, *Search for the Ultimate Sink,* 94, 97; McCormick, "Progressivism: A Contemporary Reassessment," 273–87.

Chapter 3: Political and Moral Choices in Pushcart Policy

1. Department of Agriculture, Bureau of Agricultural Economics, *Push Cart Markets in New York City* (Washington, D.C.: U.S. Department of Agriculture, 1925), 4–7, 31–32, 57; New York State Food Investigation Commission, *Report of the Committee on Markets, Prices and Costs of the New York State Food Investigation Commission* (New York: Chas. P. Young Co., Printers, 1912), 45–48; Mayor's Push-Cart Commission, *Report of the Mayor's Push-Cart Commission* (New York: City of New York, 1906), 89–90; Harry Morton Goldberg, *Pushcart Peddling in New York,* East Side Chamber of Commerce Research Studies of Community Problems, no. 1 (New York, 1929), in Pushcarts file, NYC City Hall Library (formerly Municipal Reference Library); transcript of radio talk by New York City Department of Markets Commissioner William Fellowes Morgan Jr., WNYC, November 28, 1941, in Pushcarts file, NYC City Hall Library; *New York Times,* July 26, 1912; Suzanne Rachel Wasserman, "The Good Old Days of Poverty: The Battle over the Fate of New York City's Lower East Side during the Depression" (Ph.D. diss., New York University, 1990), 166–227; Andrew R. Heinze, *Adapting to Abundance: Jewish Immigrants, Mass Consumption, and the Search for American Identity* (New York: Columbia University Press, 1990), 195; John Duffy, *A History of Public Health in New York City,* vol. 1: *1625–1866* (New York: Russell Sage Foundation, 1968), 420–39; John Duffy, *A History of Public Health in New York City,*

vol. 2: *1866–1966* (New York: Russell Sage Foundation, 1974), 25–26; Karen F. Beall, *Cries and Itinerant Trades: A Bibliography* (Hamburg, Ger.: Dr. Ernst Hauswedell, 1975), 525–29; "When the Old Streets Talked," *American Heritage* 6 (June 1955): 46–49.

2. Mayor's Push-Cart Commission, *Report,* 11–13, 22–38; City of New York, Office of the Commissioner of Accounts, *The Pushcart Problem in New York City* (New York, 1917); *Board of Aldermen Proceedings* (April 22, 1913), 239; Wendell P. Dodge, "The Push-Cart Industry," *New Age* 12 (1910): 408; J. W. Sullivan, *Markets for the People* (New York: Macmillan, 1913), 88; Bertha H. Smith, "The Way of the Pushcart Man," *Craftsman* 9 (1905): 228; *New York City Record* 32 (January 21, 1904): 401–4; *Times,* January 29, 1899, November 28, 1920; *New York Daily Tribune,* July 1, 1905; Moses Rischin, *The Promised City: New York's Jews, 1870–1914* (Cambridge, Mass.: Harvard University Press, 1962), 56.

3. *Evening Post,* August 20, 1898; *Craftsman,* September 15, 1898, December 28, 1909; Department of Agriculture, *Push Cart Markets,* 35; Alan M. Kraut, "The Butcher, the Baker, the Pushcart Peddler: Jewish Foodways and Entrepreneurial Opportunity in the East European Immigrant Community 1880–1940," *Journal of American Culture* 6 (Winter 1983): 75.

4. Maurice Fishberg, "Health and Sanitation of the Immigrant Jewish Population of New York," *Menorah* 33 (July–September 1902): 76; Smith, "Way of the Pushcart," 225; Marion Winthrop, "The Ethics and Aesthetics of the Push Cart," *Craftsman* 14 (September 1908): 595–96; Kraut, "Butcher, Baker, Pushcart Peddler," 72; Alan M. Kraut, *The Huddled Masses: The Immigrant in American Society, 1880–1921* (Arlington Heights, Ill.: Harlan Davidson, 1982), 105; Thomas Kessner, *The Golden Door: Italian and Jewish Mobility in New York City, 1880–1915* (New York: Oxford University Press, 1976), 59–65; Heinze, *Adapting to Abundance,* 35–39, 185.

5. David Blaustein, "The Inherent Cultural Forces of the Lower East Side," *University Settlement Society Annual Report of 1901* (New York, 1901), 20–25; Konrad Bercovici, "The Greatest Jewish City in the World," *Nation* 117 (September 12, 1923): 260; Fishberg, "Health and Sanitation," 74; *Times,* November 14, 1897, January 10, 1903, April 3, 1910, sec. 5; Kraut, *Huddled Masses,* 107, 138; Glenn Blackburn, *Western Civilization: A Concise History,* combined ed. (New York: St. Martin's, 1991), 61–62.

6. David Blaustein, "The People of the East Side before Emigration and after Immigration," *University Settlement Studies* (July 1905): 77; Department of Agriculture, *Push Cart Markets,* 35; Heinze, *Adapting to Abundance,* 33–48, 185–91; Kessner, *Golden Door,* 60–61; *Times,* July 14, 1912, sec. 5; *Tribune,* August 11, 1901.

7. Elias Tcherikower, ed., *The Early Jewish Labor Movement in the United States,* trans. and rev. by Aaron Antonovsky from original Yiddish (New York: YIVO Institute for Jewish Research, 1961), 145; Gerald Sorin, *A Time for Building: The Third Migration, 1880–1920* (Baltimore: Johns Hopkins University Press, 1992), 4; Kraut, "Butcher, Baker, Pushcart Peddler," 71; Irving Howe, *World of Our Fathers* (New York: Harcourt Brace Jovanovich, 1976), 73; Smith, "Way of the Pushcart," 223, 227; Rischin, *Promised City,* 55.

8. Wasserman, "Good Old Days," 166–227; Kraut, "Butcher, Baker, Pushcart Peddler," 75.

9. Smith, "Way of the Pushcart," 218–28; Mayor's Push-Cart Commission, *Report,* 204; Kessner, *Golden Door,* 51, 59–61; *Times,* November 30, 1924, sec. 4; *Tribune,* September 15, 1898.

10. *Times,* November 14, 1897 (magazine section); *Tribune,* September 15, 1898; Elizabeth

Ewen, *Immigrant Women in the Land of Dollars: Life and Culture on the Lower East Side, 1890–1925* (New York: Monthly Review Press, 1985), 87.

11. Sullivan, *Markets,* 61; Mayor's Push-Cart Commission, *Report,* 37; *Times,* July 3, 1912.

12. *Tribune,* August 11, 1901 (supp.); Abraham Cahan, *The Rise of David Levinsky* (New York: Harper, 1917), 125; Walter I. Trattner, *From Poor Law to Welfare State: A History of Social Welfare in America,* 5th ed. (New York: Free Press, 1994), 166 (Rumanian's quote).

13. Charles S. Bernheimer, "Lower East Side Dwellers," *University Settlement Studies* 4 (March 1908): 26 ("to and fro"); Bercovici, "Greatest Jewish City," 260; *Times,* July 27, 1895, November 14, 1897.

14. Bercovici, "Greatest Jewish City," 260; *Times,* July 27, 1895 (quote); *Tribune,* May 28, 1902.

15. Mayor's Push-Cart Commission, *Report,* 54–57; *Times,* July 23, 27, 1895; *Tribune,* September 15, 1898.

16. Food Investigation Commission, *Report,* 14, 51; Smith, "Way of the Pushcart," 223–26; Department of Agriculture, *Push Cart Markets,* 42, 54; *Times,* July 5, 1912, July 14, 1912, sec. 5, September 5, 1926, sec. 8.

17. Mayor's Push-Cart Commission, *Report,* 37–53, 90–93; Food Investigation Commission, *Report,* 51; *Tribune,* September 13, 1906; *Times,* July 14, 1912, sec. 5, November 30, 1924, sec. 4, May 25, 1925; Louise Bolard More and Robert Coit Chapin, as noted in David C. Hammack, *Power and Society: Greater New York at the Turn of the Century* (New York: Russell Sage Foundation, 1982), 341; Abraham Cahan, "Pushcarts Full of Woe," in *New York Commercial Advertiser,* June 29, 1898, reprinted in Moses Rischin, ed., *Grandma Never Lived in America: The New Journalism of Abraham Cahan* (Bloomington: Indiana University Press, 1985), 260–62.

18. Smith, "Way of the Pushcart," 226–27 ("dull hurt"); Winthrop, "Aesthetics of the Pushcart," 595–96 ("hoodlums"). On related issues, see Cahan, *Levinsky,* 105–15, 123–39; Tcherikower, *Early Jewish Labor Movement,* 145–48.

19. Smith, "Way of the Pushcart," 226–27 ("forget their sex"); Cahan, *Levinsky,* 107 ("so cheap"), and see also 105–15, 123–39. On related issues, see "Markets of the Poor," *Outlook* 101 (August 3, 1912): 750–51; *Times,* March 2, 1911, April 8, 1911, September 4, 1914, December 26, 1920, sec. 3; Abraham Cahan, "Fish, Fish, Living, Floundering, Jumping, Dancing Fish," in *New York Commercial Advertiser,* September 24, 1898, reprinted in Rischin, *Grandma,* 95–96; Kraut, "Butcher, Baker, Pushcart Peddler," 72, 76; Marvin Gelfand, "Welcome to America," *American Heritage* 43 (April 1992): 71, 95–96.

20. *Times,* March 30, 1897; *Tribune,* July 13, 1898, July 29, 1899, December 18, 1901.

21. Clipping from unidentified newspaper, circa 1906, in Lillian D. Wald Papers, box 30, Rare Books and Manuscripts Collection, Butler Library, Columbia University, New York.

22. Sullivan, *Markets,* 55–60; Mayor's Push-Cart Commission, *Report,* 66, 76.

23. Sullivan, *Markets,* 70, 88–89; Mayor's Push-Cart Commission, *Report,* 216, 224; *Times,* September 29, 1900, July 13, 1908, August 20, 1908, April 7, 1909, December 24, 1909, November 29, 1910, July 1, 7, 1912; *Tribune,* July 29, 1899, April 11, 1902.

24. *Tribune,* November 3, 1895 (quote); John J. Broesamle, "The Democrats from Bryan to Wilson," in *The Progressive Era,* ed. Lewis L. Gould (Syracuse: Syracuse University Press, 1974), 87.

25. Sullivan, *Markets,* 59–60; Department of Agriculture, *Push Cart Markets,* 16; Dodge, "Push-Cart Industry," 408–9; Mayor's Push-Cart Commission, *Report,* 215–20; Yorkville Citizens' Committee, *Brief Filed by Yorkville Citizens' Committee* (n.p., 1916), 4–7, from Pushcart file, NYC City Hall Library (formerly Municipal Reference Library); *Times,* September 29, 1900, October 10, 1900, February 5, 1918, July 30, 1925; *Tribune,* November 3, 1895; Heinze, *Adapting to Abundance,* 200.

26. Clay McShane, *Down the Asphalt Path: The Automobile and the American City* (New York: Columbia University Press, 1994), 1–80; Peter C. Baldwin, *Domesticating the Street: The Reform of Public Space in Hartford, 1850–1930* (Columbus: Ohio State University Press, 1999); Joseph P. Sullivan, "The Terror of the Trolley," *Journal of Urban Technology* 4 (1997): 11–12.

27. Sullivan, *Markets,* 59–60; Mayor's Push-Cart Commission, *Report,* 51–53; Cahan, "Pushcarts Full of Woe"; Abraham Cahan, "The Goodness of a Bad Man," *New York Commercial Advertiser,* January 18, 1900, reprinted in Rischin, *Grandma,* 354–56; *Times,* July 26, 1912, March 31, 1913; *Tribune,* August 21, 1905, September 16, 1906.

28. Mayor's Push-Cart Commission, *Report,* 220–29; *Times,* September 29, 1900, April 16, 1910, July 7 ("man of influence" quote), 26, 1912, March 31, 1913, July 27, 1922; *Tribune,* October 1, 1893, May 5 (quotes except "man of influence"), 6, 1902, June 14, 1902, August 21, 1905, September 16, 1906.

29. Sullivan, *Markets,* 54–56; Mayor's Push-Cart Commission, *Report,* 218–20; April 18, 1913, "Messages from the Mayor," in *Board of Aldermen Proceedings* (April 22, 1913), 185–89; *Times,* March 31, 1913.

30. Lillian D. Wald to Richard Neustadt, typewritten letter, May 27, 1912, Wald Papers, box 30.

31. Mayor's Push-Cart Commission, *Report,* 16 (quote).

32. Department of Street Cleaning (hereafter, DSC), *Report for the Year 1906* (New York: Martin P. Brown, 1907), 23–24; Mayor's Push-Cart Commission, *Report,* 196; *Tribune,* July 27, 1904, September 28, 1904.

33. *Times,* August 14, 1910.

34. John Shaw Billings, "Public Health and Municipal Government," *Annals of the American Academy of Political and Social Science,* supp. (February 1891): 13–18; *Times,* August 28, 1904, April 5, 1907, July 21, 1912, sec. 7, June 1, 1924, sec. 8; *Tribune,* November 27, 1904 (supp.); Nancy Tomes, *The Gospel of Germs: Men, Women, and the Microbe in American Life* (Cambridge, Mass.: Harvard University Press, 1998), 46–47, 57, 67, 96–102; Richard J. Evans, *Death in Hamburg: Society and Politics in the Cholera Years, 1830–1910* (Oxford: Oxford University Press, 1987), 503. The discomfort caused by street dust can hardly be overemphasized. To give just one example of the universality of this problem, when the City of New Orleans finally improved some municipal services for its African American residents in the late 1940s, the paving and cleaning of the streets were among those services most in demand. One woman related that before her street was paved and regularly cleaned, it was "so littered with trash, garbage, and dust that inside our homes, the dust and grime would settle over the furniture and floors. . . . [Now] the homes remain clean. And most important, we can sit on the porches without swallowing and breathing dust." Edward F. Haas, *DeLesseps S. Morrison and the Image of Reform: New Orleans Politics, 1946–1861* (Baton Rouge: Louisiana State University Press, 1974): 68.

35. Donald B. Armstrong, "The Sanitation of Public Markets," *Journal of the American*

Medical Association 68 (January 13, 1917): 103–6; F. P. Gorham, "The Bacteriology of Street Dust," *American City* 3 (1910): 174–76; Daniel Dana Jackson, *Pollution of New York Harbor as a Menace to Health by the Dissemination of Intestinal Diseases through the Agency of the Common House Fly* (New York: Merchants' Association of New York, 1907), Butler Library, Columbia University; Naomi Rogers, "A Disease of Cleanliness: Polio in New York City, 1900–1990," in *Hives of Sickness: Public Health and Epidemics in New York City,* ed. David Rosner (New Brunswick: Rutgers University Press, 1995), 117; Tomes, *Gospel of Germs,* 9, 96–100, 168–171; John Duffy, *The Sanitarians: A History of American Public Health* (Urbana: University of Illinois Press, 1990), 181–85.

36. Suellen M. Hoy, "'Municipal Housekeeping': The Role of Women in Improving Urban Sanitation Practices," in *Pollution and Reform in American Cities, 1870–1930,* ed. Martin V. Melosi (Austin: University of Texas Press, 1980), 179–81.

37. Ellen Richards, *Sanitation in Daily Life* (Boston: Whitcomb and Barrows, 1907), 12, 24–25.

38. *Tribune,* October 1, 1904 (quote), November 27 (supp.), 1904. Relatedly, see DSC, *Report for the Year 1906,* 3.

39. *Times,* August 28, 1904.

40. Morris D. Waldman to Edward T. Devine, typewritten letter and memorandum, August 29, 1911, Wald Papers, box 30 (Waldman quote); *Times,* September 7, 1895 ("health of the people").

41. Quotes are from Yorkville Citizens' Committee, *Brief,* 7–16. See also *Tribune,* November 3, 1895.

42. Armstrong, "Sanitation of Public Markets," 103–6.

43. *Times,* July 30, 1893; *Tribune,* July 1, 1905.

44. Richards, *Sanitation in Daily Life,* 17, 24–25; Mayor's Push-Cart Commission, *Report,* 57–58; Department of Agriculture, *Push Cart Markets,* 54–60; *Times,* July 14, 1912, sec. 5; *Board of Aldermen Proceedings* (April 22, 1913), 187; *Annual Report of the Board of Health of the Department of Health of the City of New York for the Year Ending December 31, 1913* (New York, 1914), 36; Daniel M. Bluestone, "'The Pushcart Evil': Peddlers, Merchants, and New York City's Streets, 1890–1940," *Journal of Urban History* 18 (November 1991): 79–80.

45. Waring hoped that the proposed market would be off-limits to peddlers after the noon hour, at which time the DSC would clean the area and give it over to children to use as a much needed playground in the afternoon. George E. Waring Jr., "How We Are to Treat the New York Push Carts (The Waring Market Play-Grounds)," with comments by Barnet Phillips, *Harper's Magazine* 39 (December 28, 1895): 1237–38; *Board of Aldermen Proceedings* (April 22, 1913), 239–41; *Vigilant,* September 12, 1901; "Markets of the Poor"; Food Investigation Commission, *Report,* 48–51; *Times,* January 4, 1895 ("licensed venders"), January 24, 1895, February 8, 1903, September 13, 1906, July 5–7, 9–10, 13, 1912, March 31, 1913; *Tribune,* December 24, 1895, March 16, 1896, October 1, 1904, January 5, 1905, September 13, 16, 1906, sec. 5; Richard Neustadt to Lillian D. Wald, typewritten letter signed, May 23, 1912, Wald Papers, box 30; Mayor's Push-Cart Commission, *Report,* 71, 89–101.

46. *Jewish Gazette,* February 21, 1896; *Times,* February 9, 1896; *Tribune,* March 13, 16, 1896. I am indebted to Renee Baigell for translating the *Jewish Gazette* article and other Yiddish-language material for this chapter.

47. *Times,* September 30, 1896, November 26, 1896, July 27, 1922; *Tribune,* March 16, 1896.

48. *Times,* February 9, 1896, August 28, 1898, July 27, 1922; *Tribune,* December 24, 1895, March 13, 1896, May 28, 1902.

49. Frank H. McLean, "An Experience in the Street-Cleaning Department," *University Settlement Society Annual Report of 1897* (New York, 1897), 21–23; Sullivan, *Markets,* 56, 71–72 (quote); *Evening Post,* August 20, 1898; *Times,* July 23, 1895, August 28, 1898, July 27, 1922; *Jewish Gazette,* February 21, 1896.

50. *Jewish Gazette,* February 21, 1896; *Times,* July 27, 1922; *Tribune,* December 24, 1895; Howe, *World of Our Fathers,* 362; Hammack, *Power and Society,* 144–53, 181, 315; Gerald W. McFarland, *Mugwumps, Morals, and Politics, 1884–1920* (Amherst: University of Massachusetts Press, 1975), 97–99; Alfred Connable and Edward Silberfarb, *Tigers of Tammany: Nine Men Who Ran New York* (New York: Holt, Rinehart, and Winston, 1967), 215; Augustus Cerillo Jr., "Reform in New York City: A Study of Urban Progressivism" (Ph. D. diss., Northwestern University, 1965), 38.

51. Sullivan, *Markets,* 59–60; Mayor's Push-Cart Commission, *Report,* 197; *Board of Aldermen Proceedings* (April 22, 1913), 187; "Markets of the Poor"; *Evening Post,* August 20, 1898; *Times,* September 29, 1900; *Tribune,* October 1, 1893, January 18, 1899, April 11, 1902, May 5, 6, 28, 1902, June 14, 1902.

52. *Vigilant,* January 29, 1901, September 12, 1901; Connable and Silberfarb, *Tigers,* 222–27.

53. Hammack, *Power and Society,* 154–55; McFarland, *Mugwumps,* 103–6.

54. *Times,* December 27, 28, 1900, September 1, 1901 (quote).

55. *Vigilant,* June 29, 1901 (quotes), September 12, 1901.

56. *New York City Record* 32 (January 21, 1904): 401–4; *Times,* August 8, 1903, July 7, 1912; *Daily News,* February 11, 1902; *World,* February 12, 1902; *Tribune,* March 29, 1902, May 28, 1902, July 9, 1903, August 7, 8, 13, 15, 16, 1903.

57. *Daily News,* February 11, 1902; *World,* February 12, 1902.

58. *Tribune,* March 29, 1902 (quote, reporter's paraphrase of Myers).

59. *Tribune,* March 29, 1902 ("poor pushcart pedler"), May 28, 1902 ("Things ain't what they used to be"); *Times,* July 7, 1912 ("the Mayor was a man").

60. Sullivan, *Markets,* 271–72; *Daily News,* March 29, 1903, July 25, 1904; *Times,* February 8, 1903, March 30, 1903, July 26, 27, 1904, August 7, 1904; *Tribune,* March 31, 1903, July 25, 26, 27, 28, 1904, September 28, 1904; *World,* March 31, 1903.

61. *Call,* July 30, 1912; *Times,* July 1, 16, 26, 1912.

62. Mayor's Push-Cart Commission, *Report,* 210–29 ("abused," "protection," 225); *Times,* July 7 ("man of influence"), 15, 16, 26, 1912.

63. Mayor's Push-Cart Commission, *Report,* 196–97 (Schwartz quote); *Times,* December 18, 1893 ("blood suckers"), September 29, 1900.

64. Mayor's Push-Cart Commission, *Report,* 220–24.

65. Lillian D. Wald to Richard Neustadt, typewritten letter, May 24, 1912, Wald Papers, box 30; Mayor's Push-Cart Commission, *Report,* 196–201; *Times,* July 1, 16, 1912; *Tribune,* October 1, 1904 ("responsible for blocking"), February 21, 1905 ("competition has become fierce").

66. *Times,* August 3, 1906; *American,* August 13, 1906 (quote).

67. *Times,* July 15, 1912.

68. *Call,* July 30, 1912; *Forward,* July 31, 1912; *Times,* July 7, 10, 26, 29, 1912, March 31, 1913, July 27, 1922; *Tribune,* October 1, 1893, April 11, 1902, May 5, 6, 1902.

69. Yorkville Citizens' Committee, *Brief,* 1–24; Bercovici, "Greatest Jewish City," 259–61; "Let's Give the Push-Carts a Push!" *Harlem Magazine* (June 1928): 4–5; *Times,* November 30, 1902 ("Girls' Technical School" article); Heinze, *Adapting to Abundance,* 4; Paul Boyer, *Urban Masses and Moral Order in America, 1820–1920* (Cambridge, Mass.: Harvard University Press, 1978), 60–61; Alan Wolfe, review of *Ethnic Identity: The Transformation of White America,* by Richard D. Alba, *New Republic* 203 (December 31, 1990): 27–34.

70. Yorkville Citizens' Committee, *Brief,* 3–5, 8.

71. Ibid., 12, 16.

72. See David Stradling, *Smokestacks and Progressives: Environmentalists, Engineers, and Air Quality in America, 1881–1951* (Baltimore: Johns Hopkins University Press, 1999), 48, and Richards, *Sanitation in Daily Life,* 24–33, for the era's common association of crowding and filthy air with a sense of claustrophobia and the erosion of health and morality. Progressive Era anxieties often resonate with those of our own times, as seen in an editorial in the October 23, 1986, edition of the *New York Times,* which pleads with city officials to remove graffiti from subway cars promptly: "The importance of cleaner cars is more than skin deep. To most straphangers, graffiti symbolize the transit system's decline and contribute to an atmosphere of fear and disorder, suggesting that the whole system is out of control."

73. Simon Schama, review of *The Foul and the Fragrant: Odor and the French Social Imagination,* by Alain Corbin, *New Republic* 196 (February 23, 1987): 27–30 (quote). See Tomes, *Gospel of Germs,* for a work that, in Tomes's words, "honors both the cultural construction of cleanliness and the biological dimension of disease" (17). For alternative viewpoints, see Samuel P. Hays, "The Changing Political Structure of the City in Industrial America," *Journal of Urban History* 1 (November 1974): 6–38; Edward T. Morman, "Scientific Medicine Comes to Philadelphia: Public Health Transformed, 1854–1899" (Ph. D. diss., University of Pennsylvania, 1986), vii–viii, 3–32, 243–56; Richard L. Bushman and Claudia L. Bushman, "The Early History of Cleanliness in America," *Journal of American History* 74 (March 1988): 1213–38; Jonas Frykman and Orvar Lofgren, *Culture Builders: A Historical Anthropology of Middle Class Life* (Liber Forlag, 1979; reprint, New Brunswick, N.J.: Rutgers University Press, 1987), 157–272.

74. Billings, "Public Health," 13 (quote); Harold L. Platt, "Invisible Gases: Smoke, Gender, and the Redefinition of Environmental Policy in Chicago, 1900–1920," *Planning Perspectives* 10 (1995): 82, 92; Tomes, *Gospel of Germs,* 18, 127–32, 205–33; David Rosner, "Introduction," in *Hives of Sickness,* 13; John C. Burnham, "The Cultural Interpretation of the Progressive Movement," in *Paths into American Culture: Psychology, Medicine, and Morals,* ed. John C. Burnham (Philadelphia: Temple University Press, 1988), 215–16; Arthur Mann, "British Social Thought and American Reformers of the Progressive Era," *Mississippi Valley Historical Review* 42 (March 1956): 678–79; Mark Haller, "Urban Vice and Civic Reform: Chicago in the Early Twentieth Century," in *Cities in American History,* ed. Kenneth T. Jackson and Stanley K. Schultz (New York: Alfred A. Knopf, 1972), 301; Stanley K. Schultz, *Constructing Urban Culture: American Cities and City Planning, 1800–1920* (Philadelphia: Temple University Press, 1989), 126–43; Paul Starr, *The Social Transformation of American Medicine* (New York: Basic Books, 1982), 55, 138.

75. *Vigilant,* June 29, 1901.

76. Ibid., (Rainsford quote); Fishberg, "Health and Sanitation," 44, 177–80.

77. McLean, "An Experience in the Street Cleaning Department," 20–25 (quote, 20).

78. Ibid., 20 ("malevolence"); James B. Reynolds, "Report of the Head Worker," *University Settlement Society Annual Report of 1901* (New York, 1901), 8 ("about as useless"); James B. Reynolds, "Report of the Head Worker," *University Settlement Society Annual Report of 1894* (New York, 1894), 7–9.

79. Gary Gerstle, "The Protean Character of American Liberalism," *American Historical Review* 99 (October 1994): 1050.

80. Waring, "How We Are to Treat," 1237–38; Dodge, "Push-Cart Industry," 409.

81. *Tribune,* May 27, 1902.

82. *Times,* July 30, 1893.

83. *Times,* August 7, 1904, October 12, 1911, July 6, 13, 15, 1912; *Tribune,* July 13, 1898, July 29, 1899, September 29, 1900, May 27, 1902, September 21, 1906, October 12, 1906.

84. Fred W. Viehe, "Almost Progressives: The Continuing Odyssey of Urban Reform," *Journal of Urban History* 19 (November 1992), 102–10; Gerstle, "Protean Character," 1046–47.

85. *Vigilant,* June 29, 1901; Mary Simkhovitch to Lillian Wald, typewritten letter, April 29, 1914, in Wald Papers, box 30; *Times,* July 6, 1912; Tomes, *Gospel of Germs,* 18, 127–30, 205–33; Gerstle, "Protean Character," 1051; John Whiteclay Chambers II, *The Tyranny of Change: America in the Progressive Era, 1890–1920,* 2d ed. (New York: St. Martin's, 1992), 139–42, 283; Burnham, "Cultural Interpretation," 215, 227; Schultz, *Constructing Urban Culture,* 138. Many also recognized that the pushcarts were an important source of employment opportunities on the Lower East Side, particularly for partially disabled men unsuited for other lines of work. For a less sanguine view than mine on the effect of the reformers' moral outlook on social problems and public health, see Ewen, *Immigrant Women,* 90–91, 139–45.

86. Casey Blake, "'The Cosmopolitan Note': Randolph Bourne and the Challenge of 'Trans-national America,'" *Culturefront* 4 (Winter 1995/96): 25–28; Gerstle, "Protean Character," 1043–54; Otis L. Graham Jr. and Elizabeth Koed, "Americanizing the Immigrant, Past and Future: History and Implications of a Social Movement," *Public Historian* 15 (Fall 1993): 24–45.

87. Mayor's Push-Cart Commission, *Report,* 93.

88. Ibid., 201–6 (quote, 203).

89. DSC, *Report for the Year 1906,* 3–4 (quote), 23–24; *Times,* July 13, 1912.

90. *Times,* June 4, 1904, July 3, 1904 (magazine section); *Tribune,* May 25, 1904 (quote); Woman's Municipal League (hereafter WML), *Bulletin* 3 (October 1904): 2.

91. *Daily News,* March 12 (quote), 29, 1903; *Times,* March 30, 1903.

92. *Forward,* March 12, 1903.

93. *Tribune,* July 25, 26, 27, 28, 1904; *Times,* July 26, 29, 1904.

94. *Daily News,* July 25, 1904 (quote); *Times,* May 30, 1904, June 4, 1904, July 3, 1904 (magazine section); *Tribune,* October 1, 1904; *Call,* July 26, 1912.

95. *Times,* August 7, 1904.

96. *Daily News,* July 25, 1904; *Times,* July 26, 1904; *Tribune,* July 26, 28 (quote), 1904, September 28, 1904.

97. *Times,* August 7, 1904 ("M.R.B." quote), May 21, 1906 ("demand").

98. The variety of opinions stated in *Times* letters during the era indirectly reflected

the type of dialogue going on within the minds of many reformers about the pushcart conundrum. *Times,* July 15, 1904, August 7 ("D.S.M." quote), 28, 1904, August 31, 1911, September 4, 1911 ("Jeanne C." quote), July 11, 1912.

99. *Tribune,* March 29, 1902, July 28, 1904; Howe, *World of Our Fathers,* 369.

100. *Our City: The Story of a Progressive People* (New York: Regular Democratic Organization of Greater New York, 1909), 86, 91; Rischin, *Promised City,* 233–34.

101. *Our City,* 87–88; Broesamle, "Democrats from Bryan to Wilson," 87.

102. *Board of Aldermen Proceedings* (April 22, 1913), 241; *Tribune,* October 1, 1904; Arthur Link and Richard L. McCormick, *Progressivism* (Arlington Heights, Ill.: Harlan Davidson, 1983), 62; Daniel P. Moynihan, "When the Irish Ran New York," in *The City Boss: An Interpretive Reader,* ed. Alexander B. Callow Jr. (New York: Oxford University Press, 1976), 118–23; Duffy, *History of Public Health in New York* 1:422–28.

103. Sullivan, *Markets,* 70, 89; WML, *Yearbook, 1912* (New York, 1912), 53–54; *Call,* July 30, 1912; *Times,* December 24, 28, 1909, July 7, 1912; *Tribune,* July 29, 1899, March 29, 1902, October 1, 1904, February 21, 1905, August 28, 1905; Howe, *World of Our Fathers,* 368.

104. *Board of Aldermen Proceedings* (April 22, 1913), 241 (quote); Sullivan, *Markets,* 70, 89; *Times,* July 1, 7, 9, 16, 23, 1912; *American,* July 15, 1912.

105. *Times,* July 6, 15, 26, 1912; *Call,* July 26, 30, 1912.

106. Mary Simkhovitch to Lillian D. Wald, TL, April 29, 1914, Wald Papers, box 30; "Markets of the Poor"; WML, *Women and the City's Work* 6 (May 31, 1921): 6; Sullivan, *Markets,* 68–71; Marcus M. Marks, *Reports on Market System for New York City and on Open Markets Established in Manhattan* (New York, 1915), 68; *Times,* June 14, 1912, July 6, 7, 1912, February 5, 1918; Bluestone, "'Pushcart Evil,'" 85–86.

107. Sullivan, *Markets,* 1–3, 65–92 (quote, 71).

108. "Markets of the Poor" (*Outlook* quotes); Sullivan, *Markets,* 69, 228, 304 (Sullivan quotes).

109. J. Joseph Huthmacher, "Charles Evans Hughes and Charles Francis Murphy: The Metamorphosis of Progressivism," *New York History* 46 (January 1965): 28–34; Broesamle, "Democrats from Bryan to Wilson," 88; John D. Buenker, "The Progressive Era: A Search for a Synthesis," *Mid-America* 51 (July 1969): 178–91; Steven P. Erie, *Rainbow's End: Irish-Americans and the Dilemmas of Urban Machine Politics, 1840–1985* (Berkeley: University of California Press, 1988), 91–104; Otis A. Pease, "Urban Reformers in the Progressive Era: A Reassessment," *Pacific Northwest Quarterly* 62 (April 1971): 49–58; Connable and Silberfarb, *Tigers,* 231–68; Augustus Cerillo Jr., "The Reform of Municipal Government in New York City from Seth Low to John Purroy Mitchel," *New-York Historical Society Quarterly* 57 (January 1973): 68–71; Duffy, *History of Public Health in New York,* 2:261; Martin Shefter, "Political Incorporation and Containment: Regime Transformation in New York City," in *Power, Culture, and Place: Essays on New York City,* ed. John Hull Mollenkopf (New York: Russell Sage Foundation, 1988), 135–57.

110. Rischin, *Promised City,* 233–34; Huthmacher, "Charles Evans Hughes," 29; Erie, *Rainbow's End,* 91–104.

111. William Edwards to William J. Gaynor, typewritten letter signed, March 29, 1912, Gaynor Papers (includes translation of the March 22, 1912, edition of the *Warheit*), Municipal Archives, New York.

112. Anzia Yezierska, "Soap and Water and the Immigrant," *New Republic* 18 (February 22, 1919): 117–19.

113. Howe, *World of Our Fathers,* 250–54, 275; Tomes, *Gospel of Germs,* 130, 193.

114. "The Federation Helps the Junk Peddlers," *Federation Review* (April 1908), in Wald Papers, box 30; WML, *Bulletin* 3 (October 1904): 2; WML, *Yearbook,* 1912, 53–54; *Times,* July 5, 6, 9, 15, 1912; Erie, *Rainbow's End,* 103–5; Buenker, "Progressive Era," 178–88; Howe, *World of Our Fathers,* 120–27; Hammack, *Power and Society,* 18–27, 88–105, 304–26. The very attitudes of many progressive reformers and their sympathizers tended to encourage input by members of working-class immigrant groups. Witness the attitude of a *Times* reporter, who dolefully commented on the sheepishness of some peddlers at a meeting in which they were invited to express their concerns about the issue of segregated markets: "[These were] Old World faces, tired, wan, and be-whiskered. A number of the poorer sort were plainly frightened at the meeting. The idea of poor men gathering to criticise [*sic*] public officials and to cry out against oppression with reporters of newspapers present made them shudder. They acted as if they already felt the knout [a whip used in tsarist Russia] across their shoulders." The reporter contrasted these men with younger peddlers present who dressed like neat middle-class Americans and were unafraid to speak up, adding that "[by] their bearing and manners [they] gave ample promise of a future when a push cart would be too small to hold their wares." *Times,* July 15, 1912.

115. Bruce M. Stave, John M. Allswang, Terence J. McDonald, and Jon C. Teaford, "A Reassessment of the Urban Political Boss," *History Teacher* 21 (May 1988): 302–8.

116. Department of Agriculture, *Push Cart Markets,* 11–29, 57–60; WML, *Women and the City's Work* 6 (May 31, 1921): 6; *Times,* November 28, 1920, December 26, 1920, sec. 3, April 18, 1922, July 27, 1922, November 30, 1924, sec. 4, May 11, 21, 23, 26, 1925, December 19, 1925.

117. Department of Agriculture, *Push Cart Markets,* 53; Bluestone, "Pushcart Evil," 81–89; Wasserman, "Good Old Days," 193–94.

118. Waring, "How We Are to Treat," 1237–38 (quote, in remarks by Barnet Phillips accompanying Waring article, 1237); *Times,* January 5, 10, 1940; Wasserman, "Good Old Days," 166–217; Bluestone, "'Pushcart Evil,'" 81–89. Peter C. Baldwin points to additional factors that eroded the peddlers' customer base, including the common perception that modern grocery stores offered higher standards of sanitation; the increasing popularity of brand name packaged products (which were primarily stocked by modern grocery stores); and the fact that with the increasing use of electric refrigerators in upwardly mobile working-class and middle-class households, many consumers could purchase greater quantities of food at a time, which obviated the need for daily marketing. Baldwin, *Domesticating the Street,* 195–99.

Chapter 4: Making Citizens with the Juvenile Street Cleaning Leagues

1. Delos F. Wilcox, *The American City: A Problem in Democracy* (New York: Macmillan, 1904), 91–120; Alexander Kaminsky, "The Jewish Big Brother Movement," *Guild Journal* (publication of the University Settlement) 1 (June 1911): 39–40; James H. Hamilton, "The Relation of Social Settlements to Social Progress," address before the People's Institute, Mt. Vernon, New York, 1904, *Papers of the University Settlement Society of New York City* (Madison: State Historical Society of Wisconsin, 1972), microfilm, reel 7; *Educational Alliance Fourth Annual Report, 1896* (New York: D. A. Huebsch, 1897), 23; *Educational Alliance Third Annual Report, 1895* (New York: Philip Cowen, Printer, 1896), 11–15; Paul Boyer, *Urban*

Masses and Moral Order in America, 1820–1920 (Cambridge, Mass.: Harvard University Press, 1978), 233–51; Dominick Cavallo, *Muscles and Morals: Organized Playgrounds and Urban Reform, 1880–1920* (Philadelphia: University of Pennsylvania Press, 1981), 16–25.

2. Department of Education of the City of New York, Report on Vacation Schools and Playgrounds, 83–87 (researcher's quotes). (I examined the department of education material cited in this chapter at the Special Collections division of the Milbank Memorial Library, Teachers' College, New York City. Much if not all of this material has more recently been moved to the New York City Municipal Archives.) John W. Martin, "Social Life in the Street," *University Settlement Society Annual Report of 1899* (New York, 1899), 22–24 ("always dangerous"); Frank Simonds, "The Relation of Children to Immoral Conditions," *University Settlement Society Annual Report of 1900* (New York, 1900), 33–35 ("foul mud"); Woman's Municipal League (hereafter, WML), *Bulletin* (February 1915): 12.

3. Department of Education, Report on Vacation Schools and Playgrounds, 83–87.

4. Martin, "Social Life in the Street," 22–24; Frederick A. King, "Influences in Street Life," *University Settlement Society Annual Report of 1900*, 29–32 (quotes); Jacob S. Eisinger, "Senior Club Work—Report on Young Men's Work," *University Settlement Society Annual Report of 1915–16* (New York, 1916), 13–16; Richard M. Neustadt, "Work with Our Boys' Clubs," *University Settlement Society Annual Report of 1912* (New York, 1912), 17–21; *Tribune,* September 2, 1900; Irving Howe, *World of Our Fathers* (New York: Harcourt Brace Jovanovich, 1976): 263–64; Luc Sante, "*These* Are the Good Old Days," *New York* 24 (August 12, 1991): 31–32.

5. King, "Influences in Street Life," 29–32.

6. Charles S. Bernheimer and Jacob M. Cohen, *Boys' Clubs* (New York: Baker and Taylor, 1914), 81–94; King, "Influences in Street Life," 29–32; Grace H. Dodge, *A Private Letter to Girls* (New York: The Philanthropist, 1889); Simonds, "Relation of Children to Immoral Conditions," 33–35 (quotes); Arthur Link and Richard L. McCormick, *Progressivism* (Arlington Heights, Ill.: Harlan Davidson, 1983), 79–82; Allan M. Brandt, *No Magic Bullet: A Social History of Venereal Disease in the United States Since 1880,* expanded ed. (New York: Oxford University Press, 1987), 29–34.

7. King, "Influences in Street Life," 29–32; Bernheimer and Cohen, *Boys' Clubs,* 7–94; Simonds, "Relation of Children to Immoral Conditions," 33–35 ("citizens of a few years hence," 35); Neustadt, "Work with Our Boys' Clubs," 17–21 ("moral nature," 18); Robert A. Crosby, "Foreword," *University Settlement Society Annual Report, 1915–1916,* 5–6; Wilcox, *American City,* 91–120; J. H. Chase, "Child Ethics in the Street and Settlement," *University Settlement Society Annual Report of 1901* (New York, 1901), 34–39; Kaminsky, "Jewish Big Brother Movement"; Cavallo, *Muscles,* 25; LeRoy Ashby, *Saving the Waifs: Reformers and Dependent Children, 1890–1917* (Philadelphia: Temple University Press, 1984), 7; Ruth Schwartz Cowan, *More Work for Mother: The Ironies of Household Technology from the Open Hearth to the Microwave* (New York: Basic Books, 1983), 168–72.

8. Eisinger, "Senior Club Work," 13–16; Neustadt, "Work with Our Boys Clubs," 17–21 (quotes); Bernheimer and Cohen, *Boys' Clubs,* 7–81; Howe, *World of Our Fathers,* 263.

9. Wilcox, *American City,* 110–13.

10. Mrs. Julius Henry (Ida) Cohen, *What We Should All Know about Our Streets* (New York: Woman's Municipal League of the City of New York, 1916); Frank H. McLean, "An Experience in the Street-Cleaning Department," *University Settlement Society Annual*

Report of 1897 (New York, 1897), 20–25; H. de B. Parsons, *The Disposal of Municipal Refuse* (New York: John Wiley, 1906), 6; *Times,* April 26, 1922 (quote); Steven Hunt Corey, "King Garbage: A History of Solid Waste Management in New York City, 1881–1970: (Ph.D. diss., New York University, 1994), 54; Cowan, *More Work,* 162–66; Susan Strasser, "Waste and Want: The Other Side of Consumption," paper presented to the Rutgers Center for Historical Analysis, New Brunswick, New Jersey, November 19, 1991; Adolf F. Meisen, "History of Street Cleaning in New York City, 1860–1872" (Master's thesis, Columbia University, 1939), 5–6.

11. New York City Department of Street Cleaning (hereafter, DSC), *Clean Streets through Education and Cooperation: Report of Exhibition and Tests of Street-Cleaning Appliances* (New York, 1914), 32.

12. WML, *Bulletin* 5 (August 1906): 1–10; 5 (November 1906): 1–3. These WML *Bulletin* articles reprinted Crane's September 1905 *Woman's Forum* article.

13. Wilcox, *American City,* 91–120; First Convention of the Ladies Health Protective Association of the City of New York, 9–11, New York Public Library; Report of the Second National Convention of the Women's Health Protective Associations of the United States, 40–45 (quotes), New York Public Library; WML, *Bulletin* 6 (April 1908): 6; 8 (November 1910): 4–6; Martin V. Melosi, *Garbage in the Cities: Refuse, Reform, and the Environment, 1880–1980* (College Station: Texas A & M University Press, 1981), 109–12; Stanley K. Schultz, *Constructing Urban Culture: American Cities and City Planning, 1800–1920* (Philadelphia: Temple University Press, 1989), 148–49. The demoralizing effects of civic filth on tenement dwellers can be imagined by reading a passage from one of Abraham Cahan's novels, in which his protagonist, walking the tenement streets in the heat of the summer, "had to pick and nudge his way through dense swarms of bedraggled half-naked humanity; past garbage barrels rearing their overflowing contents in sickening piles, and lining the streets in malicious suggestion of rows of trees; underneath tiers and tiers of fire escapes, barricaded and festooned with mattresses, pillows, and featherbeds not yet gathered in for the night. The pent-up sultry atmosphere was laden with nausea." Cahan, as quoted in Raymond A. Mohl, *The New City: Urban America in the Industrial Age, 1860–1920* (Arlington Heights, Ill.: Harlan Davidson, 1985), 51.

14. Wilcox, *American City,* 91–120; Hamilton, "Relation of Social Settlements"; Children's Aid Society, "An Americanizing Influence: An Attractive Study of the New York Boy Problem," pamphlet (n.p., ca. 1920), Russell Sage Collection, City University of New York Library; Melosi, *Garbage in the Cities,* 124–26.

15. Department of Education of the City of New York, Courses of Study and Syllabuses in History/Civics (New York, 1914), section on civics, 3–18; First Convention, 9–11 (Scrimgeour quote); Crosby, "Foreword," 5–6; Wilcox, *American City,* 92, 118–20; Chase, "Child Ethics in the Street," 34–39; James H. Cassedy, *Charles V. Chapin and the Public Health Movement* (Cambridge, Mass.: Harvard University Press, 1962), 139; Paula S. Fass, *Outside In: Minorities and the Transformation of American Education* (New York: Oxford University Press, 1989), 21–35; Ashby, *Saving the Waifs,* 4–7m 89.

16. Department of Education of the City of New York, Minutes of the Board of Superintendents, 1915, 321–22, 645; Department of Education of the City of New York, General Circular, number 21, item 3, March 23, 1917; DSC, *Clean Streets through Education,* 43–52; DSC, *Report for the Year 1908* (New York: Martin B. Brown Press, 1909), 9–10; DSC, *Report for the Year 1915* (New York: J. J. Little and Ives, 1916), 44–46; WML, *Bulletin* 1 (April 1902):

3 (quote); 7 (April 1909): 7; (April 1914): 7–10; WML, *Women and the City's Work* 2 (May 29, 1917): 2, 15–19; *Times,* November 23, 1916, March 12, 1917, February 16, 1919.

17. William Potts, "George Edwin Waring, Jr.," *Charities Review* 8 (1898): 467; George E. Waring Jr., *Street-Cleaning and the Disposal of a City's Wastes: Methods and Results and the Effect Upon Public Health, Public Morals, and Municipal Prosperity* (New York: Doubleday and McClure, 1898), 179, 186; F. H. McLean, "The Sanitary Union," *University Settlement Society Annual Report of 1895* (New York, 1895), 19–22; Reuben S. Simons, "The Juvenile Street Cleaning Leagues of New York," *American City* 3 (October and November 1910): 163–66, 239–43; DSC, *Report for the Year 1915,* 45–46; Educational Alliance, *Souvenir Book of the Fair* (New York, 1895), 114–15, Butler Library, Columbia University, New York City.

18. Simons, "Juvenile Street Cleaning," 163–66, 239–43; DSC, *Report for the Year 1899* (New York: W. P. Mitchell, 1901), 7; DSC, *Report for the Year 1900* (New York: W. P. Mitchell, n.d.), 7–8; *Times,* July 27, 1899, February 9, 11 ("Monte Carlo"), 1900; Benjamin Miller, *Fat of the Land: Garbage in New York the Last Two Hundred Years* (New York: Four Walls Eight Windows, 2000), 87, 105, 115.

19. Wilcox, *American City,* 118–20; Mary Ritter Beard, *Woman's Work in Municipalities* (New York: Appleton, 1915), 84–88, 216; Melosi, *Garbage in the Cities,* 76; Waring, *Street-Cleaning and Disposal,* 179.

20. Clinton Rogers Woodruff, "A Year's Disclosure and Development," in *Proceedings of the Chicago Conference for Good City Government and the Tenth Annual Meeting of the National Municipal League,* ed. Clinton Rogers Woodruff (Philadelphia: National Municipal League, 1904), 113; WML, *Bulletin* 1 (June 1902): 3–4; 2 (October 1903): 3–4; 2 (December 1903): 5–7; 2 (February 1904); 5 (March 1907): 5.

21. Simons, "Juvenile Street Cleaning," 163–66, 239–43; "Street Cleaning League," *Guild Review* (publication of the University Settlement) 1 (March 1907): 19; WML, *Bulletin* 5 (March 1907): 5; 7 (February 1909): 1–3.

22. DSC, *Report for the Year 1908,* 9–10; DSC, *Report for the Year 1909* (New York: W. P. Mitchell, 1910), 11; DSC, *Report for the Year 1915,* 44–46; DSC, *Clean Streets through Education,* 33; *Times,* July 8, 1909; *Tribune,* July 8, 1909.

23. WML, *Bulletin* (April 1914): 7–10; DSC, *Clean Streets through Education,* 46.

24. *Times,* November 23, 1916, January 3, 1917, March 12, 1917, February 16, 1919; "Anti-Litter League," *American City* 15 (July 1916): 67.

25. William Byron Forbush, *The Boy Problem* (Boston: Pilgrim Press, 1913), 59–61 (quote, 61).

26. On the common practices of the juvenile league clubs and related matters, see Waring, *Street-Cleaning and Disposal,* 177–86; WML, *Bulletin* 7 (April 1909): 8; 7 (May 1909): 8; WML, *Yearbook, 1911* (New York, 1911), 75; Simons, "Juvenile Street Cleaning," 163–66, 239–43; DSC, *Report for the Year 1915,* 45–46; DSC, *Clean Streets through Education,* 33, 46.

27. *Tribune,* June 21, 1908.

28. Waring, *Street-Cleaning and Disposal,* 183–85.

29. Ibid.; Simons, "Juvenile Street Cleaning," 163; *Times,* August 1, 1895; Eric F. Goldman, *Rendezvous with Destiny: A History of Modern American Reform,* rev. ed. (New York: Vintage, 1955), 157; John Whiteclay Chambers II, *The Tyranny of Change: America in the Progressive Era, 1890–1920,* 2d ed. (New York: St. Martin's, 1992), 151, 285; Orlando Figes, *A People's Tragedy: The Russian Revolution, 1891–1924* (New York: Penguin Books,

1996), 725–26. Some juvenile league practices may seem strange now because prosocial normative pressure has often become so very attenuated in the present day. From fear of causing offense or gaining the contempt of peers, adolescents today often fail to speak up when their more uncivil companions express antisocial attitudes or engage in antisocial or unhealthy behaviors. Thus, young people who deride intellectual achievement can become trendsetters. The movement to teach children to resist negative peer pressure is a positive sign, though that is not quite the same as speaking out to help instill a healthy sense of guilt in peers as well. Somewhat relatedly, while the movement to instill "politically correct" language and behavior is in some ways a positive assertion of normative pressures, its more extreme protagonists at times inhibit valuable traditional cultural norms—making it more difficult, for example, to speak out against public spitting (in a period when we are witnessing the recrudescence of tuberculosis), for fear of garnering the condemnation of those claiming that it is a cultural expression of nondominant social groups.

30. The Woman's Health Protective Association, Brooklyn, *Children's Aid to the Woman's Health Protective Association, Brooklyn* (Brooklyn: Eagle Book Printing, 1896), 12–13 (song lyrics); Waring, *Street-Cleaning and Disposal*, 177–86.

31. DSC, *Clean Streets through Education*, 46; Waring, *Street-Cleaning and Disposal*, 183 ("Civic Pledge"); Simons, "Juvenile Street Cleaning," 241.

32. WML, *Bulletin* 7 (February 1909): 1–3; 7 (April 1909): 8 (quote); 8 (November 1910): 4–6; 8 (May 1911): 9–12; (February 1915): 5–6.

33. Department of Education of the City of New York, Thirteenth Annual Report of the City Superintendent of Schools, 1910–1911—Vacation Schools, Recreation Centers, Vacation Playgrounds, 29, 46.

34. "The Settlement: A Builder of Character," *Guild Journal* 3 (November 1912): 21; Martin, "Social Life in the Street," 22–24; Chase, "Child Ethics in the Street," 34–39; Charles H. Warner, "Tendencies in East Side Boys' Clubs," *University Settlement Society Annual Report of 1901*, 50–53; James H. Hamilton, "What the Settlement Stands For," *University Settlement Society Annual Report of 1904* (New York, 1904), 7–16; Neustadt, "Work with Our Boys' Clubs," 17–21; Ethel Burns, "Spirit of Our Evening Club Work," *University Settlement Annual Report of 1912*, 26–31; WML, *Bulletin* (April 1914): 6–7 (quote); Boyer, *Urban Masses*, 246; Cavallo, *Muscles*, 4–6.

35. Simons, "Juvenile Street Cleaning," 241; WML, *Bulletin* 7 (May 1909): 8; 8 (November 1910): 5.

36. DSC, *Report for the Year 1909*, 11; DSC, *Report for the Year 1910* (New York: Lecouver Press, 1911), 7; Woodruff, "A Year's Disclosure," 113–14; Simons, "Juvenile Street Cleaning," 163–66, 239–43; WML, *Bulletin* 5 (May 1907): 4; 7 (May 1909): 8; *Times*, May 28, 1897, July 8, 1909, June 4, 1910; *New York Herald*, May 27, 1896.

37. *Times*, August 1, 1895.

38. Ibid., (quote); Waring, *Street-Cleaning and Disposal*, 177–86; Potts, "George Edwin Waring, Jr.," 468; George E. Waring Jr., "The Cleaning of a Great City," *McClure's Magazine* 9 (September 1897): 911–24.

39. *Educational Alliance Fourth Annual Report, 1896*, 23 (quote). On related matters, see Josiah Quincy, "Municipal Progress in Boston," *Independent* 52 (February 15, 1900): 424–26; Howe, *World of Our Fathers*, 235.

40. *Times*, May 5, 1891.

41. *Times,* November 24, 1895.

42. WML, *Yearbook, 1912,* 61.

43. Chase, "Child Ethics in the Street," 34–39.

44. Department of Education, Thirteenth Annual Report, 3–46; Department of Education, Courses of Study, 3–18; Waring, *Street-Cleaning and Disposal,* 179.

45. Julia Richman and Isabel Richman Wallach, *Good Citizenship* (New York: American Book Co., 1908), 126–29 (quote, 129); Howe, *World of Our Fathers,* 275–78.

46. Richman and Wallach, *Good Citizenship,* 126–29 (quote, 126).

47. Educational Alliance, *Book of the Fair,* 114–15 ("citizen in embryo" and "Citizen Factories"); Waring, "The Cleaning of a Great City," 911–24 ("citizens who will be interested"). On related matters, see Michael J. Sandel, *Democracy's Discontent: America in Search of a Public Philosophy* (Cambridge, Mass.: Belknap Press of Harvard University Press, 1996), 203–27.

48. *Educational Alliance Third Annual Report, 1895,* 18–20, 33 ("main object"); *Educational Alliance Seventh Annual Report, 1899* (New York, 1900), 21, 46–48 ("religious obligations"); *Educational Alliance Fourth Annual Report, 1896,* 44 ("Alliance Americanizes").

49. *Educational Alliance Eleventh Annual Report, 1903* (New York, 1904), 67–70 ("moral rectitude"); *Educational Alliance Sixth Annual Report, 1898* (New York, 1899), 19–21 ("purity of mind"). See also Neustadt, "Work with Our Boys' Clubs," 17–21. Isidor Straus was the co-owner, with his brother Nathan, of Macy's Department Store. Along with his wife, Ida, who chose to remain on board with him, Isidor went down with the *Titanic* in 1912.

50. *Times,* February 23, 1913, May 18, 1913, sec. 5; Melosi, *Garbage in the Cities,* 124–33.

51. Beard, *Woman's Work,* 84–88; "Children in City Clean-Up Work," *American City* 14 (February 1916): 156–61.

52. "Children in City Clean-Up Work" (quotes); Peter C. Baldwin, *Domesticating the Street: The Reform of Public Space in Hartford, 1850–1930* (Columbus: Ohio State University Press, 1999), 57–58.

53. Beard, *Woman's Work,* 86; "Can the East Side Be Clean," 4–5, typewritten document, 1930, Wald Papers, box 31, Street and Outdoor Cleanliness folder, Rare Books and Manuscripts Collection, Butler Library, Columbia University, New York; *Times,* February 23, 1913.

54. Beard, *Woman's Work,* 84–88, 216 (quotes, 85, 88); "Notes and Events," *National Municipal Review* 3 (July 1914): 600; "Can the East Side Be Clean," 4–5; "Syllabus in Civics and Patriotism," *University of the State of New York Bulletin* (February 15, 1920): 57–70; *Times,* February 23, 1913; Melosi, *Garbage in the Cities,* 132.

55. Philip J. Ethington, "Recasting Urban Political History: Gender, the Public, the Household, and Political Participation in Boston and San Francisco during the Progressive Era," *Social Science History* 16 (Summer 1992): 303–9.

56. Beard, *Woman's Work,* 84; "Women and Civics," *National Municipal Review* 3 (October 1914): 714; Nancy Tomes, *The Gospel of Germs: Men, Women, and the Microbe in American Life* (Cambridge, Mass.: Harvard University Press, 1998), 66.

57. Report of the Second National Convention, 45–47.

58. WML, *Yearbook, 1911,* 9.

59. WML, *Bulletin* 7 (February 1909): 4 (WML quote); Report of the Second National Convention, 40–45 (Scrimgeour quote).

60. WML, *Bulletin* 7 (February 1909): 4.

61. Jon A. Peterson, "The City Beautiful Movement: Forgotten Origins and Lost Meanings," *Journal of Urban History* 2 (August 1976): 415–34; Jon A. Peterson, "The Impact of Sanitary Reform upon American Urban Planning, 1840–1890," *Journal of Social History* 13 (Fall 1979): 90–95; Jon A. Peterson, *The Birth of City Planning in the United States, 1840–1917* (Baltimore: Johns Hopkins University Press, 2003); Melosi, *Garbage in the Cities,* 110–33; Schultz, *Constructing Urban Culture,* 211–15; David Stradling, *Smokestacks and Progressives: Environmentalists, Engineers, and Air Quality in America, 1881–1951* (Baltimore: Johns Hopkins University Press, 1999), 25, 45, 59. The City Beautiful concern for the effect of aesthetics on human health resonates with the modern-day field known as "environmental aesthetics." See *Environmental Aesthetics: Theory, Research, and Applications,* ed. Jack L. Nasar (Cambridge: Cambridge University Press, 1988).

62. Department of Education of the City of New York, Digest of Matter of Current Value from Circulars Issued by the Superintendent of Schools, 1902–1915, 43, in 1912–13 section ("maintenance"); WML, *Yearbook, 1914* (New York, 1914), 37–41 ("health and uplift," 38); WML, *Bulletin* 8 (May 1911): 3–4 ("essential"); (April 1914): 19 ("body and spirit").

63. WML, *Women and the City's Work* 2 (May 29, 1917): 10 (quote); WML, *Bulletin* 8 (May 1911): 6–7; *Times,* November 24, 1895.

64. Report of the Second National Convention, 40–45 ("ridicule"); First Convention, 9–11 ("ears polite").

65. Report of the Second National Convention, 32–36 ("even the women" and "courage") 37–40 ("bulwarks"). The New York Ladies Health Protective Association inspired the organization of several other branches nationwide during the late 1800s. Despite criticism of unladylike conduct, by the early 1890s the national umbrella organization did not feel the need to prove the feminine identity of its members, replacing the word "Ladies" with "Women's" in the group's title. The New York City group, which chose to remain only loosely associated with the national organization, then adopted the "Women's" moniker in 1897 or 1898. A member of the New York group commented that the new name seemed better suited to "a good work-a-day society." (The changes did not, however, prevent members from switching "Woman's" and "Women's" almost interchangeably in referring to these groups.) Report of the Women's Health Protective Association of New York, 1896–1900, 19–22; Anne Firor Scott, "On Seeing and Not Seeing: A Case of Historical Invisibility," *Journal of American History* 71 (June 1984): 13.

66. First Convention, 9–11. "Terrible as an army with banners" is a biblical phrase from Song of Songs 6:4, American Bible Society's King James Version.

67. Suzanne Lebsock, "Women and American Politics, 1880–1920," in *Women, Politics, and Change,* ed. Louise A. Tilly and Patricia Gurin (New York: Russell Sage Foundation, 1990), 35–62; Stradling, *Smokestacks,* 42–46.

68. Bernheimer and Cohen, *Boys' Clubs,* 7–33 ("aims" and "self-restraint," 25, 33); WML, *Bulletin* 7 (February 1909): 4 ("Goliath"); Tomes, *Gospel of Germs,* 215–25.

69. William H. Allen, "Teaching Civics by Giving Pupils Civic Work to Do," *American City* 14 (February 1916): 154–55 (quotes); WML, *Women and the City's Work* 2 (May 29, 1917): 15; Michael P. McCarthy, "Urban Optimism and Reform Thought in the Progressive Era," *The Historian* 51 (February 1989): 257–59; Chambers, *Tyranny of Change,* 210–11.

70. David Rosenstein, "Citizenship," *The Emersonian* (May 1912): 2–3 ("two obligations"), periodical in the Papers of the University Settlement Society of New York City, reel 16; Department of Education, Courses of Study, 3 (all other quotes).

71. Department of Education, Courses of Study, 4, 6, 11.

72. Richman and Wallach, *Good Citizenship*, 102.

73. WML, *Bulletin* (September 1914): 5. Relatedly, see "Municipal Departments," *University Settlement Society Annual Report of 1896* (New York, 1896), 16.

74. WML, *Bulletin* (February 1915): 3 (quote); *Times*, May 4, 1913, sec. 7.

75. DSC, *Report for the Year 1914*, 13; WML, *Bulletin* 8 (June 1910): 3–4 (Soper quote).

76. Report of the Second National Convention, 40–45.

77. WML, *Bulletin* (April 1914): 20.

78. Ibid.

79. Wilcox, *American City*, 94–95, 102, 112, 120 (quotes); Hamilton, "Relation of Social Settlements"; *Educational Alliance Fourth Annual Report, 1896*, 23; WML, *Bulletin* (September 1914): 3–5; (February 1915): 1–4; Tomes, *Gospel of Germs*, 215–25; Mark Haller, "Urban Vice and Civic Reform: Chicago in the Early Twentieth Century," in *Cities in American History*, ed. Kenneth T. Jackson and Stanley K. Schultz (New York: Knopf, 1972), 301.

80. Department of Education, Courses of Study, 3, 4, 6, 13, 15, 17 (quote, 17); Jonah J. Goldstein, "A Neighborhood Organization," *University Settlement Annual Report of 1912*, 40–43; Jean Bethke Elshtain, *Jane Addams and the Dream of American Democracy: A Life* (New York: Basic Books, 2002), 158.

81. Burns, "Spirit of Our Evening Club Work," 26–31 (non-Kelley quotes); Blanche L. Kelley, "Report on Girls' Work," *University Settlement Society Annual Report of 1915–16*, 9–11 (Kelley quotes); Howe, *World of Our Fathers*, 120–22; John C. Burnham, "The Cultural Interpretation of the Progressive Movement," in *Paths into American Culture: Psychology, Medicine, and Morals*, ed. John C. Burnham (Philadelphia: Temple University Press, 1988), 215–16; Baldwin, *Domesticating the Street*, 147–76. Baldwin does not emphasize as much as this study how often the children (or at least their parents) related positively to the reformers' agenda.

82. "What the Settlement Stands For," 7–16; Goldstein, "A Neighborhood Organization," 40–43; WML, *Bulletin* 3 (September 1904): 4 (quotes).

83. DSC, *Clean Streets through Education*, 38 (Fetherston quote); WML, *Bulletin* 6 (December 1907): 18 (WML quote); Thomas Jesse Jones, "Report of Work in the University Settlement House," *University Settlement Society Annual Report of 1901* (New York, 1901), 19; Hamilton, "What the Settlement Stands For," 7–16; Goldstein, "A Neighborhood Organization," 40–43; Augustus Cerillo Jr., "Reform in New York City: A Study of Urban Progressivism" (Ph.D. diss., Northwestern University, 1965), 97–100, 195, 214.

84. Boyer, *Urban Masses*, 221–32; Cavallo, *Muscles*, 15–23; Tomes, *Gospel of Germs*, 188–89.

85. *Times*, May 4, 1913, sec. 5.

86. Ibid.

87. Ibid.; Forbush, *The Boy Problem*, 68.

88. Diane Ravitch, *The Great School Wars: New York City, 1805–1973, A History of the Public Schools as Battlefield of Social Change* (New York: Basic Books, 1974), 110–11; Howe, *World of Our Fathers*, 276; David C. Hammack, *Power and Society: Greater New York at the Turn of the Century* (New York: Russell Sage Foundation, 1982), 275–76.

89. Waring, *Street-Cleaning and Disposal*, 177–86 (Willard quote, 185); *Times*, March 12, 1917 (Merchants' Association quote).

90. DSC, *Clean Streets through Education*, 28–29.

91. George E. Waring Jr., *Letter to the Presidents of Juvenile Leagues of the Department of Street Cleaning* (New York, [1897]).

92. Ibid.

93. Ibid. ("newsboys"); Waring, *Street-Cleaning and Disposal*, 184–85 ("inflammation").

94. Philip Brickman, Vita Carulli Rabinowitz, Jurgis Karuza Jr., Dan Coates, Ellen Cohn, and Louise Kidder, "Models of Helping and Coping," *American Psychologist* 37 (April 1982): 368–84. Relatedly, see Ravitch, *School Wars*, 170–71.

95. On the social reform progressives' work to counteract the rigid moral model viewpoint, see *Educational Alliance Third Annual Report, 1895*, 15; *Educational Alliance Fourth Annual Report, 1896*, 23; Wilcox, *American City*, 110–12; *Times*, August 20, 1911, sec. 5; Lebsock, "Women and American Politics," 48; Robert H. Bremner, *From the Depths: The Discovery of Poverty in the United States* (New York: New York University Press, 1956), 135.

96. Brickman et al., "Models of Helping," 373.

97. Glenda Gilmore, "Responding to the Challenges of the Progressive Era," in *Who Were the Progressives?* ed. Glenda Gilmore (Boston: Bedford/St. Martin's, 2002), 3–24; James Livingston, "Historians and Corporate Capitalism," *Historically Speaking* 4 (November 2002): 26–27; Robert D. Johnston, review of *Roots of Reform: Farmers, Workers, and the American State, 1877–1917*, by Elizabeth Sanders, *Reviews in American History* 28 (September 2000): 393–98; Robert D. Johnston, *The Radical Middle Class: Populist Democracy and the Question of Capitalism in Progressive Era Portland, Oregon* (Princeton University Press, 2003); Kathryn Kish Sklar, "The Historical Foundations of Women's Power in the Creation of the American Welfare State, 1830–1930," in *Mothers of a New World: Maternalist Politics and the Origins of Welfare States*, ed. Seth Koven and Sonya Michel (New York: Routledge, 1993), 43–93.

98. Walter I. Trattner, *From Poor Law to Welfare State: A History of Social Welfare in America*, 5th ed. (New York: Free Press, 1994), 167–69, and Elshtain, *Jane Addams*, 286–87, provide some examples of this type of viewpoint regarding social control, and they also offer some countervailing thoughts on the issue.

99. Goldman, *Rendezvous*, 150–67; Arthur M. Schlesinger Jr., *The Cycles of American History* (Boston: Houghton Mifflin, 1986), 219–38; John Duffy, *A History of Public Health in New York City*, vol. 1: *1625–1866* (New York: Russell Sage Foundation, 1968), 422–28.

100. Richard L. McCormick, "Ethno-Cultural Interpretations of Nineteenth-Century American Voting Behavior," *Political Science Quarterly* 89 (June 1974): 351–77; John B. Judis, "Top Down: Whatever Happened to Noblesse Oblige?" *New Republic Online* (March 27, 2000), http://www.tnr.com/032700/judis032700.html (accessed April 13, 2005); Daniel Walker Howe, *The Political Culture of the American Whigs* (Chicago: University of Chicago Press, 1979), 1–42; Daniel Feller, *The Jacksonian Promise: America, 1815–1840* (Baltimore: Johns Hopkins University Press, 1995), 187–88; Harry L. Watson, *Andrew Jackson vs. Henry Clay: Democracy and Development in Antebellum America* (Boston: Bedford/St. Martin's, 1998), 19–22.

101. Howe, *Political Culture of American Whigs*, 36; Feller, *Jacksonian Promise*, 187–88.

102. McCormick, "Ethno-Cultural Interpretations," 41–55; Howe, *Political Culture of American Whigs*, 16–20, 34–36; Duffy, *History of Public Health in New York*, 1:422–28; John

D. Buenker, John C. Burnham, and Robert M. Crunden, *Progressivism* (Cambridge, Mass.: Schenkman, 1977), 39.

103. Michael Perman, *Emancipation and Reconstruction, 1862–1879* (Wheeling, Ill.: Harlan Davidson, 1987), 107–28.

104. Buenker et al., *Progressivism,* 46–59; Gary Gerstle, "The Protean Character of American Liberalism," *American Historical Review* 99 (October 1994): 1047–48.

105. *Times,* October 27, 1912 (quote), August 21, 1914; Tomes, *Gospel of Germs,* 123–29.

106. WML, *Yearbook, 1912,* 43 (Cohen quotes); Tomes, *Gospel of Germs,* 123–32. The concept of street cleaning morals resonates with some authors' usage in the current day of the term "social capital." See Robert D. Putnam, "The Prosperous Community: Social Capital and Public Life," *The American Prospect* no. 13 (Spring 1993): 35–42; Ichiro Kawachi, Bruce P. Kennedy, and Kimberly Lochner, "Long Live Community: Social Capital as Public Health," *American Prospect* no. 35 (November–December 1997): 56–59.

107. Howe, *Political Culture of American Whigs,* 1–42; Robert M. Crunden, *Ministers of Reform: The Progressives' Achievement in American Civilization, 1889–1920* (New York: Basic Books, 1982), 3–38; Hammack, *Power and Society,* 281; Gerstle, "Protean Character," 1050; Judis, "Top Down"; Joseph P. Sullivan, "The Terror of the Trolley," *Journal of Urban Technology* 4 (1997): 1–2.

108. Jane S. Dahlberg, *The New York Bureau of Municipal Research: Pioneer in Government Administration* (New York: New York University Press, 1966), 237–38; Lebsock, "Women and American Politics," 47–48; G. Edward White, "The Social Values of the Progressives: Some New Perspectives," *South Atlantic Quarterly* 70 (Winter 1971): 69–74; Arthur Mann, "British Social Thought and American Reformers of the Progressive Era," *Mississippi Valley Historical Review* 42 (March 1956): 677–78; Kenneth Finegold, *Experts and Politicians: Reform Challenges to Machine Politics in New York, Cleveland, and Chicago* (Princeton: Princeton University Press, 1995), 33–34, 54–67 (Moses quote, 33).

109. "Junior Improvements," *American City* 3 (October 1910): 196–97.

110. Gerald W. McFarland, *Mugwumps, Morals, and Politics, 1884–1920* (Amherst: University of Massachusetts Press, 1975), 104.

111. Potts, "George Edwin Waring, Jr.," 461–62.

112. Schlesinger, *Cycles,* 219–38; Goldman, *Rendezvous,* 144–67.

113. Martin, "Social Life in the Street," 23 ("future voters"); *Times,* May 13, 1926 (Walker quote). On related matters, see *Times,* May 14, 1919; WML, *Bulletin* 8 (June 1910): 4–6.

114. *Times,* April 5, 1907, July 9, 1919 (O'Neill quote); WML, *Bulletin* 6 (June 1908): 8–9 (on Finn); 8 (November 1910): 4.

115. *Tammany Times,* December 23, 1895; Gerald N. Grob, "The Political System and Social Policy in the Nineteenth Century: Legacy of the Revolution," *Mid-America* 58 (January 1976): 5–19; Richard L. McCormick, "The Discovery That Business Corrupts Politics: A Reappraisal of the Origins of Progressivism," in *The Party Period and Public Policy: American Politics from the Age of Jackson to the Progressive Era,* ed. Richard L. McCormick (New York: Oxford University Press, 1986), 318, 329, 346.

116. *Sun* letter dated April 1897, reprinted in Report of the Second National Convention, 45–47.

117. Ibid.; *Tammany Times,* July 6, 1895, August 10, 1895 ("Sissy Waring"), September 14, 1895 ("better and purer"), December 16, 1895. Tammany's attempts to stigmatize Waring

as prissy and feminine can be seen as part of a broader late nineteenth-century political drama, in which a rigid demarcation between "masculine" politics and the "feminine" concerns of hearth and home gradually gave way to a certain blurring of these lines as the social reform concerns of women's groups and men like Waring came to the fore in political life, and as more people accepted the idea of women's participation in public life. See Paula Baker, "The Domestication of Politics: Women and American Political Society, 1780–1920," *American Historical Review* 89 (June 1984): 620–647; Lebsock, "Women and American Politics," 57–58; Rebecca Edwards, *Angels in the Machinery: Gender in American Party Politics from the Civil War to the Progressive Era* (New York: Oxford University Press, 1997), 21–27. At least during the early part of the Progressive Era, some of the articles in the *Tammany Times* reflected the racist character of the Jacksonian ethos. In commenting, for example, on the passage of a New York State law mandating equal access to public accommodations for African Americans, the paper editorialized: "In this country the white men . . . object to the proximity of the Negro. . . . [This is] not a law to preserve equal rights, but was designed for the purpose of setting one class of citizens against another in the hope of getting votes." And in response to progressive Republican critics of lynchings in Democratically controlled southern states, the paper reminded its readers of recent lynchings in Republican-controlled northern states and, while noting that these were regrettable, asserted: "One fact . . . is that white men, regardless of latitude, will protect their women and children from the brutal lust of the Senegambian [African]." *Tammany Times,* June 29, 1895 ("proximity"), September 13, 1897 ("Senegambian").

118. John A. Kouwenhoven, "Waste Not, Have Not: A Clue to American Prosperity," *Harper's Magazine* 218 (March 1959): 72–81. (A collection of articles by Kouwenhoven, entitled *The Beer Can by the Highway* [Baltimore: Johns Hopkins University Press, repr. 1988], 215–42, also contains this piece.); *Times,* September 8, 1926; Duffy, *History of Public Health in New York,* 1:422, 428; John Duffy, *A History of Public Health in New York City,* vol. 2: *1866–1966* (New York: Russell Sage Foundation, 1974), 32; William G. McLoughlin, "Pietism and the American Character," *American Quarterly* 17 (Summer 1965): 165–74. An essay by the novelist James Lee Burke ("Hammering Down I-25," *The Nation* 276 [May 12, 2003]: 22–27) resonates with Kouwenhoven's observations. In describing "the new world of Wal-Mart and the ubiquitous strip mall" that is part of the landscape of his home state of Louisiana, Burke observes, "The state roads and the parking lots of discount stores are literally layered with trash, thrown there by the cavalier, whose self-congratulatory hedonism is a form of anti-confiteor" (24).

119. WML, *Bulletin* 8 (February 1911): 4 (Cohen quote); Richman and Wallach, *Good Citizenship,* 5, 6, 127 (Richman quote).

120. Richman and Wallach, *Good Citizenship,* 134 (Richman quote); *Times,* August 1, 1895 (Waring quote), October 27, 1912, sec. 7.

121. WML, *Bulletin* 1 (June 1902): 3–4 ("manly way"); *Times,* July 21, 1895 (Bernstein quote).

122. *Times,* May 24, 1896; Howe, *World of Our Fathers,* 370.

123. *Times,* June 30, 1896.

124. Waring, *Letter to the Presidents of Juvenile Leagues.*

125. DSC, *Clean Streets through Education,* 30; WML, *Bulletin* (February 1915): 9–10; *Times,* August 1, 1895.

126. WML, *Bulletin* 7 (February 1909): 1–3 ("in touch"); 8 (November 1910): 5; (February 1915): 6 ("gradually persuading").

127. James H. Hamilton to B. Ogden Chisholm, August 1, 1907, *Papers of the University Settlement Society of New York City*, microfilm, reel 7.

128. Cohen, *What We Should All Know*; DSC, *Clean Streets through Education*, 16–38; WML, *Bulletin* 6 (December 1907): 18; (February 1915): 8–11; *Times*, November 24, 1895, October 27, 1912, sec. 7.

129. Cohen, *What We Should All Know*, 10.

130. Kouwenhoven, "Waste Not, Have Not," 72–81; Burnham, "Cultural Interpretation," 227. It is interesting to compare Cohen's statement (in the previous paragraph of the present text) with the remarks of Mayor Walker in the May 13, 1926, *Times* article previously noted. By 1926, Tammany Hall had moved closer to the progressive ideal, as seen in its promotion of community programs to foster the type of civic pride that would preclude the need for enforcement of litter laws. Nevertheless, the underlying message given by the Jacksonian-leaning Walker was that such laws should not be enforced if broken. Cohen, the progressive, was willing to countenance state coercion when needed to diminish behaviors that violated the rights of other individuals and the community as a whole; but she also envisioned a society in which social and educational programs would inspire children to adopt a civic ethic that would obviate the need for large doses of state coercion.

131. Hamilton to Chisholm, August 1, 1907 (quote); Burnham, "Cultural Interpretation," 219–20; Chambers, *Tyranny of Change*, 151, 285.

132. Burnham, "Cultural Interpretation," 215–27; Tomes, *Gospel of Germs*, 115–16; Boyer, *Urban Masses*, 281–83; Robert L. Buroker, "From Voluntary Association to Welfare State: The Illinois Immigrants' Protective League, 1908–1926," *Journal of American History* 58 (December 1971): 649; *Educational Alliance Tenth Annual Report, 1902* (New York, 1903), 21–22.

133. James B. Reynolds, "Report of the Head Worker," *University Settlement Society Annual Report of 1894* (New York, 1894), 7–10; James B. Reynolds, "Report of the Head Worker," *University Settlement Society Annual Report of 1901*, 8; McLean, "An Experience in the Street-Cleaning Department," 23; David Blaustein, "The Inherent Cultural Forces of the Lower East Side," *University Settlement Society Annual Report of 1901*, 20–25 (Blaustein's "tyranny has taught"); David Blaustein, "The People of the East Side before Emigration and after Immigration," *University Settlement Studies* (July 1905): 74–78 (other Blaustein quotes); Hamilton, "Relation of Social Settlements"; *Times*, May 4, 1913, sec. 5.

134. Crosby, "Foreword," 5–6; "Preventing Crime," *Guild Journal* 3 (December 1912): 28; *Educational Alliance Fourth Annual Report, 1896*, 44; Hamilton, "What the Settlement Stands For," 9–11; "Report of the Head Worker [of 1894]"; McLean, "An Experience in the Street-Cleaning Department," 21–22; Ravitch, *School Wars*, 123; Howe, *World of Our Fathers*, 231; Otis L. Graham Jr. and Elizabeth Koed, "Americanizing the Immigrant, Past and Future: History and Implications of a Social Movement," *Public Historian* 15 (Fall 1993): 24–45; Macaulay, as referred to in Arthur M. Schlesinger Jr., "Sources of the New Deal," in *The New Deal: The Critical Issues*, ed. Otis L. Graham, Jr. (Boston: Little, Brown, 1971), 120.

135. White, "Social Values of the Progressives," 72–73; McCarthy, "Urban Optimism," 239–62; Burnham, "Cultural Interpretation," 215; "Women and Civics," 713. While histo-

rians such as Dominick Cavallo, Paul Boyer, and Peter C. Baldwin have done fine work on the history of Progressive Era childhood recreation, I tend to emphasize more than they do the extent to which reformers shared values concerning child-rearing (and other topics) with working-class parents; encouraged creativity, self-expression, and self-actualization in children; and attempted to reach children through reasoning rather than through a more controlling approach to learning (akin to conditioning). Moreover, I tend to treat more sympathetically the reformers' anxieties about the dangers that the streets held for children, and their related perception that many parents in slum districts were at times unable to adequately supervise their children. Likewise, I am more sympathetic to the reformers' desire to foster among children a desire to cooperate, and the reformers' concomitant belief that this would help build social capital and a more involved citizenry for the future. See Cavallo, *Muscles;* Hammack, *Power and Society,* 259–99; Boyer, *Urban Masses,* 171–74, 233–51, 277–83; Baldwin, *Domesticating the Street,* 147–76; Joel Spring, *Education and the Rise of the Corporate State* (Boston: Beacon Press, 1972), 1–21.

136. Howe, *World of Our Fathers,* 234, 252–63; Alan M. Kraut, *The Huddled Masses: The Immigrant in American Society, 1880–1921* (Arlington Heights, Ill.: Harlan Davidson, 1982), 111–47.

137. WML, *Yearbook, 1911,* 67–68.

138. Report of the Second National Convention, 45–47.

139. Wilcox, *American City,* 97–98 (quote); Cowan, *More Work,* 160–68; Howe, *World of Our Fathers,* 229–34, 249–80; Boyer, *Urban Masses,* 157–59; Constance Classen, David Howes, and Anthony Synnott, *Aroma: The Cultural History of Smell* (London: Routledge, 1994), 165–69. Wilcox, like many of his contemporaries, often used the term "race" to denote that which in the current day would be termed "ethnic."

140. See Richman and Wallach, *Good Citizenship,* 139–94, for examples of occasional conflicts between working-class New Yorkers and city officials who were concerned about civic sanitation or related issues.

141. Blaustein, "Inherent Cultural Forces," 20–25.

142. "Children in City Clean-Up Work," 157–58; Blaustein, "Inherent Cultural Forces," 20–25; *Educational Alliance Fourth Annual Report, 1896,* 23.

143. Macdonough Craven to University Settlement Society Sub-Committee on Streets, March 14, 1907, *Papers of the University Settlement Society of New York City,* microfilm, reel 7.

144. *Educational Alliance Third Annual Report,* 1895, 15; *Times,* August 20, 1911, sec. 5.

145. *Educational Alliance Fourth Annual Report, 1896,* 23; "The Settlement: A Builder of Character," 21; Haller, "Urban Vice and Civic Reform," 301.

146. "Address of Jane Addams," *University Settlement Society Annual Report of 1902* (New York, 1902), 51–56 (Addams quotes).

147. Minutes of Executive Meeting of Riverside Branch of WML, January 5, 1914, in folder entitled "Minutes of Meetings," Louise and Birdie Morgenstern Papers, New-York Historical Society Library, New York City; WML, *Bulletin* (April 1914): 7–10 (quotes).

148. WML, *Bulletin* (June 1910): 8; (April 1914): 13–14; (September 1914): 3–5; (February 1915): 12–16 (title quotes); WML, *Yearbook, 1913* (New York, 1913), 40–42; *Yearbook, 1914,* 18–20, 31–33; WML, *Women and the City's Work* 2 (May 29, 1917): 11, 25; Jo Freeman, "'One Man, One Vote; One Woman, One Throat': Women in New York City Politics, 1890–1910," *American Nineteenth Century History* 1 (Autumn 2001): 101–23.

149. Herbert L. Wright, "Health Leagues in the Schools," *American City* 17 (August 1917): 152–53; Department of Education of the City of New York, Division of Educational Hygiene, *How to Safeguard the Health of the Child* (New York, 1915), pamphlet attached to Department of Education, Minutes of the Committee on Studies and Textbooks, March 4, 1913–July 25, 1917; WML, *Bulletin* (April 1914): 13–14; (February 1915): 12–13 (quote).

150. WML, *Bulletin* (April 1914): 16–17; (September 1914): 5; (February 1915): 8–11; WML, *Yearbook, 1911,* 74–78 (quotes); *Yearbook, 1912,* 39–47; *Yearbook, 1913,* 24–25, 38–41; *Yearbook, 1914,* 22–25.

151. Department of Education, Report on Vacation Schools and Playgrounds, 83 (quotes); Sadie American, "Vacation Schools and Their Function," *Kindergarten Magazine* 8 (June 1896): 706; Simonds, "Relation of Children to Immoral Conditions," 34; Howe, *World of Our Fathers,* 284; Steven J. Diner, *A Very Different Age: Americans of the Progressive Era* (New York: Hill and Wang, 1998), 78, 101.

152. Beard, *Woman's Work,* 86; WML, *Bulletin* (April 1914): 7–14; Hammack, *Power and Society,* 142; Howe, *World of Our Fathers,* 271–80; *New York Vigilant,* September 12, 1901; Abraham Cahan, "The Bolt of Israel" and "The Poor in Terror," *New York Commercial Advertiser,* November 11, 1898, October 24, 1901, respectively, reprinted in Moses Rischin, ed., *Grandma Never Lived in America: The New Journalism of Abraham Cahan* (Bloomington: Indiana University Press, 1985), 352–54, 364–68.

153. Walter Vincent Romanoff, "Americanization," *Crescent Owl* (1920), newsletter of Crescent Club, *Papers of the University Settlement Society of New York City,* microfilm, reel 17 ("our forefathers"), and see similar phrasing in Elias Lieberman, "I Am an American" (n.d.), in H. W. Smith Club section of reel 16; "'America' Breaks Strike in School," *Herald,* May 6, 1913; Howe, *World of Our Fathers,* 229–35, 252–78.

154. Abraham Cahan, "I Can't Stand Him," *New York Commercial Advertiser,* October 12, 1900, reprinted in Rischin, *Grandma,* 447–48; Kaminsky, "Jewish Big Brother Movement," 39–40; Howe, *World of Our Fathers,* 197–204, 256–71; Graham and Koed, "Americanizing the Immigrant," 39; Cavallo, *Muscles,* 105–6; Alan Wolfe, review of *Ethnic Identity: The Transformation of White America,* by Richard D. Alba, *The American Kaleidoscope: Race, Ethnicity, and the Civic Culture,* by Lawrence H. Fuchs, *Immigrant America: A Portrait,* by Alejandro Portes and Ruben G. Rumbaut, and *Ethnic Options: Choosing Identities in America,* by Mary C. Waters, *New Republic* 203 (December 31, 1990): 27–34.

155. Hamilton, "What the Settlement Stands For," 10–11.

156. See Judith Walzer Leavitt, *The Healthiest City: Milwaukee and the Politics of Health Reform* (Princeton: Princeton University Press, 1982), 76–121.

157. Kouwenhoven, "Waste Not, Have Not," 72–81.

Conclusion

1. *Times,* August 21, 1914; Rene Dubos, *Mirage of Health: Utopias, Progress, and Biological Change* (New York: Harper, 1959; repr., New Brunswick, N.J.: Rutgers University Press, 1987), 195–219 (Dubos quotes).

2. "Women and Civics," *National Municipal Review* 3 (October 1914): 716–717; Nancy Tomes, *The Gospel of Germs: Men, Women, and the Microbe in American Life* (Cambridge, Mass.: Harvard University Press, 1998), 12, 205–33.

3. Glenda Elizabeth Gilmore, ed., *Who Were the Progressives?* (Boston: Bedford/St.

Martin's, 2002), 3–24; John D. Buenker, "The Progressive Era: A Search for a Synthesis," *Mid-America* 51 (1969): 175–93; John C. Burnham, "The Cultural Interpretation of the Progressive Movement," in *Paths into American Culture: Psychology, Medicine, and Morals,* ed. John C. Burnham (Philadelphia: Temple University Press, 1988), 212, 221–22.

4. Leo P. Ribuffo, "From Carter to Clinton: The Latest Crisis of American Liberalism," *American Studies International* 35 (June 1997): 4–29; Leo P. Ribuffo, "Why Is There So Much Conservatism in the United States and Why Do So Few Historians Know Anything about It?" *American Historical Review* 99 (April 1994): 445–49; Otis L. Graham Jr. and Elizabeth Koed, "Americanizing the Immigrant, Past and Future: History and Implications of a Social Movement," *Public Historian* 15 (Fall 1993): 24–45.

5. Eleanor Roosevelt, *Tomorrow Is Now* (New York: Harper and Row, 1963), 60.

6. Ibid., 59–60.

7. Ibid., 126.

8. Anna Greenberg and Stanley Greenberg, "Adding Values," *American Prospect* 11 (August 28, 2000): 28–31; James A. Morone, "Enemies of the People: The Moral Dimension to Public Health," *Journal of Health Politics, Policy and Law* 22 (August 1997): 993–1020; *Times,* March 27, 2003 (Moynihan quote).

9. *Times,* Op-ed, January 13, 2003; David L. Kirp and Marshall S. Smith, "Scandalous Schools," *American Prospect* 14 (November 2003): 27–29; Ayelish McGarvey, "The Best Investment We Can Make," *American Prospect* 15 (February 2004): 42–44.

10. Morone, "Enemies of the People." Also, for the Progressive Era emphasis on the moral culpability of the wealthy and privileged who used their political influence to maintain unjust conditions, see Richard L. McCormick, "The Discovery That Business Corrupts Politics: A Reappraisal of the Origins of Progressivism," in *The Party Period and Public Policy: American Politics from the Age of Jackson to the Progressive Era,* ed. Richard L. McCormick (New York: Oxford University Press, 1986), 311–56.

11. Jean Bethke Elshtain, *Jane Addams and the Dream of American Democracy: A Life* (New York: Basic Books, 2002), 127.

12. Kathryn Kish Sklar, "The Historical Foundations of Women's Power in the Creation of the American Welfare State," in *Mothers of a New World: Maternalist Politics and the Origins of Welfare States,* ed. Seth Koven and Sonya Michel (New York: Routledge, 1993), 45, 75–78.

INDEX

DANIEL ELI BURNSTEIN is an associate professor of history at Seattle University. His articles have appeared in *New York History* and the *Journal of Urban History*.

The University of Illinois Press
is a founding member of the
Association of American University Presses.

Composed in 10.5/13 Adobe Minion
with Minion display
by Celia Shapland
for the University of Illinois Press
Designed by Paula Newcombe
Manufactured by Thomson-Shore, Inc.

University of Illinois Press
1325 South Oak Street
Champaign, IL 61820-6903
www.press.uillinois.edu